3/4/16

VICTORIAN
PARSON

The
VICTORIAN
PARSON

BARRY TURNER

Foreword by Richard Chartres
Bishop of London

AMBERLEY

First published 2015

Amberley Publishing
The Hill, Stroud
Gloucestershire, GL5 4EP

www.amberley-books.com

British Library Cataloguing in Publication Data.
A catalogue record for this book is available from the British Library.

ISBN 978 1 4456 4443 1 (hardback)
ISBN 978 1 4456 4444 8 (ebook)

Typeset in 11.5pt on 13pt Sabon.
Typesetting and Origination by Amberley Publishing.
Printed in the UK.

CONTENTS

Foreword
by the Bishop of London

'Would that these foolish ordinations would cease!' These words, spoken by the Radical MP Joseph Hume in 1832, issue from a period when the very existence of the Church of England was under threat.

The old system in church and state was struggling with the implications of new wealth, urbanisation and a rapid rise in population. The church was among those institutions savagely criticised but resistant to reform. 'I would that these foolish ordinations would cease now that the Church of England is recognised as being not useless only but positively deleterious.' But as Joseph Hume was speaking, the sleeping giant was waking up; the result is described in the following pages of this book, in a catena of sparkling anecdotes and quotations.

In the North, the Brontës noticed a 'shower' of curates descending on the Yorkshire Dales. In London, profiting from the ideas of the Scottish minister Thomas Chalmers, one of the most underestimated opinion formers of the nineteenth century, my predecessor Bishop Blomfield set about building new parish churches, schools and dispensaries, all financed by voluntary giving.

The United Kingdom ceased to be a confessional state in the late 1820s with Catholic Emancipation and the repeal of the

Test and Corporation Acts. The political sphere was opened to all Christians and, very soon, with the City of London in the lead, to Jews and members of other faiths. The consequence was that even the Conservative government of Robert Peel, a devout churchman, refused to assist the programme of church extension as it had done previously in the immediate aftermath of Waterloo.

There was a free market in religious ideas. The attempt to create a religious monopoly had failed – thank God. On the Continent, wherever some branch of the Christian Church succeeded in achieving a legal monopoly and a close relationship with the political status quo, those who were agitating for change tended to see the Christian Church as an enemy. In France, Italy, Spain, Prussia and Russia there developed large left-wing atheist political movements. In England, the Tolpuddle Martyrs were led not by Marxist agitators but by Methodist lay preachers, and the membership of the British Communist Party has at no time ever exceeded that of the Lord's Day Observance Society.

Still, the transition that distanced the Church of England from the State led to a reconstruction of the identity of the Church through the work of Evangelicals and members of the Oxford Movement. The effort put into the education of the young was prodigious; before the Foster Education Act of 1870 the Church was educating a million young Britons a day.

The Church of England recovered its nerve. These were the years of apparent triumph, of a church sharing in the prestige of a supremely self-confident culture. There were intellectual rumblings, but the Church felt very much at home in the Age of Improvement, in which missions to the heathens at home and abroad flourished.

The First World War was the end of the first age of globalisation, in which Britain had played such a crucial part. We are currently in the midst of a season of commemoration of

The War that Ended Peace, as the title of Margaret MacMillan's book describes 1914–18. We cannot change the past, but how we remember it is desperately important. The myth of progress was dealt a mighty blow. The laboratory of European civilisation was transformed into a vast graveyard.

The First World War dented confidence within the Church, and there followed a period of bewilderment and numerical decline. Many Church people internalised the secular narrative that the story of God could only have one end – relegation to the leisure sector. Now, however, at a time when the Editor of *The Economist* has co-authored a book entitled *God is Back*, Barry Turner's book helps us to see that there are surprises and no inevitabilities in history. His account of the astonishing world of the Victorian parson is a cordial for drooping spirits and recognition of the significance of the Church as a social institution in Victorian England.

Now is the time when the contemporary community of faith needs to refresh its understanding of the way the Church has travelled, or we shall lurch between unreasonable optimism and unwarranted despair. The past does not teach directly applicable lessons, but it rhymes and serves to reveal perennial themes and temptations. A sense of the history in which we are involved can help us to see more clearly the contemporary roles we are being called to play.

The person who has a sense of history and no sense of destiny is doubtless a very tedious fellow. But the person or community with a sense of destiny and no sense of history is very wasteful, even dangerous.

Introduction

The Victorian parson is an unsung hero. Legend and literature portray him as a buffoon or a charlatan. At best, he is the bearer of a thin veneer of piety as a cover for hypocrisy. It is true that stories of louche, lazy or plain loony vicars are easy to come by, though many of these date from pre-Victorian days when the Church was going through one of its phases of self-doubt. Having failed to take seriously or, rather, to respond constructively to the profound scepticism of the Enlightenment thinkers, it misunderstood and rejected the achievement of John Wesley in building what was to become a compelling, Nonconformist alternative to the established Church.

But not long into the new century, as Britain emerged victorious from the Napoleonic Wars and attention shifted to the social impact of an unprecedented technological and commercial revolution, the Church moved to the centre of the nation's affairs. Setting up schools across the country, it was the clergy who were largely responsible for the dramatic rise in literacy. They campaigned for better sanitation and healthier living. Above all, the Church took the lead in promoting respect and responsibility, inculcating spiritual and humanitarian values even among those who rarely entered a church. At the same time a boom in church building and decoration was accompanied by a reshaping of public worship to create the services we know today.

In the age of entrepreneurial free-for-all with self-reliance promoted as the cardinal virtue, the parish clergy were the closest the Victorians came to a national network to support the poor and the weak. Thus was created the scaffolding for the welfare state. While there were fools and mavericks in the clerical ranks, the good parson was at the heart of his community, a spiritual and civic leader who set standards of devotion, energy and commitment. We should salute him.

CHAPTER ONE

The Locust Years

At the start of the nineteenth century, the Church was in a sad state. Years of neglect had left it shabby and lethargic. The dedicated parson was a rarity.

How far regression had set in could be seen in a visit to almost any parish. At the core of medieval society, the village church was once a thing of beauty. The plastered walls carried paintings from the scriptures and the lives of the saints; the windows were filled with stained glass; wood carvings decorated the chancel screen while the altar was a blaze of coloured hangings, resplendent by candlelight.

By the eighteenth century, the puritan loathing of idolatrous images had made an ecclesiastical wasteland. While in some parishes there were patchwork repairs to fabric and fittings, many churches were left to rot. Leaking roofs, flaking walls and overgrown graveyards were a familiar part of the rural scene. By way of inspiration, the Ten Commandments flanked by the Lord's Prayer and the Apostles' Creed might be on display, but the wall paintings had long disappeared under layers of whitewash. At Lenton, near Nottingham, the altar was screened off to protect the modesty of those using the attached water closet. Graveyards were dilapidated. One rector converted his churchyard into a vegetable patch. At Chipping Norton, it was let to a local butcher for sheep grazing.

As for worship, the best that most parishes could hope for was a single, regular Sunday service, usually held in the mid-afternoon so that the congregation could return home before dark. The earlier part of the day might start with prayers but was otherwise occupied with baptisms, marriages and burials. The conduct of those ceremonials was perfunctory. Dr George Horne (later Bishop of Norwich) made note of his visit to a dilapidated country church.

> The Minister of this noble edifice was answerable to it in dress and manner. Having entered the church, he made the best of his way to the chancel where he changed his wig; put on a dirty iron moulded ragged surplice; and after a short angry dialogue with the clerk, entered his desk and began immediately without looking into the book. He read as if he had ten other churches to serve that day, at as many miles distant from each other. The clerk sang a melancholy solo – neither tune nor words of which I ever heard before.[1]

When a young curate arrived in Bloxham on the edge of the Cotswolds, he found installed a ninety-year-old vicar who had been in the parish for half a century. Communion was held with a loaf of bread and a dusty black bottle of wine on a stained cloth. Before the service began, the vicar turned to the congregation to ask if anyone had a corkscrew.[2]

With services that were sporadic and trite, attendance was correspondingly low. At Alderley in Cheshire, where Edward Stanley took over the family living in 1805, he found that his predecessor had rarely bothered to turn up to Sunday service. He had his clerk on watch for a congregation and when, as invariably happened, nobody appeared, the parson stayed at home.

Here is an account of the Revd Joshua Brooks, chaplain of the old collegiate church of Manchester until his death in 1821.

Once he was expelled from the chapter house on account of some fiery and hasty speech, and was not allowed to return until he made an apology. This he refused to do, but he put on his surplice in an adjoining chapel of the church, and then, standing outside the chapter-house door, exclaimed to all the persons who were passing on to attend the service, 'They won't let me in; they say I can't behave myself.' Sometimes he would during service box the ears of a chorister for coming late; and once he clouted a boy who was singing the Kyrie after the Fifth Commandment, saying 'Hold thy noise, lad; what hast though to do with the Fifth Commandment? Thou'st got neither father nor mother.'

When reading the Burial Service he would break off in the middle, go to the neighbouring confectioner's shop, procure a supply of hore-hound drops, and then return to his neglected duties and conclude the service. Easter Monday was the great day for weddings at the old church, and large numbers flocked to be married, and with so many couples it was rather difficult to get them properly sorted, as one reading of the service sufficed for all. It was on one of these occasions that some of the bridegrooms got married to the wrong brides and the parson shouted out, 'Sort yourselves when you go out.'[3]

The practical requirements for becoming a parson were a good social background and a working knowledge of the Classics gained at Oxford or Cambridge. The status of gentleman was deemed essential for acceptance at all levels of society. Those who aspired to holy orders were expected to know the basic tenets of the Church and to preside over its rituals. But beyond familiarity with the Bible, few parsons or curates had more than a superficial knowledge of theology. What one knew was less important than who one knew. For the most part, the power of appointment was exercised by wealthy individuals and institutions.

At the highest level, patronage was exercised by the Crown, archbishops and bishops, deans and chapters and the Oxbridge colleges. Christ Church College alone had fifteen livings at its disposal. But it was the landed gentry who were paramount. Over half the livings in the Church of England were theirs to give.

While there were patrons who took their power of appointment seriously, more often the parson was chosen from the ranks of family friends and relations, those in need of an income and a social standing that carried an invitation to the best dining tables. Compliant nonentities were commonplace. Allowing for journalistic licence, Washington Irving's portrait of the vicar of Bracebridge, a university friend of the squire, has the ring of truth. While all else at Bracebridge Hall delighted Irving, the parson, an obsessive pedant, was beyond endurance.

[He] was a little, meagre, black-looking man, with a grizzled wig that was too wide, and stood off from each ear; so that his head seemed to have shrunk away within it, like a dried filbert in its shell. He wore a rusty coat, with great skirts, and pockets that would have held the church Bible and prayer-book; and his small legs seemed still smaller, from being planted in large shoes decorated with enormous buckles. ... He would scarcely read a work printed in the Roman character. The editions of Caxton and Wynkin de Worde were his delight; and he was indefatigable in his researches ... into ... the festive rites and holiday customs of former times; but it was merely with that plodding spirit with which men of a just temperament follow up any track of study, merely because it is denominated learning; indifferent to its intrinsic nature ... He had pored over these old volumes so intensely, that they seemed to have been reflected into his countenance.[4]

Though falling well short of Irving's ideal of a 'sleek well conditioned pastor, such as is often found in a snug living in the vicinity of a rich patron's table', the Bracebridge vicar was at least respectable. No such claim could be made for the candidates of the 8th Earl of Scarborough, who held patronage over eleven livings. One of his nominees was considered so undesirable that no one could be persuaded to sign his testimonials. But then, the earl, with his five illegitimate children, was, himself, unconventional.

Regarded as an inalienable right, patronage was equated with property to be sold and bought on the open market. The regional press regularly invited offers for livings, pointing out added attractions such as the proximity of a famous hunt with plenty of game. In London there were agents who sold livings by auction, even when they were occupied. 'The biddings appeared to be governed by the age and health of the incumbents, residence, situation and other local circumstances,' wrote Sabine Baring-Gould, who was able to add a tale of double dealing.

The incumbent, [who] owned the presentation, put a price on the living which was so high that a would-be purchaser demurred. One day the latter received a telegram from the Rector's lawyer urging him to come down at once. He did so, and was told that the Rector was very ill, and had been prayed for in church, and was not expected to live. The lawyer accompanied the would-be purchaser to the parsonage, where he was entreated to make as little noise as possible, and to stay but for a short time in the room of the dying man. He and the lawyer saw the old man in bed so prostrate as to be scarce able to speak. No demur ensued as to the price, and the contract of sale was rapidly drawn and signed, and a deposit paid. Then the purchaser went down and walked about the grounds and glebe. Two hours must elapse before the train would reconduct him to town. Presently the Rector's wife emerged from the house into the garden and begged him to come in and have some dinner. This he declined, as, under the circumstances, he did not wish to give trouble. 'Not at all,' came the answer. 'The Rector would be glad of your society. The crisis is happily past and he is risen, dressed and impatient for his dinner.'

The dying Rector and patron lived on for 20 years, and bought back the presentation and advowson for his son ... The old rogue cleared £2000 by the transaction.[5]

Patrons did not have it all their own way. The last word on suitability for ordination was with the bishops, though that last word was barely heard if the candidate came from a leading family.

When, in 1822, the Hon. George Spencer, the youngest son of the 2nd Earl, sought ordination in Peterborough, he wrote to the diocesan examiner asking what books he should read. That reverend gentleman modestly declined to advise. 'It is impossible that I could ever entertain any idea of subjecting a gentleman with whose tastes and good qualities I am so well acquainted as I am with yours, to any examination except one as a matter of form, for which a verse in the Greek Testament and an Article of the Church of England returned into Latin, will be amply sufficient.'[6]

The chaplain and son-in-law of Bishop North once examined two candidates for orders at a cricket match while waiting to go in to bat.[7]

John Sharp of Horbury dined out on the story of his ordination. 'Well, Mr Sharp,' said the archbishop in his only interview with the candidate, 'so you are going to be curate to your father, Mr Sharp of Wakefield. Make my compliments to him when you go home. My secretary has your testimonials; he will give you full instructions. Be sure to be at the Minster in good time. Good morning.'

It was said of Bishop Pelham of Exeter that he examined a candidate by sending a message to him by his butler to write an essay on some given subject, then post it to him.[8] Having given his blessing, a dedicated bishop would try to keep track of his incumbents, but personal visits were sporadic and a parson might continue on his way for years without ever again seeing a diocesan representative.

In 1823, Richard Yates, Chaplain of Chelsea Hospital, compiled tables to show that over 5,300 of the estimated 12,000 beneficed clergy in England and Wales did not ordinarily live in their parishes.[9] Sunday 'duties' were frequently delegated to peripatetic curates, who rode out from market towns to serve numerous churches at half a guinea a time. Called 'gallopers', the weekly exodus of curates under Magdalen Bridge was one of the sights of Oxford. Lewes in Sussex was known as the Rookery from the number of clergy who rode out in black coats to do Sunday duty. Some even failed to measure up to that simple requirement. The curate of Berwick never once saw his parson in six years, though he lived in Lewes, less than six miles away.

Excuses were not hard to come by. The parish might be too small, too poor or too remote to warrant more than an occasional visit from a parson shared with another parish. While then, as now, the practice of one clergyman having two or more churches in his charge helped to cover gaps in the system, the administration was wide open to abuse. There was no shame. At Stradishall in Suffolk the rector, Dr Valpy, who doubled as headmaster of Reading School, limited his clerical involvement to an open letter to his parishioners in which he assured them that he would 'receive great comfort from the consideration that this address will give me, at least, an imaginary presence among you'.

The foremost pluralist in terms of notoriety was the Revd Francis Egerton, eighth and last Earl of Bridgewater. A Fellow of All Souls, prebendary of Durham and rector of the Shropshire livings of Whitechurch and Middle, he went to live in Paris where he adopted a dissolute lifestyle encompassing five illegitimate daughters and a house full of dogs, two of which he dressed in yellow coats and napkins and had them sit at his table, where they were fed by servants. For relaxation he shot pheasants and rabbits let loose in his garden.

In death Bridgewater made some recompense, with a bequest to the British Museum, which allowed for the purchase of rare manuscripts, and a grant to the Royal Society to provide what became known as the Bridgewater Treatises, essays on the 'Power, Wisdom and Goodness of God as manifested in the Creation'.

In a series of letters to the *Morning Chronicle*, a former secretary to the bishops of London, Norwich and Ely revealed the lengths some parsons would go to avoid their responsibilities.

> Ill-health of the incumbent, or his wife or daughter, is a common pretext, when no other legal cause can be found of avoiding residence. Of *twenty-two* licences granted in one diocese for this reason, *three* only of the persons are in a state of health to warrant it, and the benefices from which they absent themselves are very valuable. Some (of these incumbents) live in town during the winter; and although night air certainly cannot benefit a valetudinarian, they may be constantly seen at card-parties, routs, or the theatres; in summer enjoying the amusements of fashionable watering places, whilst too often their curates, by the parsimonious stipends they afford them, are with a numerous family in a state of the greatest poverty.[10]

Among those who doubled or trebled their livings were some who grew rich, especially in the early part of the century when the rise in farm prices during the Napoleonic Wars increased the value of glebe land attached to the Church and of the land on which they could claim tithe – 10 per cent of the produce or the cash equivalent. At Duddington in the Cambridgeshire fens, the parson drew the largest stipend in the country, £8,000 or more from reclaimed land. A long liver, he hung on to his unjust reward until 1860.

In the scramble for worldly goods, the senior clergy did themselves particularly well. Greed and ambition for preferment went together. 'What a snivelling, trickling set of rogues they were, those right reverend guardians of the court and nation ... Blessed truly in those days were the poor in spirit – they were sure to get on in the Church.'[11] At a time when the average parson was lucky to have an annual income of £250, the Archbishop of Canterbury could draw on £28,000 a year, well over £1 million by current values. As the last representative of the old regime, Archbishop William Howley was driven to Westminster from Lambeth in a coach flanked by outriders. Guests at his dinners were expected to wear court dress.

But there were many parsons whose income was barely at subsistence level. At the far end of the ecclesiastical pay scale were the curates. Parliamentary returns for 1813 put their number at just over 4,300. Often the sons of the aspiring lower middle class – farmers and tradesmen – curates might be candidates for ordination, ordinands in hope of finding a charitable patron, or simply the possessors of a bishop's licence to conduct services. Even this basic qualification was frequently ignored. Competition for placements depressed their income, which was determined by the parsons who engaged them. Many a hard bargain was struck.

Thomas Denton, who served St Mary's in Kirk Branwith near Doncaster, had to make do on a stipend of £30, out of which the absentee rector 'stops four guineas as a rent for the parsonage house and the premises, tho' all the proceeding curates had these things rent-free'.[12] Another Yorkshire curate enlisted the support of his parishioners in appealing to the archbishop for more generous terms. Henry Bond had just £25 a year to support his family. However, his employer, who was making at least £250 from his two livings of Bransby and Terrington, stood firm. He told the archbishop that Bond was receiving 'more than any person of my acquaintance allows his curate out of a living of equal value', adding that he resented the ingratitude for 'my charitable intention in preserving him and his family from starving'.[13]

In 1796 Parliament set a target of £75 plus the use of the parsonage for curates serving parishes of non-resident parsons. However, there was no way of enforcing the law, and no provision was made where the incumbent was resident and engaged an assistant. By 1800, the average income for curates was less than £50.

To make ends meet, the more fortunate took in pupils or farmed parcels of land. Occasionally, there was a curate who managed to put together a decent living. Lionel Lampett not only did duty at Duns Tew and Barford St Michael but held the mastership of the grammar school at Steeple Aston. Moreover, he continued in those offices 'all long after the infirmities of age had compelled him to travel in a sedan chair between two stalwart labourers'.[14]

Just how far unscrupulous parsons were prepared to go in exploiting their curates was recorded by Augustus Hare.

On Friday we went a long drive, passing St Buryan's, one of the three parishes of the Deanery of St Levan. A Mr Stanhope was long the rector there, having also a rich living, where he resided, in Essex. At St Buryan's he kept a curate, to whom it was only necessary to give a very small stipend indeed, because he was – a harmless maniac! He used to be fastened to the altar or the reading-desk. When once there, he was quite sane enough to go through the service perfectly! On weekday evenings he earned his subsistence by playing the fiddle at the village taverns; but he continued to be the officiating clergyman at St Buryan's till his death in 1808.[15]

James Palmer, curate of Headington, wrote to a Balliol friend in 1806: 'If I had been the 19th cousin of a lord I might have attained hopes of a living; but I have not one drop of Duke's blood in me that I know of, and have no-one to patronise or assist me, so that probably I shall continue as a curate.'[16]

He did, but not for long. He died young, falling from a horse.

Of course, there were parsons who carried out their duties conscientiously while doing their best, in adverse circumstances, to ameliorate the hardships of their parishioners. One such was the Revd James Woodforde, who, having led a relatively uneventful life, achieved immortality with his copious diaries, now, courtesy of the Parson Woodforde Society, edited down to seventeen volumes. The flavour of the diaries is of unhurried rural life (Woodforde was vicar of Weston Longville in Norfolk) with the parsonage as the first port of call in times of distress. A preoccupation with culinary delights can be forgiven when there was little else to divert from the perennial round of births, marriages and deaths.

MAR. 7, [1791], MONDAY. ... The small-Pox spreads much in the Parish. Abigail Roberts's Husband was very bad in it ... His Children are inoculated as are also Richmonds Children near me. It is a pity that all the Poor in the Parish were not inoculated also. I am entirely for it.

MAR. 8, TUESDAY. ... Gave poor Roberts one of my old Shirts to put on in the small-Pox – His, poor Fellow, being so extremely coarse and rough, that his having the small-Pox so very full, his coarse Shirt makes it very painful to him. I sent his Family a Basket of Apples and some black Currant Robb. There are many, many People in the Parish yet [who] have never had the small-Pox. Pray God all may do well that have it or shall have it. Went this Afternoon and saw poor old John Peachman Who is very lame, found him unable to walk and having no relief from the Parish gave him money. Called also at Tom Carys Shop and left some money for Roberts's Familys Use for such useful things as they might want.

If Woodforde was fixated on the contents of his larder, the Revd William Cole, vicar of Blecheley (now Bletchley) was obsessed with the weather. Almost every diary entry begins with a meteorological report. But like Woodforde, this gentle, easygoing parson worked assiduously on behalf of his parish and did what he could for the poor.

> SAT. JAN. 10. Excessive Frost. Sent Money & Victuals to the poor People & a Bottle of Wine to Will Hebbes. Could not buy wood for them. Mr Cartwright told me that Richard Braund of Shenley was killed by a Shot in his Head, supposed to be received on Robbing somebody. I sent to buy Wood for the poor People on Thursday, but could get none, as the Snow lay so thick on the Faggots of Rickley Wood. Froze in the Bed-Chamber where the Bottle of Water was set for washing. Put off washing on Monday on Account of the Severity of the Weather.[17]

The wood was eventually gathered in. Meanwhile, Cole welcomed villagers into his home for a decent meal.

How many other Woodfordes and Coles there were it is impossible to tell, though it is hard to believe that they were alone. Then again, the evidence from visitation records shows that in some dioceses, serious efforts were made to raise the level of church care and maintenance.[18] But there are exceptions to every rule, and the fact remains that the Church was noted more for its abuses than for its dedication to the Christian message. The time for renewal was long overdue.

CHAPTER TWO

A Promise of Change

How the Church went about its mission had long been a matter of debate. Canon law was plain enough. The clergy

> shall not give themselves to any base or servile labour, or to drinking or riot, spending their time idly by day or by night, playing at dice, cards or tables, or any other unlawful games: but at all times convenient they shall hear or read somewhat of Holy Scriptures, or shall occupy themselves with some other honest study or exercise, always doing the things which shall appertain to honesty, and endeavouring to profit the church of God; having always in mind that they ought to excel all others in purity of life, and should be examples to the people to live well and Christianly, under pain of ecclesiastical censures.

But this left much room for arguments about Christian fundamentals, not least Church customs and ritual. On one side were the Evangelicals, the heirs to John Wesley and his 'simple childlike faith' as the way to salvation. Many Evangelicals had hived off into one of the Nonconformist sects (by mid-nineteenth century they had well over a thousand meeting places), but they remained a powerful lobby within the Church. About one in eight of the clergy could be classed as Evangelical.[1] Anglicans and Methodists overlapped for much of our period.

High Churchmen distrusted the 'enthusiasm' of their Evangelical colleagues. They had more regard for what they saw as the dignity of the Church, which distanced the clergy from the common herd. Respect and deference were the twin pillars of Church orthodoxy. But while the theological battle lines were clearly drawn by the turn of the century neither side had much time for internecine warfare while the Church as a whole was under attack. By 1817, the year of Victoria's birth, the Church was in crisis as, indeed, was the entire country.

Ideas of liberty and equality, promoted by the French Revolution, were reinvigorated after Napoleon's failure to dominate Europe. The celebration of victory did not mark a return to passivity. While working people feared the loss of their livelihoods to machine-led mass production, a rising middle class wanted more say in the running of the country. The old nobility foresaw anarchy and bloodletting.

Reform was in the air but few, least of all in the two leading state institutions – Parliament and the Church – understood how it could be made palpable. While Parliament relied on hereditary rights and an electoral system that was as corrupt as it was unrepresentative, the established Church managed its affairs with exaggerated respect for tired practices. The fear of change was greater than the need to change. The Church saw itself as the guardian of timeless values and eternal truths. To start tinkering with the system was, in the view of many, to risk undermining the foundations of all that was sacrosanct. The result would be anarchic individualism.

But despite the fears of social breakdown it was not long before the ecclesiastical fault lines became too wide to ignore. Clerical abuses, which for generations had been accepted as part of the natural order of things, came under aggressive attack.

Free thinkers, dissenters and radicals of all stripes rushed into print with their denunciations of a crumbling monolith. If the critics failed to present a united front, they were agreed that the Church had such an air of neglect and decline as to put into question the future of established religion.

The general mood of disenchantment with the clergy grew apace. Ending his tour of Hampshire, Berkshire, Surrey and Sussex in 1823, William Cobbett felt unable to sign off 'without noticing the sort of language I hear everywhere made use of with regard to parsons, but which language I do not care to repeat'. With the introduction of the paper-making machine and steam-powered printing, Cobbett's style of vituperate journalism flourished.

In 1820 appeared the first instalments of a coruscating attack on the establishment, called *Corruption Unmasked*. Later republished as *The Extraordinary Black Book*, its author, John Wade, a *Unitarian* and *Spectator* leader writer, sniped at royalty, the judiciary and the military. But the Church was his bull's eye. Though his statistics were suspect (he had a tendency to double the number he first thought of) his charge of nepotism and maladministration on a massive scale could not easily be refuted.

Bishop Sparke of Ely was accused of handing out jobs to his son and son-in-law to achieve a combined income of £31,000. The figure was exaggerated but the family links were real enough. And there could be no denying that Manners-Sutton, as Archbishop of Canterbury, appointed his grandson, aged twelve, to the office of Registrar of the Prerogative Court of Canterbury, a sinecure worth £9,000 to £12,000 a year. The Bishop of Bangor, who died in 1830, held no fewer than eleven parochial offices.

Wealthy prelates, nearly all linked to the aristocracy by birth or marriage, were not above manipulating charities to favour their relatives. Wade claimed that the rental from 650 acres near

Lincoln left to support six poor men produced just £24 for the main beneficiaries while the rest, well over £2000, was pocketed by a warden who turned out to be the bishop's nephew.

The Black Book inspired other publications, two of which, the *Episcopal Gazette* and the *Church Examiner*, were given over entirely to anti-clerical diatribes.

All this rattled the governing class. Fear of revolution was ever present. The Britain of Victoria's infancy was in a fragile state. Unemployment was high; so too was the price of bread. A poor harvest in 1816 came hard on the introduction of the Corn Laws, which sought to protect the landed interest (and, incidentally, those who worked the land) by cutting out cheap, foreign competition. Violent protests against the new industrial machinery that displaced skilled workers in the Midlands, Lancashire, Cheshire and Yorkshire extended to the countryside, where rick burnings had parties of armed vigilantes out at night to protect threshing machines and other steam-powered innovations. The East Anglian 'blood and bread' riots were particularly ferocious.

In 1817, shortly after the mass meetings at Spa Fields, Islington, against rising food prices, Richard Yates sent a timely open letter to the Prime Minister, Lord Liverpool.

> It is not only the absence of Religious Instruction that the danger to our existing institutions must be estimated, we must also take into account the positive introduction of licentious, irreligious and blasphemous principles [with] no religious impressions to contrast them.[2]

Yates overstated his case. But his apocalyptic view of society, first expressed in *The Church in Danger*, published in 1815, gained wide circulation and he persuaded many of those who sat at Westminster that the established Church was falling short of its spiritual and political duties. The rhetorical question put by the seventeenth-century divine, Archbishop John Tillotson, echoed down the years.

> What's religion good for but to reform the manners and dispositions of men, to refrain human nature from violence and cruelty, from falsehood and treachery, from sedition and rebellion?

Put like this, the failure of the Church was manifest. The clergy were all for discipline and obedience but, for the most part, they went about achieving this in quite the wrong way. Instead of setting examples, they lent their authority to archaic laws which bore heavily on the poor. With as many as one parson in six doubling as a Justice of the Peace, we can easily imagine how a parishioner might feel about his church when he was punished unduly for poaching a rabbit or selling vegetables on Sunday.

The clergy were swept along in the fear of contagion from the French Revolution. In the days before railways and the telegraph, rural parsons were beset by rumours of imminent insurrection. In February 1817, the Revd Benjamin Newton, in his Yorkshire parish of Wath, sat down to 'read the report of the secret Committee setting forth the treasonable attempts to overthrow the Government and divide all the property'. If this was not alarming enough, 'Mr Lascelles, the grandson of Lord Harewood, said that all public meetings in England ought to be dispersed by grapeshot and that all petitions either to the Lords or Commons ought to be considered treason.'[3]

That he was not alone in his opinion was highlighted two years later when a demonstration for parliamentary reform in St Peter's Fields, Manchester, was broken up by sabre-waving cavalry. In what became known as the Peterloo Massacre, at least eleven were killed and 700 injured. The magistrates who summoned the military were both clergy, one of whom, W. R. Hay, was to be presented with a good living at Rochdale, his patron being the Archbishop of Canterbury. It was a misjudgement not easily forgotten by the radical press.

But even the most diehard reactionary had to acknowledge that repression was not enough. The appeal was for the Church to discharge its role in bringing contentment to the people and reasserting respect for authority. The starting point was for the Church to heal itself. Any rational observer knew what had to be done, starting with limits on pluralism and lay patronage, introducing order to diocesan geography and tightening clerical discipline. But since the Church derived its authority from Parliament, structural reform depended on political initiative and sanction. Until 1842, even creating a new parish required legislation. The pace of Church reform thus matched the pace of political reform. Both moved slowly. Clerics on substantial incomes and in positions of authority were no more willing to surrender their advantages than politicians whose election depended on buying votes from a tightly restricted franchise.

While the Tories were in power – and they had an almost uninterrupted run of fifty years, leading up to 1830 – little could be expected. Half-hearted attempts to raise standards had produced a Residence Act (1803) to require a parson to live in his parish or persuade his bishop that absenteeism was justified. The bishops were disinclined to cooperate, though few went so far as the eighty-eight-year-old Bishop of Worcester, who refused point blank to enforce a law that would 'cause the clergy such inconvenience'. Presumably, this included the incumbent of Dittisham, who lived in Penang, and the parson of Honeychurch, who resided in Brazil.[4] The Rector of Emberton was absent from his parish for fifteen years on doctor's orders. He died in 1860, aged eighty-seven. When the Canterbury clergy warned Archbishop Howley against hasty reform, *The Times* was quick to point out that the leading light of the petition held three highly profitable offices.

The Residence Act was followed by bits and pieces of legislation that, if not of much practical value, at least recognised that there were deficiencies to be remedied. Renewed attempts to settle on a guaranteed wage for curates culminated in the Stipendiary Curates Act (1813). It targeted those livings with absentee parsons. When one of those parishes fell vacant and was taken over by another non-resident, the bishop was empowered to engage a curate at the appropriate salary. But vacancies were slow to appear. Clergy with the poorest records for attending to their duties had a disturbing tendency to longevity. Half a century later, there was still a scattering of places where the non-resident incumbent had held the living before 1813. In any case, wrote Sydney Smith in the *Edinburgh Review*, 'The law cannot arm clergyman against clergyman ... Men laugh at such prohibitions.' Some relief was provided by two associations, the Evangelical-led Church Pastoral Aid Society and its High Church rival, the Additional Curates Society. Both set a reasonable salary at between £80 and £100.

In 1817 the law was changed; it limited the amount of land a parson could farm, imposed restrictions on holding parallel occupations, required the clergy to keep their parsonages in good repair and gave bishops the power to appoint curates for parishes where the incumbents were too old or too infirm to carry out their duties. But lack of consensus within the Church drained reform of real substance. As Archbishop Manners-Sutton observed euphemistically, there were difficulties in 'making a suit of clothes to fit the moon in all its changes'.

Not surprisingly, agreement was easiest when there was a financial inducement. The precedent for subsidising the established Church was set early in the eighteenth century when Queen Anne's Bounty was created to support poor livings. Almost a century later, as part of its effort to put the ecclesiastical lid on insurrection, Parliament increased the bounty by £100,000, a grant that was renewed every year but one from 1809 to 1820.

By the same reasoning there was a good case for building churches where no churches had been before. The initiative came from a group of High Church friends and relatives who lived in what was then the village of Hackney, north of London. What was known as the Hackney Phalanx was led by Joshua Watson, a wine merchant who had spread his interest during the Napoleonic Wars to make a large fortune as a government contractor. Possessed of a strong philanthropic conscience, Watson retired from business at the age of forty-three to dedicate the rest of his long life to extending the reach of the Church.

Witnessing at first hand London's burgeoning population – at over one million in 1800, it grew by 20 per cent in each of the five following decades – the Hackney Phalanx set up the Church Building Society as a fundraising body while lobbying the government to match its efforts. The result was the 1818 Church Building Act, supported by £1 million of taxpayers' money. The grant was increased by half as much again in 1824.

Led by the Crown Architects – John Nash, John Soane and Robert Smirke – what became known as Commissioners' Churches were built, 214 of them over twelve years, mostly in London and the new towns that had sprung from villages in Lancashire, Yorkshire and the Midlands. The brief was to accommodate 'the greatest number of persons at the smallest expense within the compass of an ordinary voice'. A maximum of 20 inches for each worshipper was stipulated. Within these severe constraints there were some remarkable achievements, though at the time critics were not impressed.

The now revered All Souls, on Langham Place, the only surviving church by John Nash (his other Commissioners' church in Haggeston was destroyed in the 1941 Blitz), was attacked for its 'puny proportions and scantiness of decoration' and was said to be 'one of the most miserable structures in the metropolis'. Baring-Gould called it a 'hideous erection ... with its caryatids, copied from the Erechtheum at Athens'.[5] There was nothing but ridicule for the inverted cone-shaped steeple, today one of the more attractively distinctive features of that part of London. It would have comforted Nash to know that a century later, the façade of Broadcasting House was made to harmonise with All Souls.

Familiarity with existing forms gave the edge to neoclassical and Gothic designs. At Workington the concept was 'Roman of the Tuscan Order with a Portico and Cupola', while St George's, Hanover Square, was to be 'Ionic of the Temple of Minerva Polias at Prieni, with two Belfries, Portico and Cupola'. Such confections were the despair of the connoisseurs.

Happy to go along with whatever the client demanded was Thomas Rickman, a Quaker architect from Liverpool, who was equally at home with the Gothic or Grecian style. He built twenty-one churches for the Commission, more than any other architect.[6] The consensus at the time held that Rickman was too ready to sacrifice quality to economy. Even so, three of his churches are now Grade 1 listed. His finest achievement, the neoclassical St Thomas's, in Birmingham, was lost to bombs in 1940.

In London, one of the more successful neo-classical structures was St John the Evangelist, on the south side of Waterloo Bridge. Built between 1822 and 1824 to accommodate 2,000 worshippers, it was one of four Commissioners' churches for new parishes carved out of Lambeth. Because it was too close to the Thames crossing to the more salubrious north side of the city, 'a more imposing design was selected than would otherwise have been chosen'. This was in the Greek style with six Doric columns facing Waterloo Road. The architect, Francis Octavius Bedford, was responsible for four other Greek inspired churches in south London, though later, almost certainly more for economic than aesthetic reasons, he was converted to Gothic.

Surrounded by an acre or two of open land enclosed by a low wall, St John's must have made an imposing sight to those more used to overcrowded tenements.

But pride of place in the catalogue of Commissioners' churches goes to St Luke's in Chelsea, where more than two-thirds of the higher-than-average cost came from voluntary subscriptions. The architect, James Savage, better known as a civil engineer and bridge designer, used his engineering skills to erect a stone rib vault, complete with flying buttresses, over a neo-Gothic church, the first since the Reformation.

Many of the new churches had the look of being cobbled together by committee, which was very often the case. But with barely two dozen new churches in the eighteenth century, Joshua Watson, with state support, may be credited with starting a new age of church building, that most visible sign of a Church revival. When the Exchequer grant ran out, the society struggled to keep afloat. Among the many appeals for support that had to be rejected because of the 'exhausted state of the Society's funds'[7] was one from Keighley, where a population of 10,000 was served by one church. All but thirty-six seats were rented out. Noting the profusion of Nonconformist chapels, the parson observed, 'The poor must become dissenters or nothing.'

Even when finance was not a problem, the society could be thwarted by local prejudice. A strong plea from William Wordsworth to bring Christian enlightenment to Cockermouth, his birthplace on the edge of the Lake District, incurred the opposition of a jealous incumbent and from a wealthy Evangelical who would only give his support if appointments of clergy were subject to his approval. Wordsworth eventually relinquished his attempt to visit on Cockermouth 'a church of which the present generation at least appears to be unworthy'.

On the plus side, senior clerics were ready to take up the challenge. In 1836 Bishop Blomfield began his project for building fifty new churches in London, ten of them in Bethnal

Green, one of the city's poorest districts, while Bishop Kaye presided over a scheme to provide church accommodation for two thirds of the inhabitants of the rapidly growing Nottingham.[8] At Leeds, Dean Hook raised the funds for twenty-one new churches. And this was only a small part of the church building boom.

Other forces for change within the Church were beginning to make themselves felt. Leading the spiritual revival, Evangelical church services were more frequent and better managed. They insisted on two services on Sunday and often held a third to compete with the chapels. Early in the century, John Venn instituted a Sunday evening service at Clapham, described as 'a great novelty', while Daniel Wilson insisted that at his evening service in Islington the tradition of renting out pews to the superior social set should be dropped. All pews were allocated on the principle of first come, first served, at a time when the best pews were generally reserved for those who could afford to pay.[9]

This was more radical than might have first appeared. Pew rents were an important part of Church income (the collecting plate was not common until much later in the century). Conservatives feared that Wilson's initiative, if followed widely, would not only offend social mores but, more seriously, undermine the financial structure of the Church. Wilson may well have responded by arguing that it was the duty of the clergy to reach out to the spiritually dispossessed. Any increase in church attendance was to be welcomed.

Another encouraging pointer was the increase in the annual output of ordinands, a doubling in the first twenty years of the new century. Even allowing for the scarcity of other openings to professional status – the law, teaching and medicine still had to make their mark – the appeal of the rectory reflected a growing demand for an active body of clergy, ready to take its responsibilities seriously and to do its best, often in unfavourable circumstances, to serve the people.

It could be a busy life. Benjamin Newton, who was from 1814 the rector of Wath, a few miles north of Ripon in Yorkshire, spent at least a day a week on what he described as 'justicing', while holding regular services and christenings, marrying, visiting, burying, even vaccinating his parishioners against smallpox, an exercise in preventative medicine that had to wait until 1858 to be made compulsory by law. Having married well, Newton was indeed a bit of a snob, not caring to socialise with tenant farmers or tradesmen. But as a JP, he wisely declined to hear cases against his own parishioners.

The Revd Francis Witts, Rector of Upper Slaughter from 1808 to 1854, suffered no inhibitions in exercising his judicial responsibilities. He was a regular attender at petty sessions and occasionally presided at one of the court of quarter sessions. Offences which fell within his brief ranged from poaching to assault and threats of murder. It was in his power to order a convicted offender to be whipped, placed in the stocks or be committed to the house of correction.

Though generally a kindly man, Witts was no soft touch when it came to administering the law, especially when public order was threatened. This was his diary entry for 13 January, 1826.

The business at hand at the Sessions, was the trial of several weavers who, acting under the delusion so prevalent in all manufacturing districts, have been guilty of very serious riots and acts of disturbance at Wotton-under-Edge and its neighbourhood some weeks ago. They proceeded to great violence, assaulting the operatives who undertook work at a lower rate than was approved by them, proceeding to the demolition of workshops and factories, meeting in large companies and debating in their clubs measures to obtain higher wages and control over their masters. Of these misguided men several were of very decent appearance; one had been a serjeant and enjoyed a pension.

They must be punished with severity since the indulgence shown
to the Stroud rioters has failed in its effect. The worse cases now
will receive two years incarceration in one of the Houses of
Correction.[10]

A stickler for detail, Francis Witts was ever ready to check that
the punishments he handed down were conducted in a proper
manner.

I inspected the treadwheel at Northleach Bridewell, recently put
up. The machinery still requires some alterations. The velocity
with which the wheel revolved was too great so that the fatigue
exceeded the strength of the prisoners. The revolutions should
be limited to about 52 steps in a minute. A regulator must be
applied to the machine in such a manner as to compensate for
any difference in the weight of the gangs on the wheel, whether
grown men or boys. The millwright was in attendance. It is
intended to keep the machine going, should there at any time be
a failure of corn to grind. Nine or ten prisoners were on the mill
at once, they worked each 4½ or 5 minutes, one descending from
the extremity of the wheel every half minute. A relay of prisoners
is kept in an adjacent yard, walking in a circle.[11]

The number of clerical magistrates was in decline as parsons
came to recognise that they had more to do than simply keep
their parishioners in place. Charles Jerram, Rector of Witney
from 1834 to 1853, noted in his journal that while 'serving on
the Surrey bench had enabled him to tackle social evils linked to
the licensing of public houses, Sunday observance and the Poor
Law, the habit of suspicion he had acquired was ill-suited to the
practice of Christian charity'.[12] It was widely recognised that
by enforcing archaic laws, the parson could make himself look
sinister or ridiculous as when, in 1847, the Revd W. S. Bricknell
fined a man for selling a pennyworth of walnuts on a Sunday.

Benjamin Newton was punctilious in visiting those who needed him, handing out advice on decent living while, along the way, noting life's little oddities such as a Mrs Barry who 'has just been seized with a violent longing to see her mother though no one knew she had a mother and she has never seen or mentioned her till within a few days'. That same day, 1 July 1817, Newton was told of a man 'leaning against a bank ... who appeared to be dying or dead ... it turned out to be Squire Peacock of Carthorpe almost dead drunk, fallen from his horse which had run away'.[13] The demon drink is a recurring theme in clerical memoirs.

How parsons should go about their work was largely a matter of individual choice, though there were generally accepted standards. The historian James Froude, son of a West Country clergyman, described what he regarded as a typical parson. He was

a man of private fortune ... His professional duties were his services on Sundays, funerals and weddings on week-days, and visits when needed among the sick. In other respects he lived like his neighbours ... He farmed his own glebe; he kept horses ... he attended public meetings and his education enabled him to take a leading part in country business. His wife and daughters looked after the poor, taught in the Sunday-school, and managed the penny clubs and clothing clubs. He himself was spoken of in the parish as 'the master' – the person who was responsible for keeping order there, and who knew how to keep it. The labourers and the farmers looked up to him. The 'family' in the great house could hardly look down upon him.

As the likeliest candidate to chair the parish vestry, the representative body of ratepayers, the good parson undertook a range of administrative and charitable duties. He was liable to be called upon to pronounce on fair wages, to fix the price of bread, to supervise the maintenance of roads and bridges, to arbitrate on the poor rates imposed by the vestry and to be the final arbiter on how funds should be distributed. Since much of the work was concentrated on reconciling conflicting interests, the greatest virtue for a parson was the possession of sound, practical common sense and the power of persuasion.

It was a sign of the times, however, that parsons, particularly those with private incomes, were increasingly mindful of their public image. Benjamin Newton lived well, dining regularly on venison, turtle and champagne. In 1818, after visiting a man in the last stages of consumption, he hurried away to go coursing with a neighbouring incumbent. Before long, this was thought to be not quite the thing to do.

There were those who were unable to adapt. As a hard-working and generous parson, Archer Clive felt the pressure. He had got off to a good start when his wealthy father presented him with the living at Solihull. True to his family's lifestyle, he enjoyed hunting and regularly attended race meetings. But he did so knowing that many of his parishioners would 'think me little better than a Heathen if they heard of it'.[14] Unable to reconcile what he was – a person of means – and what he wanted to be – a man of the people – Clive abandoned the Church to become a reforming landowner.

Much criticism was directed at parsons who lived in the pockets of the squirearchy, lending their authority to the establishment in its efforts to keep the lower orders in submission. A well-worn tale had the squire telling his clerical crony, 'You keep 'em ignorant and I'll keep 'em poor.' But to do a good job, the parson needed to have a working relationship with his squire. It was he who was assumed to set the social and political tone, while the parson promoted spiritual values, embracing honesty, decency and clean living.

When the squire and parson were at odds, it was nearly always to the detriment of the community they were supposed to serve.

It happened in Kettering in Norfolk, where the Revd William Wayte Andrew (dedicated, devout, dour) confronted Sir John Boileau (jovial, easily bored and none too tolerant of anyone who challenged his authority).[15] An early skirmish had Sir John making clear that one Sunday sermon was 'quite enough for us' and Andrew complaining that the squire, 'a designing man', was given to talking too much of secular matters on the Sabbath. Andrew's frustration boiled over when, in 1839, Sir John accepted the office of steward at the Norwich races. His written protest encompassed a full range of grievances. 'What must the people think if on the authority of God's word I condemn the pleasures of the world and they hear that you advocate bells and plays.'

Andrew was not someone to meet on a long journey. He was given to handing out moralistic tracts and lecturing on the evils of the world. His favourite pitch was a railway coach, where there was no escape. But his style of preaching, spontaneous and energetic, had a wide appeal, attracting worshippers from neighbouring villages, who packed the church full. Sir John was one of the few dissidents, shuffling in his pew and making frequent, pointed references to his watch. He thought Andrew's sermons incoherent and rambling. Further, he objected to Ketteringham playing host to Sunday visitors who had their own churches to go to. His benevolence to villagers on hard times came with the proviso that the community was run on the lines he stipulated.

An enthusiast for elementary education, he built a school and paid for a trained teacher, but he flatly refused to allow Andrew to use the premises as a lecture hall. More tactlessly, he treated the church as his property, making alterations that seemed to him beneficial and even erecting a monument to a late employee without consulting the vicar. Angry letters were exchanged. The long-running discord – it lasted all of twenty-seven years – was not good for Ketteringham, except as a source of gossip.

'If the squire and the vicar were a little afraid of each other, the cottagers were more than a little afraid of both.'[16]

Open warfare between the squire and his parson was not unknown. When James Banks Stanhope, who held the patronage for the Lincolnshire parish of Revesby, gave the Revd Andrew Veitch notice to quit, he was met by a blank refusal to go. Defiant to the last, Veitch continued to hold services until, one Sunday, he arrived to find Stanhope's gamekeepers in occupation. Refused admittance, he entered as one of the congregation and began reading the service in competition with another parson favoured by the lord of the manor. The upshot was his forcible removal from the church. It was reported in the local press that he continued to read the service as he was carried bodily along the nave and thrown out at the door.

'This disgraceful scene ... caused the utmost excitement among the congregation. In the afternoon a large crowd assembled, expecting a repetition of the scene at the evening service but Mr Veitch did not appear.'[17]

Occasionally, along came a clerical personality so strong as to defy all attempts to force him into line. Sydney Smith was one such. In an age when wit and humour, or that of it handed down to us, was heavy weighted, Smith was the master of the pithy response and the sharp put down. A large, jovial man, he delighted in good company in the best houses and was much sought after for his table talk.

Ordained in 1794, 'without apparent enthusiasm' and having no resources of his own, he had to start from the bottom, in his case the curacy at Netheravon on Salisbury Plain, where he was thoroughly miserable. 'Nothing,' he wrote, 'can equal ... the awful dullness of this place.' Nonetheless, he established a Sunday school, found a teacher and laid down a study programme. Publishing a book of sermons helped to widen his reputation, but his comments on the 'low state of pulpit eloquence'[18] were not appreciated by his superiors, who decided that he was too clever by half. As if to prove the point, in 1802 Smith founded the *Edinburgh Review*, a journal of trenchant criticism of social and political conventions, which set the standard for serious journalism.

Relegated to another rural living, this time Foston-le-Clay, 'twelve miles from a lemon' between York and Malton, Smith decided to make the best of it. With no resident parson for 150 years, Foston church was said to be a 'miserable little hovel with a wooden belfry'. Having to find his own accommodation, Smith designed and built his own parsonage with the help of a loan from Queen Anne's Bounty. He was the first to do so. With characteristic energy, he was village parson, doctor, magistrate and general comforter all in one. He spoke up for toleration for Roman Catholics and Dissenters and was an advocate of prison reform. 'Not knowing a turnip from a carrot,' he taught himself farming and others the virtue of self help, arguing that his poor parishioners would be better off learning how to make best use of available resources than depending on charitable doles of food. With this aim he divided up several acres of his glebe for cheap rents. His daughter recalled these small plots, each sufficient to supply a cottager with vegetables with space left over for a pigsty, 'filled at dawn with women and children cultivating them before they went to their day's labours'.

Smith ended his career as one of the better-paid clergy, a canon of St Paul's, where he reformed the administration and embarked on restoring the fabric 'as cheaply as we can, consistently with it being done well'.[19] We are left to wonder what he could have achieved if the Church had been bold enough to appoint him to higher office.

With the spread of industrialisation, Britain's population doubled to 21 million in the first half of the century. But it was still a country where agriculture occupied over a quarter of the population. Villages were growing into towns but rural seclusion, primitive living at best, was the lot of many, and loneliness was an occupational hazard for young ordinands.

It was with much trepidation that Richard William Church gave up his Oriel fellowship for the living of Whatley, a small parish in Somerset. His Oxford friends missed him, but not so much as he missed them. 'The weather is very fine,' he assured one of his correspondents, 'and the country looking very pretty; but it does not reconcile me to my transplanting. I think all day long of ... my den, cold and dirty as it was, at Oriel.'[20]

But Church soon adapted and when, twenty years later, he was persuaded to accept the Deanery of St Paul's, he was sad to leave. 'I have not the least notion how far I can bear the huge change from the country, with its fresh air and simple ways of life, to the gloomy atmosphere and big dinners and late hours of London.'[21]

Church came to terms with his circumstances, but others were less accommodating. The parson at Kirton in North Lincolnshire withstood seven years of loneliness and hostility before departing a disillusioned idealist.

> I know and feel I have within me the power of being satisfied in obscurity and in poverty if I am cheered by the consciousness of usefulness and by the affection of those whose good opinion I have never deserved to lose. [But] all my prospects of usefulness, all bright visions which cheered the obscurity of my lot ... have closed in utter darkness.

His consolation was a fresh start in a well endowed parish, described as a 'comfortable sinecure'.[22]

Not so fortunate was John Skinner. After two curacies, he moved to Camerton near Bath where his clerical uncle had promised him a 'comfortable independence'. He was twenty-eight, and about to be disabused. Camerton was no longer a rural backwater. The discovery of rich veins of coal had transformed a village that was now out of kilter with its past and facing an uncertain future. The life of the miner was rough, tough and driven by alcohol. The attentions of a devout parson were rejected, though it is clear from his own words that Skinner was less than tactful in his approach.

He made the arrogant assumption that his strictures on morality and decency were not to be questioned. Conflict with his parishioners was inevitable and, because Skinner was acutely sensitive to opposition and insult, the daily round was agony for him. He had no success in his one-man campaign against the public houses, 'the principal causes of all the licentiousness and insubordination, poverty and consequent misery of the lower orders'.[23] He simply could not comprehend why, as one drink-induced tragedy followed another, he remained a lone voice for temperance.

A stranger from Ireland named Culling Macnab, who worked in the coal pits, being much intoxicated on Saturday night was drowned by falling into the Canal, and afterwards a collier of the name of Cook killed by some loose earth as the bottom of the pit falling upon him, his two sons who were working close by providentially escaped, and endeavoured to dig away the earth from their father, but could not do it in time to save his life, but were near enough to hear him exclaim, 'My poor lads, it will soon be over with me.'

Aaron Horler, another collier, was killed in a very extraordinary manner. He had been drinking at the public house, whence, after behaving in a violent manner by dancing on the tables and stools, etc., and insulting some of his associates there assembled, he walked to the Lower Pit and, it is supposed, endeavoured to slide down the rope (by which the coal is hauled) to the bottom; but going too quick, not being able to retain his hold, he fell down many fathoms and was dashed to pieces, his hands being much burned by the velocity with which the rope passed through them before he let go his hold. A person going down the pit about ten o'clock to feed the asses kept under-ground was presented with this horrid spectacle on his descent, and was so much frightened as not to recover himself for some time.

Skinner went out of his way to meet his parishioners, visiting the sick and tending to the dying. He supported free education for the poor and stood up for the miners when he felt that they were being treated unfairly. He spoke out against the employment of children.

A little boy of the name of Cottle, son of the Schoolmistress, was killed in the coal pit by some loose ground falling upon him. He was only eight years old, and had worked a year.

Skinner blamed the parents for 'permitting such little boys to work, who cannot possibly take care of themselves and must be ignorant of the dangers they are exposed to'. He made no secret of his opinion that the Cottles made 'everything which is sacred subservient to their own interest'.[24]

While his heart was in the right place, Skinner's self-righteous, hectoring tone, forever finding fault, grated on those he sought to influence. Regaling a persistent imbiber, he threatened that unless the offender repented, 'he would be condemned to lasting torments in Hell, and what would he do then?'

The reply, 'Why, I must do what the rest do,' was not a bad response, but Skinner failed to see the joke. He was shouted at in the street and heckled in church.

I performed Evening Service at Timsbury. Whilst reading the Prayers I experienced an open insult from some of the congregation in the gallery, as the people made such a constant hawking, in the manner the audience at a theatre expresses disapproval of an actor on the stage, I was obliged to tell them to leave off, otherwise I could not proceed with the Service. Then they stopped.

There were bouts of depression. 'I am sick of the vineyard it is my lot to cultivate ... [I am in] a continued state of irritation and disappointment.' And later, 'I clearly see I cannot live longer with this people, I am so continually disgusted with their conduct.'

He found some comfort in writing his journal, joining archaeological digs and in long rambles over the countryside, using the woods as a protection against unwelcome encounters. Recognising a depressive, his bishop began taking an interest in someone he had hitherto tried to avoid. But he was too late. One day, Skinner loaded his pistol, left the house and walked into the woods for the last time.

A more resilient character, who knew a thing or two about loneliness, was Robert Stephen Hawker. A hasty biography, published soon after his subject's death, secured the posthumous reputation of Hawker as one of the clerical eccentrics. But he was more than that. Three years after his ordination in 1831, Hawker was appointed to Morwenstow in North Cornwall, 'an awesomely bleak place, hemmed in by rough moorland to the east and so ravaged by storms from the Atlantic on its western border that the trees ... bend inland to avoid the blast'.[25] On a clear day the view from the cliffs was of the Welsh mountains to the north and Lundy to the north-west. To the west, as Hawker told visitors, 'There is not a speck of land between Morwenstow and the coast of Labrador.'

When Hawker arrived in Morwenstow, then not so much a village as a collection of scattered hamlets, there had been no resident parson for over a century. His parishioners he described as 'a mixed multitude of smugglers, wreckers and dissenters of various hue'. This was a misrepresentation. Smugglers there had been but, like the wreckers, those who had lured ships on to the rocks, they were part of folklore. Rather more typical were farmers, labourers, servants and craftsmen such as masons and thatchers. They led a simple and precarious life in overcrowded cottages on a diet of bread, potatoes and hard liquor.

Hawker was appalled by the drunkenness, the random cruelties to animals and the rejection of common decencies. He mounted a one-man crusade for reform. Spending freely of his wife's dowry, he started on the physical amenities. His first undertaking was to bridge a dangerous ford which had deterred anyone venturing far out of Morwenstow. He then built a rectory and a school with a house for the schoolmaster and restored the church. He was generous to a fault and, though he earned a decent stipend, he was always short of money.

Thus far, Hawker was in the mainstream of good parsons. But, like many of his breed, he was also a performer; he loved to make an impression. He dressed extravagantly, sporting a claret-coloured long-tailed coat over a fisherman's blue jersey with a red cross embroidered at the side to remind him of his Master's wounds. Like his parishioners, he wore tall fishing boots. For extra warmth he wrapped himself in a yellow poncho. He studied folklore and became obsessed with ancient superstitions of ghosts and goblins. At one time he kept a pet pig called Gyp which followed him about the parish like a dog. His flock were only too happy to inflate his idiosyncrasies. There was a story of him taking his six cats to church and excommunicating one of them when it caught a mouse on Sunday.[26]

On a cliff path he built a hut out of timber from wrecked ships where he composed mystical verse, little of which is remembered. Hawker is best known today for *The Song of the Western Men*, a ballad he composed before he came to Morwenstow. In a good mood, Hawker welcomed the loneliness of his clerical outpost as an inspiration for his literary efforts. More frequently and as he got older, 'this bleak, bare shore of the Bristol Channel' filled him with despair.

After storms, the waters of the Bristol Channel were often, as Hawker graphically put it, 'peopled with corpses', and his 'nervous terrors' about what each tide would bring in were accordingly 'great'. Sometimes it was a bloated body which had only become light enough to rise to the surface and float, after ten days or more of decomposing in the water. More often though, and this was the second circumstance which tormented Hawker, the sailors had been mutilated, literally cut to pieces on the rocks. Frequently, dismembered limbs were found – an arm, a leg, a hand. When the *Caledonia* was wrecked, 'a mangled seaman's heart' was discovered. After a wreck in 1859 five out of seven corpses buried by Hawker 'had no Heads – cut off by jagged rocks!!' Unrecognizable lumps of human flesh, known locally as 'gobbets', were collected in baskets. All were buried with decency.[27]

In his later years Hawker, like so many others, took opium as a medicine, in his case to relieve stomach pains. But, again, like many others, he became addicted and his aberrations multiplied.

Many a lonely or disillusioned parson turned to drink. While Bishop of Chester, Charles Blomfield had to reprimand a cleric who turned up drunk at a funeral and fell into the grave. Another miscreant defended his conduct by protesting that he had never been drunk on duty.[28]

There were encouraging signs of tighter discipline with a new generation of bishops ready to crack down on indolent parsons. The High Church and highly opinionated Henry Phillpotts at Exeter from 1830 (it was said that he ruled his diocese with an iron hand undisguised by any sort of glove) had a particular aversion to the hunting and shooting fraternity, though his success rate in containing their sporting instincts was patchy. A formidable bearing was of little avail when he took on John Froude, vicar of Knowstone. Many of the stories about Froude and his hunting prowess are apocryphal but it is on the bishop's own word that the miscreant avoided interview by feigning serious illness, on one occasion persuading his housekeeper to tell Phillpotts that he had typhus. The same afternoon he was out with his hounds. On another visit to Knowstone, Phillpotts gained entry to the vicarage where, in the dining room, he found 'six foxes' brushes, two of them bell-pulls with a fox engraved, and tally-ho! upon them'.[29]

There was a case to be made for the clergy who mixed with the community rather than standing aloof. In the hunting shires, a parson counted for little unless he could hold his own in the saddle. Much loved was the Revd Sir Henry Bate Dudley, who was master of an Essex hunt while rector of Bradwell-on-Sea. His most famous run ended in the churchyard of Cricksea or, rather, on the church roof, the fox having scrambled up an ivy-covered buttress followed by Sir Henry and six hounds. The kill took place on the leads of the chancel.[30]

Jack Russell, whose name lives on as a breed of Scottish terrier, was revered by his Swimbridge parishioners as much for his hunting exploits as for his force as a preacher. He was a sporting byword in Devon but, more to the point, in the words of one of his flock, he was 'as good a Christian, as worthy a pastor and as true a gentleman as I ever seed'.[31] One who was persuaded that hunting was unfitting for a clergyman, Bartholomew Edwards, rector of Ashill in Norfolk, remained an excellent judge of a horse. In a long career (he died within nine days of his hundredth birthday) he was absent from his church on only three Sundays.[32] In the Home Counties it was cricket that gave a parson the edge. If he was a good man at the wicket his popularity was assured. It was all a matter of degree. 'I am told, my lord, that you object to my hunting,' said a parson who confronted Bishop Phillpotts. Back came a snappy response. 'Dear me, who could have told you so? What I object to is that you seem never to do anything else.'

Phillpotts, the son of a Gloucester innkeeper, was conscious of his status and with a taste for the good life. On his appointment to Exeter, he sent ahead his newly employed secretary with the injunction 'to purchase for me some dozens of port, claret or sherry ... really old and good'.[33] A Tory of the far right, he could be fiercely confrontational, particularly when it came to disputes with the Evangelical tendency over Church ritual. But he was tireless in raising standards and encouraging the younger clergy who 'are deserving of all praise'.[34]

More liberal than Phillpotts but equally hostile to field sports was Charles Blomfield, who went to Chester in 1824 and later, as Bishop of London, was to be the front man of Church reform. He moaned that in Cheshire fox hunting was almost a religion in itself. His aversion had its origins in the days when he was the parson at Chesterford, on the road from London to Newmarket. Travellers stopped to change horses at a large inn close by the church. It happened that the first day of the Newmarket Spring Meeting coincided with Easter Monday, when hundreds were attracted to a riotous fair held in the open space in front of the inn, while Blomfield and his congregation were celebrating Holy Communion. As a result of his hard lobbying, the start of the Spring Meeting was changed to a Tuesday.[35]

A classical scholar of note, Blomfield was highly intelligent and not afraid to show it. He was a forceful if arrogant debater. His colleagues, as much as his adversaries, lived in fear of him. Sydney Smith, no mean judge of character, said of Blomfield that he enjoyed more power than any churchman since the days of Laud. He 'is passionately fond of labour, is of a quick temper, great ability, and thoroughly versed in ecclesiastical law'. By common consent, if Blomfield was late for a meeting no business was done until he arrived. Though a great believer in self-help and generally opposed to what had yet to be called 'welfare legislation', Blomfield campaigned for penal reform, arguing that young criminals needed special treatment, that those convicted of minor offences ought not to be confined with hardened criminals and that every prisoner should be helped to return to society.

Edward Stanley was a model parson of his day. When he took on the family living at Alderley in Cheshire, the parish had been neglected so badly that the former rector could boast of never having set foot in a sick person's cottage. Stanley laboured for thirty-two years to create a caring community before his appointment as Bishop of Norwich in 1837. Since his predecessor, the 'lazy and indulgent' Henry Bathurst, had died in harness at the age of ninety-three, it is not surprising that Stanley made an early impression as a more active bishop. He was also more of a reformer than Bathurst, though that worthy had once been reputed to be the only liberal bishop in the House of Lords.

Stanley spoke out for elementary education for all and refused to join in the clamour against dissenters. At his inaugural service at Norwich Cathedral before the mayor and civic dignitaries, priority seating went to 1,200 charity school children. Conservative parsons, who were thick on the ground in Norfolk, were mostly won over when they were invited to the palace to meet the leading men of the county. It sounds little enough, but, in the days when social divisions were sharp, it came as a pleasant surprise to the rural clergy to be treated as equals.

Then there was Samuel Wilberforce, who entered the history books as the chief protagonist for Church orthodoxy in the debate with T. H. Huxley ('Darwin's bulldog') on evolution as a religion-busting science. A forceful speaker, Wilberforce was also a skilled politician who was hard to pin down. The third son of William Wilberforce, who had led the campaign against slavery, he was raised in a strong Evangelical environment, but in his career, first as Bishop of Oxford from 1846, then of Winchester, he leaned towards the High Church – if not so far as his three brothers, all of whom converted to Rome. In his first speech to the House of Lords, Wilberforce defended the repeal of the Corn Laws, urging the clergy to put the welfare of the country before their own interest in maintaining the value of their tithe. He opposed public hangings and transportation, and had no time for the British tendency to rush into conflict to further its commercial power.[36]

In the popular press, Wilberforce was known as 'Soapy' or 'Slippery' Sam, possibly because he refused to be labelled, because, as he liked to say, he came out of every transaction with clean hands, or simply because he had the habit, when in full voice, of wringing his hands. Among the first of the bishops to take advantage of the railways, he was constantly on the move, urging his clergy to greater efforts, raising funds for new churches or sponsoring bright young ordinands for his diocese. One of his lasting achievements was to transform his bishop's palace at Cuddesdon into a theological college.

Lazy and ineffectual bishops were still a powerful contingent. Spending up to eight months a year in London as representatives of the Church at Westminster, they were delighted to hold forth on any subject while giving little attention to diocesan matters. That said, the trend of new appointments was in the right direction. What remained deficient was the manner in which the bishops were allowed to exercise authority. The Church Discipline Act of 1840 was supposed to extend the power of the bishops to rid the Church of incompetent, corrupt or dissolute clergy. But it remained near impossible to break the tradition of the parson's freehold. John Willis, rector of Haddenham in Buckinghamshire, was one of the first miscreants to test the law. A commission of enquiry found Willis guilty of having visited a brothel in Aylesbury and of being drunk in the pulpit. Willis made no attempt to deny the charges, which represented the least of his offences. His bishop was keen to act against him but ecclesiastical lawyers warned against expensive and probably abortive action. Willis was suspended for one year.[37] When William Cockburn, Dean of York, sold lead from the Minster roof and pocketed the proceeds, the archbishop deprived him of his office. But the archbishop was overruled by the Court of the Queen's Bench and Cockburn continued to serve as Dean until his death in 1858.

Clerical misdeeds were the lifeblood of the radical press, and it never went short of material. Charles Bampfylde, rector of Dunkerton in Cornwall from 1820 for thirty-five years, was known as the Devil of Dunkerton and was described by a fellow parson as a 'worthless, unprincipled man'. When local farmers called at the rectory to pay their tithes, Bampfylde sat at table with a bottle by his side and a brace of loaded pistols in front of him.

In 1829, Edward Drax Free, rector of Sutton in Bedfordshire, was another who took lead from the roof of his church to sell for scrap. But he was also found guilty of grazing cattle in the churchyard, using profane language, processing indecent books and prints, drunkenness and having illicit relationships with his maids. After twenty-two years of bad behaviour, he took a step too far when he attempted to have his squire fined for non-attendance at church. For this breach of etiquette, he was deprived of his living.

CHAPTER THREE

Reform

In the year of the future queen's birth, Robert Southey found reasons to believe that 'the state of religion in these kingdoms is better at this time than it has been at any other since the first fervour of the Reformation'. Lord Liverpool agreed, noting 'a great improvement in the clergy in the last twenty or thirty years', while John Hobhouse, elected as a radical MP in 1820, told the House of Commons that 'the religious feelings of the people had very much increased' since the start of the century.

But there was still a long way to go before the Church could claim to have put its house in order. Moreover, the likelihood of the Church, by its own volition, engaging in energetic reform was remote. Fortunately, the clamour for political reform, growing louder by the week, carried the Church along in its wake. When the Tories split over Catholic emancipation – an attempt to quieten Ireland, where seven-eighths of the people remained outside the Protestant embrace – a Whig government led by Lord Grey pledged modest changes in the constitution. After a struggle with the House of Lords, the 1832 Reform Act did away with rotten boroughs (some were controlled by the Church; in at least one constituency the parson was the only voter), increased the representation of growing towns and extended the franchise to one in six male adults.

This was hardly the stuff of revolution. Yet the substantial parliamentary vote against the Bill included all but two of the bishops. The fear was an encroaching democracy, that devil in waiting. It was not just diehard conservatives who had nightmares of mob rule. Even Thomas Babington Macaulay, a supreme optimist who believed the English to be the 'greatest and most highly civilized people', regarded universal suffrage with 'dread and aversion'. Democracy, he argued, was 'incompatible with property and ... consequently incompatible with civilization'.

Church leaders agreed. Speaking for the Hackney Phalanx, Joshua Watson appealed for clerical appointments by merit, restrictions on the movement of bishops to richer dioceses and the redistribution of Church property to make for a more effective administration. But he made clear his view that 'appointments are safest in the hands of high and responsible authorities', adding, 'I hate democracy in any shape, but of all shapes the worst is an ecclesiastical democracy.'[1]

The risks of broadening the constitutional power base had been demonstrated in 1830 by the overthrow of the French monarchy, or rather the overthrow of the Bourbon monarchy in favour of the House of Orléans. The after-effects in Britain caused near panic. Unrest was restricted largely to the south and east of the country, where farm workers took to breaking up threshers and other agricultural machinery, which they claimed would threaten their livelihoods. But official reaction was savage. Traditional loyalties put the clergy on the side of the landowners. There was no shortage of clerical volunteers to serve as magistrates.

There were even those who were ready to act as the local sheriff. In 1830, Robert Wright, rector of Itchin in Hampshire, rallied the tenants of the Duke of Buckingham to mount a guard on Avington House. When a mob, 300-strong, advanced on the mansion, they were met by Wright at the head of his private army. The confrontation was brief, prisoners were sent off to jail and the parson had his moment of fame in the national press. Radical anger erupted again when clerical intransigence threatened the Reform Bill. Ridicule and abuse rolled off the radical presses and there were disturbances whenever an eminent churchman appeared in public. The Archbishop of Canterbury was well advised to sit tight when his coach was hit by a shower of rotten vegetables. In Bristol, the bishop's palace was lost to arsonists. Modest reforms could no longer be resisted.

Bills to restrict pluralism and non-residence failed in 1835, but by then the Ecclesiastical Revenues Commission, set up in the year of the Reform Bill, had begun an exhaustive investigation into the value of every clerical living in England and Wales. The chief finding in a comprehensive thousand-page report was of gross inequality. While there was no denying the wealth of the Church, it was concentrated in few hands. To the surprise of the secular lobby, it was concluded that while a third of the clergy were doing very nicely, the majority were struggling. True, they were as well or better off than ordinary working parishioners, but the social conventions could not be ignored. The good parson was expected to maintain a standard of living that allowed for support to a variety of charitable causes, ranging from winter blankets for the poor to helping to pay for a village teacher. He could not do this and raise a family on the £100 a year or less earned by nearly a fifth of the English incumbents and over a quarter of Welsh parsons. Nearly 5,000 livings even lacked habitable parsonages. Norfolk and Kent were two of the richest counties, Cumbria was the poorest. Lumping all incumbents and curates together, their total income was estimated at £3.4 million. This contrasted sharply with the much-bandied guesses of the opposition, which ranged from £5 to £20 million.

The way forward had already been set out by Lord Henley,

the brother-in-law of Sir Robert Peel, who was raised to the premiership in 1834. In plain English (Henley was a lawyer who favoured the blunt approach) he proposed diverting money from the cathedrals and collegiate establishments to the poorer clergy. The practical details were to be left to a body of ecclesiastical and lay commissioners who would report annually to Parliament.

As that most pragmatic of politicians, Peel supported the Ecclesiastical Commissioners but, not wanting to commit too early, waited for them to come up with their own ideas on how reform might be achieved. The first Commissioners were senior clergy, with the Lord Chancellor heading a group of government ministers. Of the five clerical representatives, archbishops Howley and Harcourt played little part in the proceedings. This was fortunate, since both were given to waffle and indecision. 'That which at first sight offends us is not always wrong,' was one of Howley's pithier comments. And again, 'A system far short of theoretical perfection may be exquisitely adapted to the combination of circumstances in this mixed state of things.' Fortunately, the driving force of the Commissioners was Charles Blomfield, Bishop of London from 1829, supported by his two friends from Cambridge days, John Kaye, Bishop of Lincoln, and James Mark, Bishop of Gloucester. All three were reformers but Blomfield led the way.

A weaker man might have felt inhibited by the reminder that he had achieved high office by patronage, absenteeism and pluralism – the pillars of the Church he now seemed determined to demolish. But like his political mentor, Robert Peel, who had changed his mind over Catholic emancipation and was to do so again over the Corn Laws, Blomfield deserves credit for having the courage of his conversion. He put in train measures that, whatever their limitations, amounted to the biggest administrative overhaul of the Church since the Norman Conquest.

Change started at the top. For the first time, bishops' salaries were fixed and made more equitable. Canterbury headed the list at £15,000, while the lower ranks were put in the £4,000 to £5,000 bracket. The industrial rise of Lancashire and the West Riding was recognised with the creation of two new dioceses, while numbers were kept level by merging Bangor with St Asaph and Gloucester with Bristol. Savings of around £360,000 were found to support poor livings and new parishes in the cities. The downside was the protection offered to existing office holders, who, however incompetent or idle, were assured of a lifetime enjoyment of their privileges. This was one reason why expectations of a state subsidy were disappointed.[2] Taxpayers were not inclined to support more handouts when there were centres of clerical riches still to be tapped.

The realisation that popular opinion was not to be fobbed off served as a warning to those cathedrals harbouring conspicuous wealth. Durham was the first to act. Pre-empting moves to requisition its income from coal mining, which supported twelve canons, three of whom doubled as bishops, on a combined income of £40,000, the chapter resolved to found a theological college. This was soon to become Durham University, with the bishop's palace as part of its campus.

There was at least one immediate benefit for the ordinary parson. An attempt was made to introduce order into contentious payment of tithes, a major source of income for the clergy but one that was beset by angry disputes and interminable ill feeling. Until 1836, unless the farmers and their parson had agreed on a money payment in lieu of payment in kind, the tithe was literally a tenth of whatever the parish produced. Devious were the ways in which farmers tried to get the best of the deal. In 1822, the rector of Camerton in Somerset complained of 'shabby manoeuvring', having been given sixteen lambs as tithe only to find that one had a broken back.[3] It was not unknown for disputes to end in blows. By the Tithe Commutation Act the tithe was calculated on the average crop prices over the past seven years. There was an allowance for inflation but not for the fall in prices that followed the advent of the steam ship and the opening up of the American prairies. Still, the formula worked well enough for the best part of half a century.

Debate was at its hottest over the number of livings that could be held by one person. The compromise was to permit no more than two livings to be held jointly, their combined income to be under £1,000 and the distance between them a maximum of ten miles.[4] The measure was less revisionist than it at first appeared. Of the clergy with more than two livings, only 5 per cent exceeded the £1,000 barrier.

Again, the figures came as a surprise to the anti-clerical party. They expected them to be much higher. When enlightenment dawned they called for a ruling that in 'no case ought there to be more than one living vested in the same person'. That was a step too far for the House of Commons. Twelve years had to pass before another attempt was made to end pluralism once and for all, but, since life interests were respected, it was not until late in the Victorian period that 90 per cent of parishes could claim a resident incumbent.

It was the proud boast of Bishop Blomfield that the reforms of the Ecclesiastical Commissioners had saved the Church. They had at least introduced changes that prepared the Church for the modern age. But for many, reform had not gone far enough. Nonconformists welcomed the civil registration of births, marriages and deaths, which allowed for marriages to be held in dissenting churches.[5] However, they were less taken with an otherwise much-needed measure to introduce order and a degree of efficiency into municipal administration.[6] Under the new rules, local authorities were no longer responsible for repairs to churches. It was up to church wardens to collect the rates and to impose them where they had not been previously collected. The inevitable consequence was a series of highly publicised prosecutions against those who refused to pay, among them John Thorogood, who, falling foul of arcane law, went to prison only to find there was no way of getting out except by Act of Parliament.[7]

There was opposition, too, from the High Church. John Keble, Oxford's professor of poetry, fellow of Oriel and, famously, author of *The Christian Year*, probably the century's most popular volume of verse, took the opportunity of a sermon before the sheriff, judge and grand jury of the Oxford assizes to attack the introduction of a mild note of reality into the Irish Church. Eight bishoprics, hardly more than sinecures, were to be dispensed with, making savings which would go to supplementing small stipends and paying for church repairs. This, according to Keble, amounted to sacrilege. How could a parliament containing Dissenters, Roman Catholics and non-believers presume to legislate for the Church? A Church, moreover, the liberties of which had been guaranteed by Magna Carta? How long would it be before it was stripped entirely of all its authority and majesty?

The cause was taken up by the man who, more than any other, came to represent the High Church resurgence in England. John Henry Newman, fellow of Oriel and the incumbent of St Mary's in Oxford, saw the Church not as an ordinary institution subject to man-made laws but as a higher sovereignty enshrining the great doctrines of the Catholic faith. He called for the restoration of ancient rituals, led by priests whose authority stemmed directly from Christ's apostles and who had the power of absolution. The enemy was 'liberalism', which, for Newman, stood for atheism, immorality and democracy.

With his base in Oxford, the academic heartland of High Church Toryism, Newman could rely on a sympathetic hearing. In July 1833, shortly after Keble's assize sermon, a gathering of friends encouraged Newman, Keble and the ascetic and charismatic Hurrell Froude to produce a series of tracts for *The Times*, setting out the doctrines of the Reformed Catholic

Church of England. The tracts broke with tradition in more ways than one. Most theological pronouncements were associated with multi-volume tedium. A series of short, direct, low-price booklets, each focusing on a single issue, came as a welcome change. Benefiting from Newman's talent for writing clearly and persuasively on complex issues, the tracts were an immediate success.

Many years later, after Newman had converted to Rome, he explained what he and his friends had set out to accomplish and what had eventually led him to Catholicism.

> I had a supreme confidence in our cause; we were upholding that primitive Christianity which was delivered for all time by the early teachers of the Church, and which was registered and attested in the Anglican formularies and by the Anglican divines. That ancient religion had well-nigh faded away out of the land, through the political changes of the last 150 years, and it must be restored. It would be in fact a second Reformation – a better Reformation.[8]

Put simply, the aim was to restore the Church to its role as interpreter of Christianity while acting as the indisputable guide to human affairs.

The Tractarian message had strong appeal to young parsons and curates, the 'labouring clergy' or 'journeyman parsons' as they were known, struggling against the odds in often isolated parishes without much recognition or support from their superiors. Newman gave them a sense of purpose. He wanted, as he said, to 'magnify' their office. Moreover, he spoke with certainty, a characteristic hitherto the preserve of the Evangelicals. There were no 'ifs' and 'buts' in Newman's teaching. The Bible was historical fact. Philosophy was only useful as a buttress to orthodox theology. The way forward was clearly indicated. It was a straight road with no diversions.

In the first effective counter-attack against dissidents and secularists, Newman looked to strengthen faith by restoring dignity and beauty to the Church. His appeal was to believers who wanted a structured Christian base that was firmer and more visible than the simple, unadorned worship of the Evangelicals.

By evoking a lost age of purity and contentment, the Oxford Movement owed more than a little to the Victorian cult of medievalism, the fashionable escape 'from the frightening implications of the present and future into the romantic if indefinable past'.[9] It was the world of Walter Scott. Published in 1819, his wildly popular *Ivanhoe* is set in the twelfth century, when chivalry, 'the stay of the oppressed, the redresser of grievances, the curb of the power of the tyrant', brought harmony and reconciliation between rulers and their people. Taking his lead from Sir Thomas Malory's *Morte d'Arthur*, Scott crafted a medieval world with a contemporary feel. Eight of his Waverley novels are set in the Middle Ages.

In his make-believe conversations with Sir Thomas More,[10] Robert Southey lauded the feudal system as a mutually beneficial relationship between lord and serf. William Cobbett went further. It is hard to imagine what, if anything, Newman and Cobbett had in common, yet both could agree that the medieval social and religious model was far superior to the contemporary order. As Cobbett would have it, in the Middle Ages 'people were better off, better fed and clad ... than they ever have been since' and that 'labouring people were most kindly treated by their superiors'. The Reformation and latterly, the Industrial Revolution, had covered England with 'pauperism, fanaticism and crime', condemning millions 'to the extreme of misery'.[11] It was a myth, of course, but one that appealed to the thousands who turned up to watch medieval pageants as much as those who were inspired by Church ritual.

The medieval tendency stands out in any cross-section of Victorian culture and politics. Literature and art thrived on medieval themes. After Scott set the tone with the Waverley novels, Tennyson quarried the Middle Ages for the chivalrous ideas of *The Lady of Shalott*, *Morte d'Arthur* and *The Idylls of the King*. The medieval novel was taken up by Edward Bulwer-Lytton, William Harrison Ainsworth and G. P. R. James. In *Past and Present*, Thomas Carlyle contrasted the equitable world of the twelfth-century monastery with the modern 'cash nexus', which assumed that people were expendable economic units to be dumped in the workhouse when they had lost their usefulness.

Artists were obsessed by medievalism. Landseer produced *Bolton Abbey in Olden Time*, Frith painted the *Coming of Age in the Olden Time* and Maclise, *Merry Christmas in the Baron's Hall*. Rossetti portrayed female virtue, beauty and passion in a medieval wrapping, while the Gothic touch is very much in evidence in most of the work of the Pre-Raphaelites. The best of Gothic belonged to Burne-Jones, who spent the best part of his life on a 'quest too sacred to be found'. After spending nearly twenty years on a vast canvas, *The Sleep of Arthur in Avalon*, he died before it was finished.

Royalty, too, caught the Gothic bug. The curiosity here is that Prince Albert, an intelligent and sophisticated consort, was in the forefront of modern thinking. Yet he loved tradition, and Gothic suited his German upbringing. Victoria was an early convert, deeply resentful that, for her coronation, the customary medieval ball in Westminster Hall was abandoned to save expense. But Windsor was made thoroughly Gothic. Landseer painted Victoria and Albert in medieval costume and the Arthurian legend decorated the queen's robing room at Westminster, where she was portrayed as the bride of Albert in the guise of King Arthur. When Albert died, his tomb at Windsor was Arthur's tomb, bearing the familiar legend, 'I have fought the good fight. I have finished my course.'

It was with the Church, however, that medievalism had its strongest links. This was not surprising, since, modest reforms notwithstanding, the Church was tied closer to medieval precedent than any other national institution. The seeds of the Oxford Movement were cast on fertile ground.

With hindsight, it is plain that the Oxford Movement was part of the Roman Catholic rejuvenation that was spreading across Europe. This was not generally admitted among Tractarians who took care, at least in the opening phases of the movement, to distance themselves from Rome. They spoke lovingly of the ancient Church, with its saints and martyrs, while attempting to show that the Catholic view of orders and sacraments, shorn of what were airily dismissed as superstitions, represented the considered mind of the Church of England. Holding scrupulously to the letter of the Prayer Book, the Tractarians put faith before reason. It was the duty of the Church to inspire awe and reverence with services enriched by vestments and ceremonials that 'act insensibly on the mind' to bring out the 'beauty of holiness'. This was from Edward Pusey, Professor of Hebrew at Oxford and a celebrated scholar whose sentiments were promoted energetically by his fellow Tractarians. Placing the ancient church at the heart of Christian belief, they proclaimed a source of authority that transcended individual minds.

The Oxford Movement was soon to overplay its hand. With a leader such as Newman, with his questing, restless intellect, as ready to provoke as to persuade, it could not have been otherwise. If Keble had stayed close to the centre of the intellectual turmoil he had initiated, he might have exercised restraint. Instead, 'humble minded and self effacing',[12] he took himself off to Hursley, a village in Hampshire, where he settled as parson of All Saints to live the life he commended in the most frequently quoted verse of *The Christian Year*.

> The trivial round, the common task,
> Would furnish all we ought to ask,
> Room to deny ourselves; a road
> To bring us daily nearer God.

Not that Keble was entirely detached. He was in frequent correspondence with his fellow Tractarians but being shy of argument or new ideas and, depending on taste, endearingly or irritatingly naïve, he was at a loss to understand the passion his cause had engendered. His particular worry was Hurrell Froude, one of his closest companions, who made no secret of his conviction that the Reformation was the work of criminals and madmen.

A devoted medievalist, tall, handsome, clever and dogmatic, Froude was one who combined 'the gravity and authority of age with all the charms of youth'.[13] But his godliness was marked by an intellectual and religious intensity that was almost paranoid. As a consumptive with the expectation of a short life, Froude was a young man in a hurry. In his quest for holiness, and mortified by his moral lapses, he poured out his heart to Keble, who warned him against too much introspection, while holding back from blunt disapproval of Froude's undermining the Anglican Church.

Superficially, there was no reason why the Oxford Movement and the Evangelicals could not coexist peacefully. Both were strenuously opposed to parliamentary meddling, both wanted tighter Church discipline and both put absolute trust in the gospels. Newman himself was of Evangelical background. But as the theological debate opened up, areas of likely conflict became glaringly obvious. For one thing, Tractarians made no secret of their elitism. Their doctrine of reserve held to a distinction between the teaching appropriate to the weak and ignorant for whom the mysteries had to be spelt out in parables. They required, said Newman, 'the nourishment of children rather than grown men'.[14]

This was not what Evangelicals wanted to hear. It was bad enough to suggest that the scriptures were in need of interpretation, but worse still to claim that the only safe interpreters were those approved by the High Church party.

Their outrage produced a sharp response from Newman, who dismissed Evangelical clergy as 'creatures of the people'. He asked, 'Can any greater evil befall Christians than for their teachers to be guided by them instead of guiding?'[15]

It did not pass notice that Newman was increasingly inclined to echo sentiments favoured by Rome. Keble was more measured but he fully supported Newman's views on reserve. Indeed, he carried it over to poetry, going so far as to defend the practice whereby the Professor of Poetry at Oxford lectured in Latin on the esoteric nature of his art to ensure that the secrets were not divulged to the unworthy.[16]

Those who feared a slide towards popery had their worst fears confirmed with the publication of *Remains*, the journals and letters of Froude, who died in 1836, aged thirty-three. Jointly edited by Newman and Keble, the first volume (three others were to follow) gave full force to Froude's 'personal example of holiness, his romantic vision of the medieval Church, his corresponding denigration of the Reformation and his ambitions to "unprotestantize" the Church'.[17]

The hostile reaction – Thomas Arnold complained of 'extraordinary impudence of language against the Reformers' – came as no surprise to Newman, who doubtless welcomed another push on his journey towards Rome. But Keble was shocked and distressed. Overwhelmed by the death of Froude, 'one of his dearest companions',[18] Keble argued, artlessly, that to refuse to identify the Church with the Reformation was not in the least an argument for Rome. Quite the opposite. Froude was appealing to the ancient universal Church that preceded the Reformation and Rome.

The Evangelicals would have none of this. It was clear to them that the Tractarian regard for crucifixes and other images, vestments, candles on brightly coloured altars, holy water, processions, the waving of incense and flowers in the sanctuary amounted to a full-frontal attack on the Reformation. A war of words dominated the religious press, which all but ignored the rather more constructive thoughts of those who were seeking an accommodation of different views within a broad Church.

Thomas Arnold is best remembered as the reforming headmaster of Rugby and the inspiration for *Tom Brown's Schooldays*, but it was not on education alone that he made his presence felt. Arnold realised that feuding within the Church made it ridiculous in the eyes of the level-headed. Along with his friend Richard Whateley, Archbishop of Dublin, a liberal churchman, deeply committed to the 'march of mind', Arnold regarded High and Low Church as 'equal bigatories'.[19] 'The Church as it now stands,' he wrote in 1833, 'no human power can save.'

Like Newman, Arnold believed that an elite cadre of Christian thinkers could bring about the spiritual and social renewal of the nation. 'Religious society is only civil society fully enlightened,' he wrote in *Principles of Church Reform*, 'the State in its highest perfection becomes the Church.' But in sharp contrast to Newman, Arnold wanted to save the Church by reuniting all Christian bodies on the basis of easily defined moral principles based on those fundamental doctrines that were beyond dispute.[20]

It was not a strategy that found favour with many opinion leaders, each of whom has his ideological sanctuary. While there was something to be said for the clash of ideas as a stimulant for reenergising the Church, giving it a relevance that had been conspicuously lacking in the earlier part of the century, the religious debate was deeply rooted in prejudice. As John Morley observed, 'Labels are devices for saving talkative persons the trouble of thinking.' This became all the more obvious with the first stirrings of a Roman Catholic revival inspired by Pope Pius IX.

'Warm of heart and weak of intellect,' was how Prince Metternich described Pius IX.[21] He started his reign as a liberal, releasing a thousand political prisoners and lifting restrictions on the press. For a short time he was seen as the embodiment of the revolutionary fervour that embraced Europe in 1848. It was widely assumed that he favoured a united Italy. In fact, he supported nothing of the sort. His first concern was to protect his own authority and that of the Papal States. He declared against unification. In the general melee that followed, Pius was chased out of Rome, returning only when his safety could be guaranteed by a French garrison. Though technically the prince of Rome, his authority was complete only within the Vatican, from which he rarely ventured.

It was from this position of weakness that Pius decided to reinstate the Roman Catholic hierarchy for England and Wales. The justification was the increased number of Catholics, from some 30,000 at the turn of the century to three-quarters of a million, largely as a result of Irish immigration. But, like all immigrants of recent vintage, the Irish were mistrusted, not least by their fellow workers, who regarded them as unfair competition for labour. Bigotry thrived on the unfounded suspicion that they were set on imposing their version of Christianity – and this on behalf of a pontiff who was diminished on his home ground.

It did not help that the newly appointed leader of English Catholics, Cardinal Archbishop Nicholas Wiseman, was given to emotional orations liable to be interpreted as declarations of open warfare to win the heart and soul of Protestantism. *The Times* spoke darkly of 'papal aggression', while Prime Minister Lord John Russell described the Catholic initiative as 'insolent and insidious'.

Parliament wasted its time on a silly piece of legislation limiting the use of ecclesiastical titles, which was forgotten as soon as it was on the statute book. But the damage had been done. Anti-Catholic sentiment was all the stronger after Pius confirmed Metternich's view of his mental capacity by claiming infallibility. Taking his stand against 'progress, liberalism and civilisation', he brought into sharper relief the doctrinal struggle between the High and Low divisions within the Church of England.

CHAPTER FOUR

The Church Revived

Fired up by the rediscovery of the splendour of public worship, the Tractarians brought colour back into the church. Though averse to such a frivolous pastime as play acting, their regard for costume and ceremony gave church-going a sense of occasion that was close to theatre. Congregations were slow to adapt. While they could be persuaded to have windows cleaned, floors swept and churchyards tidied, they were instinctively averse to anything that could be construed as idolatrous.

Thinking back to mid-century, Edward Boys Ellman recalled: 'When I was first ordained, anything like church decoration was dreaded; the cross or even the candlesticks on the altar was looked upon as Popish. Flowers were considered the same. The only decoration ever indulged in was at Christmas. The decorations consisted of pieces of holly or other evergreens stuck on the tops of high pews, holes being bored in them to hold the branches.'[1]

Moving cautiously to avoid any suggestion that he was leaning all the way towards Rome, the High Church parson was likely to signal his intentions by sacrificing the black gown, said to make him look like a large crow when he raised his arms. Instead, a white surplice was favoured. If this passed muster, other innovations soon followed. The parson's white neck cloth or tie was abandoned in favour of the dog collar, though this had distinct Roman Catholic associations. The process of change was rarely smooth. In the 1840s in Exeter and London there were 'surplice riots', when the mob occupied churches to prevent services from being held.

When funds for church decoration were short, the parson improvised. In his collection of clerical anecdotes, Ditchfield tells the story of a rector who was at a loss to know how to brighten up his church until his wife went to the village wheelwright to buy a stock of vivid red, blue, green and yellow wagon paints. The church was transformed into a riot of colour.[2]

In 1870, the Revd Armstrong reflected on the early days of his twenty years' incumbency at East Dereham in Norfolk.

> Then, the altar was a miserable mahogany table with covering 50 years old; there was a vile yellow carpet; a Grecian reredos with daubs of Moses and Aaron; no painted glass, and the rail for the communicants intersecting the sedilla. Look at it now – an altar and super-altar of full dimensions, with flower-vases always replenished with flowers; candlesticks and candles; three altar-cloths changed at the seasons; the windows painted; a stone reredos highly painted and with a central Cross; rich carpet; credence table and a Bishop's chair.[3]

Stained glass regained its popularity, though techniques long lost had to be rediscovered. William Morris and Edward Burne-Jones are closely identified with the art, but it was Charles Earner Kempe, a Tractarian deterred from taking holy orders by a pronounced stutter, who left the strongest body of work in five cathedrals, King's College Chapel and a score of parish churches. Other fine artists in glass were Henry Holiday and the partners J. R. Clayton and Alfred Bell. Based on research by Charles Winston and W. E. Chance, the production of 'antique' glass allowed artists to create more sophisticated mosaics.

Even when ornamentation proved hard to introduce, much could be done to raise the appeal of church-going. The first move in this direction was the removal of box pews, much beloved by the squire and his relations. Built with high wooden partitions, these rooms within a room might contain a sofa, table and even, occasionally, a fireplace. In churches attached to grand country estates, refreshments were likely to be taken during breaks in the service. A well-documented story has one squire reading his letters and newspapers throughout the sermon. Exclusivity was all. The occupants of a box pew, who generally sat or knelt on three sides looking inwards, could not be seen by the rest of the congregation or even by the parson, unless he happened to be standing above them on the top level of a three-decker pulpit.

At Holy Trinity in Cookham a high pew dominating the centre of the church was designated for Sir George Young, formerly an Admiral of the Fleet, who took a rather grand view of his squirearchical entitlements. Not to be outdone, other local worthies raised the floor level of their pews only to find that the admiral had followed suit. It took stern words from the bishop to end this competitive pewmanship.[4]

In some village churches, the box pew was the only seating on offer; everyone else had to remain standing or kneeling throughout the service, though the more enlightened parsons insisted on benches along the walls for the aged and infirm, the origin of the phrase 'the weakest go to the wall'.

Well before the signs of a church revival, voices were raised against the class distinction imposed by the use of box pews. As early as 1790, Anna Barbauld, the radical poet and children's writer, railed against these 'gloomy solitary cells' which 'deform the building no less to the eye of taste than to the eye of benevolence and insulating each family within its separate enclosure, favour at once the pride of rank and the laziness of indulgence'.

The best that could be said of box pews or of any sections
of the church reserved for the gentry was that their rental
value brought in much-needed revenue. Parsons of ill-endowed
churches were particularly vocal in defence of traditional
practices. That their conservation was, in effect, a rejection of
the poor seemed not to have occurred to some clergy, though
others made plain their conviction that, whatever the social
conventions, all those who entered the house of God were on an
equal sitting.

When John Mason Neale went to Crawley in Sussex he
demonstrated his strength of purpose by taking an axe to the
box pews. Hawker did the same at Morwenstow. Among their
opponents were the uncompromising defenders of the rights of
property. John Sharp, the incumbent of Harbury in Yorkshire from
1834 to his death in 1899, had to go to law to defeat the diehards.
He met his costs by selling most of the furniture in the vicarage.

Pew allocation was beset by inconsistencies and conflicts. In his
parish church in Derby, the head of the Mozley family, a prosperous
businessman, closed on an agreement to rent a pew of five sittings
'at the usual rate of a guinea a sitting'. He was surprised to be told
that a new financial arrangement was to be put in place.

> The churchwardens announced at a vestry meeting that all the
> sittings in the centre aisle would for the future be let for what
> they would fetch. Naming an early day, they brought in Mr
> Eyre, a well-known auctioneer, who went from one pew door
> to another, inviting bids, and knocking down every pew to the
> highest bidder. More than a hundred people, many of whom
> had occupied their sittings all their lives, and their fathers before
> them, had to give way to new occupants, receiving no further
> notice than that on one Sunday the beadle told them they must
> not come to that place the next. But this was not the genteel part
> of the church; the occupants were of a lower caste; and even the
> successful bidders were now told shortly that they might have

to turn out at a very brief notice in case of their sittings being wanted by their betters.[5]

Change was piecemeal. Various attempts in Parliament to 'prohibit absolutely the appropriation of seats and buying of rents' failed for fear of upsetting the bishops. But the pressure was kept up by voluntary organisations such as the Free and Open Church Association. When St Barnabas opened in Pimlico in 1850, it became the first of the new London churches to allocate pews on the principle of first come, first seated. Nine years later, St Philip's, Clerkenwell, took the lead as the first London church with rented pews to abandon the system.[6] This caused rebellion in the middle-class ranks. 'Being placed too near, or even next, to those whose habits are wanting in the ordinary decencies of life,' was too much for one church-goer, who went on to complain of 'an odious American habit [presumably, spitting] which is really distressing to people of delicacy, or even of common decorum'.[7]

Class sensitivities doubtless persuaded the Archbishop of York to declare against the churchwardens of Beverley when, in defiance of their vicar, they abolished pew allocation. The absurdity of the dispute attracted wide press coverage, climaxing in a letter to *The Times*, in which the churchwardens dismissed the verdict of 'a bishop whose voice and face we hardly know', while holding out an olive branch to a parson 'whose comparative youth and inexperience may perchance be pleaded in extenuation of his temerity'.[8]

The archbishop backed down, though the standard guide for churchwardens, telling them that seating arrangements were subject to a bishop's approval, was still in force at the end of the century. The decline of rented seats accelerated with the dismantling of box pews and, more especially, with the introduction of the weekly offertory.

The three-decker pulpit soon went the way of box pews.

Traditionally, the bottom section was occupied by the parish clerk, who read out each line of a psalm for the benefit of the illiterate, and signalled the end of a prayer with a loud 'Amen'. At the second level, the parson conducted the service, ascending to the third tier to deliver his sermon. Under the new arrangements, the pulpit and reading-desk were on opposite sides of the nave to give a clear view of the altar, while the centre of activity moved to the chancel, where it has remained.

It was the Evangelicals who recognised the inspirational power of music. When they got used to the idea, congregations loved to sing. As they lifted their voices in united affirmation, the service became properly theirs. More conservative elements deemed popular music an incitement to 'enthusiasm', only one step short of unseemly behaviour. Instrumentalists, typically led by a flautist and a fiddler, along with a few vocalists, were acceptable as long as they were decently hidden in a gallery, at the west end of the church above and out of sight of the congregation. They did duty for the psalm and, in bigger churches, an anthem, when it was customary for the congregation to look towards the gallery (hence the expression 'turn to face the music').

Washington Irving has left us with his impressions of a village Christmas celebration, starting with a public argument about decoration.

> On reaching the church-porch, we found the parson rebuking the gray-headed sexton for having used mistletoe among the greens with which the church was decorated. It was, he observed, an unholy plant, profaned by having been used by the Druids in their mystic ceremonies; and though it might be innocently employed in the festive ornamenting of halls and kitchens, yet it had been deemed by the Fathers of the Church as unhallowed, and totally unfit for sacred purposes. So obliged was he on this point, that the poor sexton was obliged to strip down a great

part of the humble trophies of his taste, before the parson would consent to enter upon the service of the day.[9]

Then there was the music.

The orchestra was in a small gallery, and presented a most whimsical grouping of heads, piled one above the other, among which I particularly noticed that of the village tailor, a pale fellow with a retreating forehead and chin, who played on the clarionet, and seemed to have blown his face to a point; and there was another, a short pursy man, stooping and labouring at a bass viol, like the egg of an ostrich. There were two or three pretty faces among the female singers, to which the keen air of a frosty morning had given a bright rosy tint; but the gentlemen choristers had evidently been chosen, like old Cremona fiddles, more for tone than looks; and as several had to sing from the same book, there were clusterings of odd physiognomies, not unlike those groups of cherubs we sometimes see on country tombstones.

The usual services of the choir were managed tolerably well, the vocal parts generally lagging a little behind the instrumental, and some loitering fiddler now and then making up for lost time by travelling over a passage with prodigious celerity, and clearing more bars than the keenest fox-hunter to be in at the death. But the great trial was an anthem. Unluckily there was a blunder at the very outset; the musicians became flurried. Everything went on lamely and irregularly until they came to a chorus beginning 'Now let us sing with one accord,' which seemed to be a signal for parting company: all became discord and confusion; each shifted for himself, and got to the end as well, or rather as soon, as he could, excepting one old chorister in a pair of horn spectacles bestriding and pinching a long sonorous nose; who, happening to stand a little apart, and being wrapped up in his own melody, kept on a quavering course, wriggling his head, ogling his book, and winding all up by a nasal solo of at least three bars' duration.[10]

Though performances, at best, were generally mediocre, musicians were notoriously sensitive to criticism. A suggestion from the parson that a new tune might be tried or an old one abandoned, or that an instrumentalist should try harder to play notes in the right order, caused vitriolic rows. Notwithstanding the troublemakers, High Church parsons soon came to realise that services without music were dull and uninviting compared to services in the Nonconformist chapels. Choirs were formed, a few including women. Their place in the church was in the chancel, but while this gave them greater involvement in the service, complaints were made that they blocked the view of the altar. New and restored churches allowed for wider chancels.

More bells were rung. The bells called worshippers to church but they also announced the arrival in the parish of important visitors and marked local or national events. The trouble with ringers was that invariably each had his own ideas on what constituted a worthy peal. At East Dereham in Norfolk, the Revd Benjamin Armstrong confessed to his diary, 'Among the numerous characters difficult to manage ... such as clerks, schoolmasters, singers and organist ... the bellringers are often conspicuous.'[11] Personal animosities were the bane of the village parson.

Some Sundays are certainly more bright and joyous than others. To-day, owing perhaps to the east winds so long prevailing, people were cranky. The senior members of the choir would not attend church because they had quarrelled with the deputy organist; the needlework teacher would not attend Sunday School because she had quarrelled with the master's wife, and means to resign her post. Such is our love of self that God's teaching and service may take care of themselves while we enjoy our pique. The church was very cold and the congregation looked nipped.[12]

By the 1850s, the choir, often of children from the parish school, was an established part of Sunday services. The singers, who wore cassocks and surplices, were led by a harmonium or barrel organ. The latter was not well favoured since someone, usually a servant from the big house, had to act as grinder. The arrival of a harmonium, powered by pedals at the feet of the player, was an occasion of great excitement. Francis Kilvert oversaw an installation at his Langley church.

> Though a small instrument it quite filled the Church with sound. We placed it in the Baptistry close to the Font. This morning was an epoch in the history of Langley Church and the first sound of an instrument within the walls an event and sensation not soon to be forgotten. How this innovation, necessary though it has become, will be received by the Squire no one can tell. He has forced us to do it himself and opened the way for the change by dismissing George Jefferies, the chief singer, from his post of leader of the Church singing, but we expect some violence of language at least.[13]

In the event, all went well. The congregation enthused and the few disaffected were pacified by the squire. Less successful was the first appearance of a small organ at Stowford in Devon.

> An announcement was made to the parishes round that on the following Sunday the organ would be 'opened'. Accordingly a large congregation assembled. But when the voluntary was being played at the entry of the clergy the organ uttered a gasp and became silent. After some fumbling, and many whispers, the clerk stood forward and said: 'This here is to give notice, that the entertainment with the orging is persponed to next Sunday, as her bellies [bellows] be bust.'[14]

At Jevington in Sussex a barrel organ, hastily installed, having played a psalm for Sunday worship, could not be stopped from following up with 'Drops of Brandy' and 'Go to the Devil and Shake Yourself', popular numbers of the day but unappreciated by the parson.[15] Modern organs began to appear in the 1850s, though they were often simple instruments, pumped by hand and exhausting to play for very long. The first electric organs were built in 1868.

The Victorians were increasingly drawn to hymns as a source of comfort and consolation, a demonstration, however brief, of a community spirit of determination to overcome all obstacles. It has been estimated that a staggering 400,000 hymns were written between 1837 and 1901, though fewer than a thousand have survived and, of these, only a hundred or so continue to appear in hymn books.[16]

Church music thrived on the business skills of Alfred Novello (of Italian Roman Catholic descent) who adopted modern printing for cheap sheet music. No longer did choirs have to rely on sharing a single well-thumbed copy of a favourite hymn. In mid-century Novello reduced the cost of the score of the *Messiah* from six shillings to one shilling and four pence. In 1878 he published *The Cathedral Psalter*, which was soon adopted by most parish churches.

Interest in choral singing was further stimulated by government support for musical education. From 1839 to 1841, public money provided for mass weekly singing classes in the Exeter Hall in London's Strand. Singing was a regular and popular Sunday School activity.[17] Hymn writers came from all walks of life. It was an Isle of Wight ironmonger, Albert Midlane, who gave us 'There's a friend for little children', a hugely popular singalong for Sunday Schools where Heaven was portrayed as a happy home crowded with contented children.

There's a home for little children
Above the bright blue sky,
Where Jesus reigns in glory,
A home of peace and joy.
No home on earth is like it,
Or can with it compare,
For every one is happy,
Nor could be happier there.

The architect James Edmeston wrote more than 2,000 hymns including the evergreen 'Lead us heavenly Father, lead us'. When a severe winter kept Oswald Allen away from his duties as a Kirby Lonsdale bank manager, he put together a collection of 148 of his own hymns. Teachers and academics were among the keenest hymn writers. 'God is working his purpose out' came from the creative mind of Arthur Campbell Ginger, an assistant master at Eton, while Henry James Buckoll of Rugby became identified with the beginning and end of school terms throughout the country with his 'Lord behold us/dismiss us with thy blessing'.

Among the hymns that have retained their popularity are several by Mrs Cecil Francis Alexander, who published her *Hymns for Little Children* in 1848. With 'All things bright and beautiful', 'There is a green hill far away' and 'Once in royal David's city', it is not surprising that the collection went through more than a hundred impressions over the next fifty years. The profits were donated to an institute for the deaf. The daughter of the agent to the Earl of Wicklow and married to William Alexander, a Tractarian who became Archbishop of Armagh and Primate of all Ireland, Mrs Alexander was very much part of the establishment. Writing 'All things bright and beautiful', it would not have occurred to her that any offence would be taken to 'the rich man in his castle' and 'the poor man at his gate' being part of

God's plan. Later generations have accused her of endorsing inequality as a natural state, but, as Ian Bradley has pointed out, she was more concerned with showing that God's grace is equally available to all.

> The poor man in his straw-roofed cottage,
> The rich man in his lordly hall,
> The old man's voice, the child's first whisper,
> He listens, and He answers all.

Simplistic it may have been, but the hymn, 'far from being about the divine ordaining of inequality, is rather about God's indifference to human distinctions of rank and wealth'.[18]

It was the clergy who were the strongest contingent of hymn writers. It is thanks to Henry Baker, vicar of Monkland in Hertfordshire, that we have 'The King of love my Shepherd is'. Sabine Baring-Gould wrote 'Through the night of dark and sorrow' and 'Onward Christian Soldiers', which gained enormous popularity when set to a march by Arthur Sullivan.

'The Church's one foundation' was by Samuel Stone, a curate of Windsor, while John Ellerton, a Cheshire vicar, was responsible for eighty-six hymns, including 'The day thou gavest, Lord, is ended', which entered the list of all-time favourites when it was chosen by the queen for the celebration of her Diamond Jubilee. For generations the most popular hymn in the English language, 'Abide with me', was written by Henry Francis Lyte, a West Country clergyman, in 1847. Suffering from tuberculosis, he set the words to music just three weeks before he died.

In 1853 Thomas Helmore published *Carols for Christmastide, set to ancient melodies*. Though 'Hark the herald angels sing' was heard at Christmas before Victoria was born, it took more than a decade for carol services to become established. A fine example was set by Hawker, who had his choir singing carols from house to house throughout Christmas Eve. Christina Rossetti wrote 'In the Bleak Midwinter' in 1870, though it was not recognised as a hymn until the next century. The carol service of nine lessons was the creation of Bishop Benson and was first heard at Truro Cathedral.

That hymns became a prominent feature of almost every church service had less to do with the words as with the accompanying tunes. The most prolific of Victorian hymn tune composers was John Bacchus Dykes, vicar of St Oswald's in Durham. The verses he set to music include 'Holy, holy, holy, Lord God Almighty', 'We plough the fields and scatter' (a translation of a German hymn, incidentally), 'Eternal Father strong to save', otherwise known as 'For those in peril on the sea', and John Henry Newman's 'Lead, kindly light'. The composer of over 300 hymn tunes, Dykes' work appears in every hymn book published between 1860 and 1900.

> No one better epitomizes the distinctive musical style of Victorian hymnody, with its lush chromatic harmonies, heavy use of repeated notes and stationary basses, close affinity to part song and parlour ballad and dramatic use of mood and melody to heighten the emotional and spiritual impact of the words.[19]

Rarely asking for payment, Dykes was happy for his tunes to be used by all denominations.

As music became an integral part of the church service, a profusion of hymn books (over 1,200 collections were published between 1837 and 1901) was consolidated into *Hymns Ancient and Modern*, first published in 1861. *The Hymnal Companion to the Book of Common Prayer* and, from the SPCK, *Church Hymns*, appeared in 1870. Some 250 hymns were shared by all three collections. The new hymnals were not always welcome.

When the curate at Middleton, near Manchester, introduced *Hymns Ancient and Modern*, the lady of the manor sent her maid to church to remove the books. 'There was a fearful row but the books were returned, and used.'[20]

Sacred music with full orchestra and choir was once again heard in the cathedrals. The tradition had almost died except in Gloucester, where an annual concert, to raise money for 'the widows and orphans of the distressed clergy', demonstrated the 'united charms of solemn strains and exquisite architecture'. The Revd Francis Witts was there in 1823 when he and his family had good seats in the choir.

> The Cathedral was extremely crowded. The orchestra is erected in front of the Organ facing the altar; the area between the pulpit and altar filled with benches, the space occupied by the altar is covered by raised sittings, one behind another in ranges, up to the top of the screen, and to-day, there were arranged here various schools, the young ladies of each being dressed uniformly, which was a very pretty sight. On each side of the inner choir, the large arches above the stalls, opening into the transepts were filled with temporary galleries, that on the right being appropriated to the friends of the lay stewards, that on the left to those of the clerical stewards. These galleries being almost wholly filled with ladies in elegant morning dresses present a most beautiful parterre to the eye. The Dettinger Te Deum, the Overture to Esther, Dr. Boyce's Anthem (Charity) and Knyvett's new Coronation anthem were the musical treats for the morning.[21]

Occasions such as this were soon part of almost every cathedral calendar. By mid-century, Llandaff was the only cathedral without choral services.

There were other less imposing but no less significant signs of changing times. Around 1883 the first lists of past vicars hanging on the walls of country churches appeared, along with the first boards for hymn numbers. By 1870, most churches had collection bags or plates, though in some rural parishes where the church rate was collected farmers protested that they were being asked to pay twice to support their church. That the Prayer Book called for a collection of alms for the poor every Sunday did not impress them.

The extent to which an individual parson could shape the style and content of church services varied from parish to parish. In January, 1865, Benjamin Armstrong visited St Mary Magdalene in London's Munster Square where Edward Stuart, the founder and chief benefactor of the church, was a dedicated Tractarian. Armstrong could hardly believe the vestments and incense.

> When one thinks of the rows caused 20 years ago by preaching in a surplice, one feels that the public mind must have undergone a great change to tolerate this. Even now, it would only go down in isolated and exceptional places.[22]

Armstrong would have dearly liked to follow Stuart's example at his own Norfolk church but while he was able to persuade his choir to wear surplices, he could not take the support of his congregation for granted.

> In my Annual Church Report I suggested chanting the psalms, and omitting the litany from the morning service on the grounds that I had the Bishop's permission, and that the litany was always used at a later service. I soon found, however, that the congregation *did* object. I gave up the idea, seeing that good generalship is seen by knowing how to retreat as well as how to advance. The remonstrances which I received were of a very kind and friendly nature, and, by yielding with a good grace, I do not think that I have lost ground. It all shows how people love a grievance for its own sake. All are complaining of the length of the service, yet, when you propose to shorten it, they object.[23]

Fear of encroaching Catholicism surfaced at intervals over many years.

A Norwich weekly paper, of a scandalous nature, and having correspondents in each town, has of late been attacking me and my son [who acted as his curate] for 'Romish' proceedings. To-day, having to go to Norwich, I determined to call on the Editor of this paper – *Daylight* – and demand the name of the contributor. I called and told him that an action would be brought if the thing was repeated. The Editor said that his only justification was the belief that the charge was true, but, on my describing the nature of our services and pointing out that the Bishop had joined in them, that I was on good terms with the parishioners, including many dissenters, he confessed that he had been labouring under a mistake, and that more caution would be observed by him for the future. It is clear that I have an enemy, and also, judging by internal evidence, that he is a regular attendant at Church![24]

High Church parsons favoured weekday services. By the 1860s, it was not uncommon to have morning and evening prayers, sometimes both.

Special services such as the Harvest Festival gained favour as an alternative to the traditional drunken celebrations, pagan in origin, that were liable to get out of hand in the absence of a restraining clerical influence. Several parsons claimed credit for introducing the Harvest Festival, among them Hawker of Morwenstow, Piers Claughton, rector of Elton in Huntingdonshire, and G. A. Davison at East Brent. An official form of service for Harvest Festival was introduced in 1862. Invariably the service and a procession with all the villagers taking part were followed by a dinner of beef and plum pudding and beer, paid for by the wealthier farmers. Women and children were given a tea, sometimes a more substantial 'knife and fork' tea.

Annual fairs were also linked to church services. Francis Kilvert has left us an Arcadian description of dressing his church for the Hay-on-Wye Fair.

Wild hops, bright red apples, boughs loaded with rosy apples and quantities of bright yellow Siberian crabs. At the school the children were busy sorting out corn from a loose heap on the floor, sitting among the straw and tying up wheat, barley and oats in small sheaves and bundles,. Gipsy Lizzie was amongst them, up to her beautiful eyes in corn and straw. The schoolmaster, the boys and I gathering stringed ivy from the trees in the Castle Clump. The Miss Baskervilles dressing the hoops for the seven window sills with flowers and fruit. Mrs Morrell undertook to dress the reading desk, pulpit, and clerk's desk, and did them beautifully. Then Cooper came down with his men carrying magnificent ferns and plants and began to work in the chancel. One fine silver fern was put in the font. Gibbins undertook the font and dressed it tastefully with moss and white asters under the sweeping fronds of the silver fern. Round the stem were twined the delicate light green sprays of white convolvulus. The pillars were wreathed and twined with wild hop vine falling in graceful careless festoons and curling tendrils from wreath and capital. St Andrew crossed sheaves of all sorts of corn were placed against the walls between the windows, wheat, barley and oats with a spray of hop vine drooping in a festoon across the sheaf butts and a spray of red barberries between the sheaf heads. Bright flowers in pots clustered round the spring of the arches upon the capital of the pillars, the flower pots veiled by a twist of hope vine. Mrs Partridge returned from Worcestershire this afternoon and brought and sent us two magnificent branches of real hops from the Worcestershire hop yards. These we hung drooping full length on either side of a text Mrs V. had made, white letters on scarlet flannel, 'I am the Vine. Ye are the branches. Without Me ye can do nothing.'[25]

CHAPTER FIVE

Doing Good

The Victorians had a passion for good causes, although popular images make this hard to believe. Benevolence does not sit easily with a society of established landed gentry, hard-headed entrepreneurs and empire builders united in their respect for property and their aversion to any sort of government interference that threatened their freedom of action.

But unfettered capitalism, promoted by Adam Smith and justifiably credited with Britain's commercial success, did not preclude charity, a cardinal principle of Christianity. The Church and, in particular, the Evangelical Church, stressed the need to reconcile rights with social responsibilities. It was the duty of the individual to help the less fortunate. As William Wilberforce wrote, it was not enough for the Christian to be 'serious' and 'earnest'. He had to be seen to be both.[1]

In the last two decades of the eighteenth century, innumerable charities were set up to provide hospitals and dispensaries for the poor, refuges for the destitute and alms houses. All of them were led by the Anglican Church or by one of the Nonconformist sects. When the Society for Bettering the Condition of the Poor was created in 1796, William Wilberforce was among the founders.

An MP from 1784 and a loyal member of the established Church, Wilberforce made his life's work one of the greatest humanitarian campaigns of his or any other century – the abolition of slavery. The first part of his objective, the ending of British participation in the shipping of slaves, he achieved in 1807, though slavery itself remained legal until 1833. In the years between, Wilberforce was the guiding spirit of the Clapham Sect, the Evangelical equivalent of the High Church Hackney Phalanx, described as 'a network of friends and relatives ... bound together by their shared moral and spiritual values'.[2] They were all well off but lived an almost monastic life, dedicating themselves to good works and noble causes. The Saints, as they were commonly known, organised petitions and public meetings, lobbied politicians, published a journal, *The Christian Observer*, and dozens of tracts against the strongly defended view that slavery was an economic cornerstone of the Empire and that owning slaves was on par with owning property and thus inviolate.

Wilberforce's early biographers bestowed on him a mantle of saintliness. 'At midnight on 31 July 1834,' wrote Sir Richard Coupland, 'eight hundred thousand slaves became free. It was more than a great event in African or British history. It was one of the greatest events in the history of the world.'[3] But Wilberforce was no revolutionary. He wanted to ameliorate conditions with schools and hospitals and less barbaric criminal laws, but not to change society out of recognition.

> The more lowly path of the poor, has been allotted to them by the hand of God ... it is their part faithfully to discharge its duties and contentedly to bear its inconveniences ... if their superiors enjoy more abundant comforts, they are also exposed to many temptations from which the inferior classes are happily exempted.[4]

This was a view shared by nearly all the clergy, whatever their liturgical persuasion. They also believed that charity was superior to intervention by a secular government. While standing for the underdog, the typical parson defended the *laissez-faire* economics of a wealth-creating society knowing that it was bound to have losers who deserved their support. It all seemed so straightforward. In practice, the philosophy was riddled with contradictions. *Laissez-faire* was not, nor could ever be, entirely comprehensive. It was all very well for Wilberforce to see the 'hand of God' directing the 'lowly path of the poor' but was it God who also subscribed to open sewers and fever-ridden tenements or approved the sweated labour of small children? Did not these offences against humanity call for a political solution?

Yet, even by modern welfare standards, the case for state intervention was not always self-evident. It could go horribly wrong, as it did with the well-intentioned attempt to update the Poor Law. The traditional system of poor relief, with its medieval roots, charged each parish with providing for the destitute who were born and lived locally. The assumption was of people living in small, detached communities where drifters were easy to identify. With a rising population and the migration to the industrial towns, this was no longer practical.

Pauperism increased, particularly in depressed rural areas, and the cost of poor relief rose precipitously, a four-fold increase between 1780 and 1830. Moreover, received opinion had it that the Poor Law did most harm to those it was supposed to help by penalising thrift, undermining self-reliance and lowering wages. In other words, poor relief was self-defeating. This is not too far from the arguments heard today against the indiscriminate handing out of welfare benefits. However, by a curious twist, the abuses of the Poor Law favoured those who paid out rather than those who received.

Tom Mozley, parson and journalist, recalled his father's appointment in 1826 as Overseer of the Poor in Gainsborough. For Mozley senior, a successful businessman, this was his first experience of local administration. He was shocked at the blatant exploitation by employers keen to keep down wages by 'throwing their old servants on the parish and receiving them back as paupers on the understanding that the parish must supplement their earnings out of public funds'. There was an easy excuse. 'Every employer found he was paying for other people's poor and subsidising his neighbour's wages-book; so, in self-defence, he demanded the same contributions in return.'[5]

A solution was provided by Edwin Chadwick, a thorough-going bureaucrat well before the term was in currency. As secretary to Jeremy Bentham, Chadwick shared his master's devotion to efficiency, conducive to 'the greatest happiness of the greatest number'. Though a public servant of talent and vision, he had the fault of many of his breed of treating people as units. Sensitivity was not his strongest suit.

As drafted by Chadwick, the Poor Law Amendment Act abolished outdoor relief except for the aged and infirm. All others could obtain relief for themselves and their families only within a workhouse, hideously misnamed, observed Carlyle, since it did not offer any work. This was meant to put an end to cheap labour subsidised by the rates and encourage able-bodied men to seek work wherever it could be found. To this end, logic dictated that workhouse conditions should be sufficiently unpleasant to make hard, ill-paid labouring a happy alternative.

The legislation was greeted angrily in the country, not least from the clergy, whose role in the parish vestries was supplanted by a new system bringing together groups of parishes under Boards of Guardians, elected by ratepayers and accountable to full-time commissioners based in London. But there was little opposition in Parliament, where prevailing opinion sided with the economist David Ricardo, who assumed that a fixed proportion of the national wealth was available for wages so that whatever was paid out in poor relief had to be deducted from the 'wages fund'. If hearts needed further hardening, the Revd Thomas Malthus had taught wrongly, if convincingly, that short of moral restraint, population growth was bound to outpace the means of subsistence.

Bishop Blomfield spoke in the House of Lords in support of the Poor Law Amendment Act. He hoped 'that the people would soon be induced to exercise a foresight which would render relief unnecessary'.[6] Education was the way forward. Parsons across the country took him at his word, throwing their energies into setting up schools but also initiating a variety of projects to mitigate what was soon seen to be a piece of retrograde legislation. Chadwick, who was not easily put down, recovered his administrative lustre at the forefront of a movement for sanitation and clean water, although, surely coincidentally, a Poor Law that saved money was more popular with politicians and vested interests than proposals for spending money to prevent the spread of disease.

As the new rule on outdoor relief began to bite, Robert Hawker of Morwenstow rose to the challenge with characteristic energy. He attacked the discrimination against poor labourers, 'who have each a wife and four children to feed and clothe on seven shillings a week, because such men are forbidden to be relieved from the parish rate,' Hawker collected enough money to pay each family a shilling a week for the three months up to Christmas.

> We anticipate a gloomy winter for the poor; the potato harvest, their chief article of food, has failed; the scantiness of the barley and oat crops will throw many threshers out of employment, and we would fain therefore make every effort for their relief.[7]

The Poor Law, said Hawker, 'made poverty a guilt and interfered with Christian alms'. That the general prohibition on outdoor relief was not more rigorously enforced was largely thanks to the humanity of parochial clergy.

At Radford in Nottinghamshire, where Samuel Cresswell had succeeded his father as rector, a gardens scheme allowed for parishioners, regardless of religious affiliation, to rent small plots of land below the market rate. A similar scheme was introduced at Sherington in Buckinghamshire, where the Revd J. C. Williams divided 11 acres of glebe land into forty-four allotments. An incidental result was that his Sunday congregation, morning and afternoon, more than doubled.[8]

When H. T. Becher was curate of Thurgarton in Nottinghamshire, he led a campaign to ensure that every labourer had a garden and enough grazing for a cow. In Northamptonshire, the practice of letting out small plots of land 'has become almost universal ... the clergyman of the parish being in general the person who has set the thing on foot'.[9]

Such enterprises, insofar as they promoted self-reliance, might have been expected to win the unanimous approval of the respectable middle class. Not so. Farmers and landlords were keen on open competition for others but not when it entered their orbits, particularly when it threatened, if ever so slightly, to undermine their bargaining power. For a labourer to keep a small garden and a pig was just about acceptable. But to permit him an allotment and a cow was to divert him from work on the farms. In Suffolk, farmers pledged to 'refuse all employment and show no favour to any day labourer who should hold an allotment'.[10]

Less contentious were the thrift clubs sponsored by the clergy. By the late 1830s, it was a rare parish that did not boast a clothing or coal club into which members paid a penny a week. Almost all were run from a parsonage. Local savings banks guaranteed by the squire and managed by the parson were increasingly common. The Revd Samuel Best, rector of Abbotts Ann in Hampshire, declared roundly that care of the poor was 'a chief object of our ministry' for 'temporal as well spiritual interests are committed to our cause'.[11]

The benevolent parson braved a torrent of criticism from those who feared that subsidising the poor would simply encourage them to remain poor. This miserly sentiment was supported by examples where money given to buy food went on drink. The remedy, increasingly adopted as the century advanced, was to substitute 'mendicity tickets' for money and gifts. The tickets, redeemable at local shops, were not a guarantee of good behaviour but they did go some way towards preventing relief money from flowing into the pub.

There were those parsons who solved the problem by actually going into retailing, for example, by buying essential goods in bulk to sell on to poorer parishioners at wholesale prices. At Stoneleigh in Warwickshire, the Revd J. W. Leigh managed a fully stocked cooperative store. Leigh belonged to a wealthy landowning family but disclaimed any suggestion that he was subsidising the shop. It was run strictly on business lines by a committee of working men, with Leigh acting as chairman. Other cooperative enterprises run under Church auspices included a store at Castle Combe in Wiltshire. At Assington in Suffolk, there was even a cooperative farm.

Many and varied were the semi-commercial activities undertaken by the clergy. In an 1837 enquiry into the working of the Poor Law in West Meon in Hampshire the curate reported:

A clothing club in which there are 50 poor people, and in addition to 5s that they subscribe, 5s is added. Archdeacon Bailey has a clothing club of his own, of 20 members. There is a clothing club in the school of 30 members. Men's Provident Society, 15 members; the men pay per week, sixpence, and have added by the rector, three pence to each shilling; that is laid out for them at Christmas in fuel and clothing. There is a sick agricultural club, with 90 members in it; there is a Trades' Union Friendly Society with 36 members in it; and I myself have started a fuel club, at which I sell coals and faggots at half price.[12]

The impact of the Evangelical conscience cannot be overrated. After Wilberforce, the leading lay churchman in the Evangelical fold was Lord Ashley, or Earl of Shaftesbury as he was to become, the epitome of Victorian philanthropy. Though saddled with heavy debts after inheriting the earldom, he spent lavishly on schemes for moral and social regeneration ranging from the Pure Literature Fund and the Cabmen's Shelter Fund to the Flower Girls' Mission and the Metropolitan Drinking Fountain Association. He fought hard for the better treatment of the mentally ill and for a ban on small boys climbing into chimneys to hack away the soot. But his greatest contribution was to put himself at the head of a campaign to limit the employment of young children in the textile mills, where they were shamelessly exploited as cheap labour. Though he did not relish government interference in commerce, it was of greater import that 'children cannot protect themselves and are therefore entitled to the protection of the public'.

With more than a little help from landowner MPs, who were only too happy to traduce upstart manufacturers, the necessary legislation was introduced in 1833. The terms were modest. Children under nine were no longer permitted to work in the textile mills, while those between nine and thirteen were limited to a maximum eight-hour day. Another four hours could be worked by children over thirteen. Two hours a day were set aside for education. With only four inspectors to check that Parliament's wishes were carried out, the law was given scant respect in some quarters. Even so, there was soon a noticeable fall in the number of child workers. Shaftesbury continued to fight for tougher rules on a wider industrial base, while encouraging attendance at one of his ragged schools.

The strongest or, at least, the most energetic movement in

the Church for the first thirty years of the nineteenth century, the Evangelicals raised standards of clerical responsibility and gave the Church a renewed sense of purpose and direction. They reached the peak of their vitality in the mid-century, when Evangelical clergy numbered 6,500, over a third of practising clergy.[13]

By the passion of their commitment, the Evangelicals influenced social behaviour way beyond the confines of chapel or church. Hundreds of philanthropic bodies, ranging from soup kitchens to mission halls, were started on their initiative. In south London, members of the congregation at the activist Evangelical parish of Christ Church, Gipsey Hill, complained of so many parochial organisations that 'one really grows bewildered among them'.[14]

The puritan ethic was 'the moral cement of English society'.[15] It defined concepts of decency and respectability. It placed work and duty at the heart of personal fulfilment and while repressing young lives it produced a strong psychological drive for success in later life. It was also responsible for much of the cant and hypocrisy that disfigured Victorian life. Wilberforce was among the more liberal of his party. He had no time for petty doctrinal differences. But he shared the meddling tendencies of self-anointed moralists.

Everyone accepted that social and family behaviour could bear improvement. It was less obvious that this could be achieved by the insidiously named Society for the Suppression of Vice. Gambling, prostitution and drunkenness were among its legitimate targets, but the society also brought prosecutions against what it regarded as immoral literature and it came down hard on such innocent pastimes as dancing and card games.

Sydney Smith was among those who took delight in pointing out the inconsistencies. The society, he wrote, 'was bent on suppressing not the vices of the rich but the pleasures of the poor', and he went on to accuse the society of wanting to wrap the nation in 'decorous gloom' while leaving untouched the gambling houses of St James. Particularly offensive was the society's use of informers to enforce laws that had wilted on the statute book, such as those on Sunday observance. This, said Smith, was not to deny, say, the evils of heavy drinking, but to deplore the society's dictatorial methods of going about its mission, which 'creates so much disgust that it almost renders vice popular'.

Wilberforce denied any problem with amusements that were 'really innocent', but deciding what fell into this category was no easy task. Until late in the century, Evangelicals were inclined to play safe by imposing blanket prohibitions on anything that might 'sanction the representation of sin'. Novels were taboo, as were stage performances. Social recreation was a moral minefield. Preachers were driven to a frenzy of denunciation against dancing. Charles Clayton, vicar of Holy Trinity, Cambridge, spoke out against the university Bachelors' Ball of 1857, contending that a murderer had been prompted to his reckless crime by the sight of six clergymen at a ball.[16]

With a faith immune to doubt or criticism, Shaftesbury was a vocal advocate of Sunday observance. There was a strong case for limiting the hours of hard toil. But Shaftesbury was among those who supported legislation to ban all Sunday trading and to prohibit 'any pastime of public indecorum, inconvenience or nuisance'. He even succeeded in stopping military bands from playing in London parks. Opponents were quick to take Sydney Smith's point that it was the poor who bore the brunt of the law. Relying on servants, private carriages and well-stocked larders, the rich could continue to treat Sunday like any other day.

Introduced to the House of Commons in 1833, a bill to reinforce Sunday observance was lost by just six votes. But this left in place laws that could be applied with greater rigour. One of the many prosecutions that became a standing joke was brought against Thames fishermen who had lowered their nets on a Sunday. It emerged that further along the banks, gentlemen fishing with rods and line were apparently beyond the law. The accused were let off without a fine but had to promise not to repeat the offence.

In 1835, when the feast day at Bardney, near Lincoln, fell on a Sunday, the squire, a sabbatarian and magistrate, forbade the sale of apples and ordered the churchwarden to prosecute a stallholder for selling gingerbread to children. This brought a letter of protest to the local newspaper. The feast was 'altogether quite a village concern'. There were 'no pickpockets, no thimble-men. ... The poverty of the place protects it from the intrusion of vice, and hard labour – a thing you know very little about – secures it from any disposition to uproar.' Children, the writer went on, enjoyed their gingerbread and lollipops, men their pipes. 'There is a luxury in it, which gentlemen like you who have nothing to do but to visit and be visited, and who have nurseries at the other end of the house, can form no idea of.' Nevertheless the gingerbread man was tried, convicted and fined.[17]

Another attempt to close down the country once a week was made in 1855, when the outrage in London was such as to persuade Karl Marx that the revolution had started. The Revd Armstrong was a witness to the mob protest. Carriages were stopped in the street and passengers told to get out and walk. They were sent on their way to cries of, 'Go to church.'[18] The bill was withdrawn but the dismal Sunday continued to encroach, particularly where the temperance movement was strong. It was a fear of the demon drink that led to the Sunday closure of the Crystal Palace. From 1881, no pub in Wales was allowed to open on a Sunday.

CHAPTER SIX

Nurturing the Mind

The Victorian parson spent as much time in the classroom as in church. What gave him his passion for education? The reasons were spiritual and social. Teaching godly ways made godly people, whose respect for authority on earth directed them towards the highest authority in Heaven. But drawing the two strands together was the conviction that knowledge brought self-awareness, the realisation of the fulfilment to be gained from the common decencies of life, of love and charity. As the radical theologian F. D. Maurice put it, 'We have a commission, and authority, and ability to educate the whole mind of the country.'[1]

Early in the century, promoting some form of popular education was a lively concern of the Society for Bettering the Condition of the Poor, though little was done beyond supporting existing charity schools or the common dame schools, many of which were not more than child-minding establishments. The typical dame school had no building of its own. Space was taken wherever it could be found – in a garret or cellar, in a barn or church vestry or a shed in the graveyard. Bare literacy, and often not even that, was required of a teacher, who was likely to be a wife or widow experienced in raising an unruly brood, or one of the army or navy wounded who had no other way of scraping a living. There were frequent reports of barbaric conditions. In one cramped room was found eleven children gathered round a teacher who was bedridden with measles. A few days earlier a child had died of the disease.[2]

There were exceptions that proved the rule. Thomas Cooper, a leading Chartist who had a chequered career as a teacher, journalist and poet, praised his dame school, where reading and spelling were 'expertly and laboriously taught'. At a young age, he could pronounce hard names from the Bible 'like the person in church'.[3] But it was stretching a point to call this education.

Among those with a voice to be heard, most held that a little more learning was a dangerous thing. The case against schools as nurseries of sedition was put in the House of Commons in 1807 when an attempt was made to legislate for the instruction of pauper children.

> The scheme would be found to be prejudicial to the morals and happiness of the labouring classes; it would teach them to despise their lot in life, instead of making them good servants in agriculture and other laborious employments to which their rank in society had destined them; instead of teaching them subordination it would render them factious and refractory as was evident in the manufacturing counties; it would enable them to read seditious pamphlets, vicious books and publications against Christianity; it would render them insolent to their superiors.

Or, as an eighteenth-century writer pithily expressed it, 'If a horse knew as much as a man I should not like to be his rider.' Such fears turned out to be groundless. By mid-century there were few signs that basic learning was an incitement for the lower orders to rise up against their betters. In 1848, the National Society monthly newsletter described education as 'the best police' and the 'one great panacea for all the evils of this country'. A decade later, Henry Newland, a High Church parson, told a diocesan education conference, 'When you have manufactured a steady, honest, God-fearing, Church-going population, then you will have done your duty as schoolmasters.'[4]

But if fear of insurrection was mellowed by experience, farmers and factory owners kept up their anti-school chorus. They were unwilling to lose their cheap child labour while parents were equally reluctant to forgo the miserable earnings brought home by their youngsters. There was more sympathy for Sunday schools, which had the virtue of keeping children off the streets and out of mischief on their only day of rest.

At the start of the century there were over a thousand Sunday schools. While the clergy kept their distance from the dame schools, except in so far as to deplore their ineptitude, they were the backbone of the Sunday schools. Their best standards were rarely matched except in the higher-grade charity schools. The curriculum was narrow but it served a wider purpose. The curate of Sandford in Oxfordshire was understandably proud of the record of the two Sunday schools under his direction.

> The scholars are taught every Sunday, from 8 in the morning till 4, 5 or 6 in the afternoon, according to the season of the year, to read and spell, and to commit to memory Watts' Hymns, the Catechism broke [into small quantities] and the Collects and Gospels for the day, after learning which a second time they proceed to the Epistles for the day, Gastrel's Institutes and Mann's Exposition of the Catechism which last books several of the scholars have gone entirely thro'.[5]

By 1815 Sunday schools were so general that one of the numerous handbooks for teachers and supervisors could find 'few parishes in the kingdom where they have not been established'.[6] The numbers attending increased to 450,000 by

1818 and to 2.5 million by mid-century. In Stockport, a single Sunday school had 5,000 on its pupil register.

The popularity of Sunday schools convinced the clergy that their teaching role should go beyond simple exhortations to be righteous. To multiply the faithful, the young had to be inculcated with the ways of the Church. Lay sentiment was moving the same way. Growing radical agitation and recurring threats of revolution suggested that general ignorance was no guarantee of peace and security. Christian morality, with its message of humility and acceptance of one's lot in life, offered the better hope of a society free of insurrection.

It was the religious element that inspired Joshua Watson, the High Church philanthropist who had launched the church building programme. As treasurer of the Society for the Promotion of Christian Knowledge, Watson arranged for the schools started by the SPCK to be transferred over to another organisation with a long-winded title – the National Society for the Education of the Poor in the Principles of the Established Church, soon to be known more congenially as the National Society. The aim was to open schools for seven- to fourteen-year-olds in deprived areas and, longer term, to open a school in every parish.

Instruction was to be given on the Prayer Book and the catechism. Beyond basic Christianity in the Anglican tradition, the children could expect to learn basic reading, writing and arithmetic. It was judged useful for girls to be taught sewing. In broad terms, the purpose of education was to reduce vice and crime and to encourage stable family life.

Inevitably, the National Society had its enemies. Snooping magistrates scoured reading material for subversive propaganda calculated to 'elevate the minds of those doomed to the drudgery of daily labour above their condition thereby rendering them discontented and unhappy in their lot'. There were senior clergy who took the same line. To include writing and arithmetic in the curriculum was wholly mistaken, said Bishop Vaughan Thomas. 'Such accomplishments would harm their retentive memories and encourage them to leave the land for precarious positions elsewhere.' But reading was acceptable as 'the key to the treasures of holy writ'.[7]

Paradoxically, among the opponents of the National Society were some of the most fervent promoters of popular education. Nonconformists had no wish to be part of a movement that was so obviously attached to the established Church. Watson was disinclined to compromise. In the Phalanx journal, the *Critic*, and elsewhere he laid down strict qualifications for a society grant, starting with regular attendance at church. The only books to be used were those published by the SPCK.

Watson attracted big names – the Prince Regent as patron, the Archbishop of Canterbury as president – to head the campaign for subscriptions. In little more than six months, £16,000 was raised, sufficient to offer grants to build schools in parishes where the squire or local businessman was willing to donate a site or offer a long lease at a peppercorn rent. The clergy responded enthusiastically, often putting their own money into projects.

In 1812 a Mr Berkis, curate of a parish in the Forest of Dean, opened a school for 350 children. The vicar of the tiny country parish of Acton Burnell in Shropshire used the chancel of his church as a schoolroom, which was soon overcrowded with ninety children coming every weekday.[8] At Reading, a parson made 'a moveable schoolroom' built 'on the principles of the houses sent out to Van Diemen's Land and the Colonies' – in other words, a prefabricated hut.

By 1815 every diocese in England was taking advice from the society, and around 100,000 children were in its schools. A decade later, the figure was closer to 400,000. Between 1811 and 1833, 7,000 schools were built or assisted by the National Society which claimed a country-wide attendance of a million children. This almost certain exaggeration was, perhaps, forgivable. Accurate figures were hard to come by when children could be pulled out of school at short notice to help bring in the harvest or otherwise to supplement the family income.

Industrial centres held out against the society until legislation against child labour was enforced. In Manchester, as late as 1834, one-third of children between five and fifteen were totally illiterate, not even able to sign their names. Overworked parsons did their best to alleviate the injustice. One of them reported: 'My only schoolroom is an empty cotton mill from which we are liable to be ejected any moment, the mill being part of a bankrupt estate. In this room, which contains neither fireplace nor stove, we have assembled throughout the winter 220 children. A great many more would have attended if a fire could have been made.'[9]

Until inspectors were appointed the quality of the schooling varied enormously. Even where there were dedicated teachers, what they had to offer could fall short for want of support by parents and employers.

There was a good school in the village. But on my return from my evening walks, generally in the Freshford direction, I used to fall in with groups of children, down to a very early age, coming from the mills; and I remember gathering from them that all through the winter they had to be at the mill, two miles off, by six in the morning, not leaving till six in the evening. Thus the journey to and fro would be in the dark for many months.[10]

This was Bath in the late 1820s. While near Chalderton, on the edge of Salisbury Plain:

The village school draws poor children from holes and corners worse than caves, and out-of-the-way places worse than deserts.

Property and agriculture distribute population often too widely and dispersedly for its good. The solitary cottage, or the very small hamlet, in the heart of the down, or the depth of the wood, or the extremity of the long alley, is very apt to produce specimens of humanity hardly credible in an age and country like ours. The children, with none to interest them by word or example except the one parent who is not always away from home, grow up savages in their instincts and in their language. When they appear in the village, they can hardly make themselves understood. I find myself using the present tense, but all this is happily less of our times than of the times gone by.[11]

There were some odd characters employed as teachers. When John Atkinson wanted to know why the schoolmaster at Danby was a total incompetent he was told, 'Wheel, he could do nowght else. He had muddled away his land, and we put him in schoolmaster that he man't get a bite o' bread'.[12] In his Cornish outpost, Robert Hawker was shocked to find that the teacher he was supposed to treat as an equal was a retired slaver from the West Indies.

With the shortage of teachers, the already entrenched monitorial system, with older and brighter pupils helping to teach the others, was widely practised. If books were a rarity, so too was paper, an expensive item that few schools could afford. Instead, sand trays and slates were used for writing. The clergy were not only active in setting up schools; they also contributed to the teaching. John Keble taught in his village school at Hursley for an hour each morning. Many parsons followed his example with regular appearances at their schools while also offering religious teaching in their own homes. In 1840, the Revd Francis Goddard paid a visit to a neighbouring vicarage where he found the drawing room full of girls being prepared for confirmation. He commented, 'It is a fact that I never before heard of classes of instruction for confirmation:

the only mode adopted by me and others was a sort of house-to-house visit to those we could pick up after their work was done.'[13]

If, by today's standards, there was an overemphasis on the Bible as a primer, it gave more stimulus to learning than the dull recitation of basic words and numbers. The Bible offered 'mystery and greatness, meat beside the dry bread of the three Rs ... nothing could keep its great rhythms from the ear'. It was a 'real' book with 'myth, legend, miracle and poetry' with a 'shining personality' at its centre.[14]

Across the country, the parson was at the forefront of the war on ignorance. At Burton Agnes, near Hull, Robert Wilberforce opened a school for boys and another for girls in his garden and, as Archdeacon of the East Riding, was active in extending the work of the National Society in Yorkshire. It was thanks to Wilberforce that a teacher training college for men was set up at York and for women at Ripon. Like father, like son. Robert's parents worried that he was 'overdoing himself on Sundays by going twice a day to the school, besides his two services and his examination of the children after evening service, and he talks of an adult school for boys and young men if he can get it together in order to occupy their evening leisure a little'.[15]

In the early days of Edward Boys Ellman's incumbency at Berwick in Sussex, he started six dame schools in each of which he taught twice a week. Later he paid for the building of a day school. Backsliders were not tolerated.

The most effectual punishment for a child (or rather the child's mother, for in her does the fault chiefly lie) for irregular attendance, or any serious fault, was to strike the name off the books, and thus I have kept a child away from school for three months, with good effect, not only to the child but also in the example to the others.[16]

As a parson with an eye for business, William Papillon, vicar at Wymondham in Norfolk, quadrupled his stipend by buying and renting out around 30 acres close by the abbey. With the income he set up two schools and paid towards the teachers' salaries. The trust he created towards the end of his life supported an extra Sunday service with a fee and expenses for visiting preachers.[17]

At Finmere, all the children attended the day school and Sunday school. Soup dinners were provided twice a week and each child was provided with a complete outfit of clothes.[18] Wheatley in Oxfordshire was blessed with a parson of indefatigable energy. Dissatisfied with the existing village school, which he said was 'unfit for purpose', Edward Elton launched a campaign to build a new one. Bishop Wilberforce was enlisted to persuade an Oxford brewer to make a gift of land close to the church. George Edmund Street was contracted to design the building with separate schoolrooms for boys and girls and a house for the schoolmaster. So successful was Elton's fundraising that he had no problem in securing a matching government grant. From inception to completion, the project took less than two years.[19]

The people of Morwenstow were told in no uncertain terms where their duty lay. 'Take Notice,' declaimed Robert Hawker. 'The Vicar will attend St Mark's schoolroom every Friday at three o'clock, to catechize the scholars, and at the Sunday school at the usual hour. He will not from henceforth show the same kindness to those who keep back their children from school as he will to those who send them.' From the pulpit he told parents, 'If you love your children do not keep them for your own indulgence away from Heaven, separate from church, absent from school. They will then breathe a thanksgiving over your grave.'[20] But Hawker gave pupils time off during the harvest.

Among the clergy were inspired teachers for whom the school

was the dominant factor of their lives. One such was Richard Dawes, a Cambridge don who went to Kings Somborne in Hampshire with no experience of elementary education. That was in 1837. There was no school until Dawes set about creating one on a site donated by the lady of the manor. His two guiding principles were self-sufficiency (the school had to pay for itself) and learning by doing. He took the pupils out on nature trips and taught them to record what they observed in the changing seasons. The standard curriculum was broadened to take in history and science. As the school grew (it started with thirty-eight children but was soon accommodating over 100) Dawes invested in a library to nourish the pleasures of reading. Families were expected to pay two pennies a week for their first child with a penny for each sibling, but there were a number of free places.

Glowing reports encouraged other parsons to take the Dawes route, which he set out in his *Suggestive Hints*, a book, said an inspector, 'which ought to be in the hands of every elementary teacher'. At Abbotts Ann, where Samuel Best followed the Dawes rule of taking in children of all denominations, the school was so popular over a wide area that some pupils were walking up to 11 miles a day or boarding in local cottages.

What was chiefly remarkable about Richard Dawes was his ability to make a successful transition from tutoring university students to teaching near illiterate youngsters while giving every impression of enjoying himself enormously. But he was by no means alone. The ordained John Henslow was professor of History at Cambridge. Such was his renown, he was first choice to be the naturalist on the survey ship HMS *Beagle*. After his wife dissuaded him from two years away from home, Henslow recommended one of his students. Charles Darwin was duly appointed. In 1837, Henslow accepted the living at Hitcham in Suffolk. It was not, as might at first have appeared, an act of self-sacrifice. Hitcham was poor, but the stipend, in the gift of the Crown, was generous. Moreover, Henslow was able to retain his Cambridge professorship. But the chief beneficiary was his rural parish, which gained a school, largely financed by its parson, and a progressive style of teaching that embraced botanic excursions, practical science and pupil-tended allotments supporting produce and flower shows. His cricket and athletic clubs became the focal points for village festivals. A catalogue of parson teachers who made a real difference in their communities would be a thick volume.

In 1846, as assistant curate at New Shoreham, Nathaniel Woodward opened a school for the poor. Two years later he raised his sights with the publication of *A Plea for the Middle Classes*. His idea was to organise a hierarchy of schools to meet the needs of the different levels of society. The schools in the higher categories were to subsidise those lower on the scale and there were to be opportunities for able boys to move up the educational ladder. Woodward fell short of his ambition to create a general system but in the south of England he founded his public school at Lancing, a school at the second level at Hurstpierpoint and the lowest at Ardingly. When he died in 1891 he was credited with eleven schools, providing for a total of 1,350 pupils.[21]

It was not all good news. When Robert Lawrence was appointed vicar of Chalgrove in 1832 he set about connecting a pair of cottages to make a school. When money ran short he hoped to persuade parents to contribute to the costs of running the school, which did not include a teacher's salary, since Lawrence himself did all the teaching. His call went unanswered. In less than a year, the school closed.[22]

There were other signs that the National Society was beginning to stall. The challenge of mounting a crusade for mass literacy was too great for a voluntarily supported institution. What the society had started, the state had to advance. Public money came on stream after a campaign by the radical MP John

Roebuck to set up a centrally controlled network of schools to provide for all children from six to twelve years of age. Roebuck could hardly have expected to win a parliamentary majority, but he did prepare the way for a major concession, a school-building grant of £20,000 to be shared between the National Society and the Nonconformist-led British and Foreign Schools Society. This was in 1833, when the best estimate was that of every ten children of school age, three went to Sunday schools only, two to dame schools or private schools, four missed out on education altogether and one attended a National Society school.

In nearly all schools, society controlled or not, the Church was dominant. But for how long? Joshua Watson was well aware of the financial restraints. Many appeals for aid had to be rejected. But eager as he was to gather in funds, he did not welcome the help of a government with strong secular leanings. It marked the beginning of the end of his attachment to the National Society. Even so, to Watson must go the chief credit for setting a pattern for elementary education, underpinned by the Church, which lasted well into the twentieth century.

Once government backing had been endorsed there could be no retreat. The grant was renewed annually until 1838, when further outlays were made conditional on a closer check on the way the money was spent. A Committee of the Privy Council 'for the consideration of all matters affecting the Education of the People' led to instituting a corps of inspectors to travel the country, reporting on standards while advising and encouraging teachers.

At this point the National Society decided that an attempt was being made to undermine the Church. The principle of inspection was not in question; the quarrel was about the power to appoint and control inspectors, which the National Society wanted to keep for itself. In the end, Church and State agreed to share the responsibility. Inspectors had to be vetted by an archbishop before they could be empowered to enter Anglican schools; the Church retained control over religious instruction while the Board of Education, in the person of its first secretary, Dr (later Sir) James Kay-Shuttleworth, conceded that 'no plan of education ought to be encouraged in which intellectual instruction is not subordinate to the regulation of the thoughts and habits of the children by the doctrine and precepts of revealed religion'.

Though some allowance must be made for political tact, inspectors were strong in their praise of the parson's role. One of them wrote,

> I can find only nine instances out of nearly 200 where I have not seen reason to think that the clergyman has a deep interest in his school, not shown by words, but by watchful care and frequent attendance. I could mention instances where after morning religious instruction in the day school, the clergyman teaches the school at night; others where the master has been ill or absent for sometime, the clergyman has cheerfully supplied his place, lest the school should suffer loss; others again where besides labouring almost beyond his strength, pecuniary help beyond his means has been cheerfully given, poor children paid for, masters' stipends made up to a certain income, repairs done, as it were by stealth, debts willingly taken upon himself, and contributions offered, liberal to excess, that others might be moved to contribute liberally ... I am convinced that no one could see what I have seen, of the truly charitable work of the clergy for the support and success of these schools, without feeling increased respect for them.[23]

From within the Church there were liberals such as Edward Stanley, Bishop of Norwich, who wanted the National Society to loosen its grip.

> It would be far more useful, and have a far better right to be called National, if it received with open arms the children of all

who acknowledge the Bible as the standard faith and the rule of practice.

His views were greeted with a chorus of approval from Nonconformists who, though curiously slow in setting up their own schools, were strongly in favour of a state system with interdenominational Christian teaching. Their case was strengthened when a parson of authoritarian temper assumed dictatorial power over a school and its teachers.

The argument was taken a stage further by Walter Farquhar Hook, vicar of Leeds, a vigorous and outspoken parson who had within his remit 'a district containing 250,000 souls, exclusive of the large towns, in which there are thousands uneducated, or receiving an education worse than none'. In an open letter to the Bishop of St Davids, a kindred spirit, Hook was highly critical of the voluntary system superintended by the National Society. While 'we have done much more than, with our scanty resources [we] could have supposed to be possible', society schools were concentrated in the more prosperous areas, 'where the clergy are not only active, but numerous and influential'.

The contrast with what was happening in the industrial towns hardly needed to be emphasised. Hook gave a vivid description of the life of a teacher starting out to earn a livelihood 'by the pence of the children'.

The poor young man having been sent to that apology for a training school at Westminster, has confided to him as a great privilege, the sole charge of 100 or 150 little dirty, ragged, ignorant urchins, assembled in the miserable building now dignified by the name of a National School Room, and he is expected, as by a miracle, to convert them, in as short a space of time as possible, into clean, well-bred, intelligent children, capable of passing a creditable examination, if by chance an inspector or organizing master pass that way.

The task, said Hook, was impossible and experience had shown it to be so. The teacher

> cannot educate all the children himself, and therefore he is obliged to have recourse to the monitorial system: the result of which is, while a portion of the children are vain, conceited and puffed-up, a larger proportion are left in their ignorance. I have known instances of children who have been for two years at a National School, and have left it unable to read.

Hook's solution was for the state to take over the work of the National Society. The Church alone could never fulfil her pastoral and educational mission. The weight of opinion was against Hook. As if in response, in 1846, the National Society raised £160,000 to create schools in heavily populated areas. By then, the National Society was accommodating 465,000 pupils while other Anglican schools accounted for 336,000, in all around half the total number of pupils in day schools.

But Hook's argument was not to be dismissed. In protesting the lack of qualified teachers to build on the initiative of the Church, he touched a sensitive nerve. There were two training schools at Westminster and forty-three others across the country but it was not until 1841 that the National Society opened its first genuine college, St Mark's in Chelsea. The following year a women's college was founded close by at Whitelands. By 1845 there were thirteen training colleges, six of them for women, most of which were run by the Church of England.

The average course for women lasted no longer than a year and was heavily biased towards domestic economy. The curriculum was justified by the emphasis on practical work in the schools and by the fact that many of the student teachers would themselves end up caring for their own homes and families, but there was also a strong suspicion that colleges favoured practical lessons as a cheap method of disposing of the housework. At Salisbury it was said that 'such work as scrubbing, cleaning shoes, etc. has a beneficial tendency in correcting faults of vanity, indolence, etc., and in giving a practical lesson in humility'.[24] Even at Whitelands, which had one of the best academic reputations, the strongest emphasis was on the ability to undertake needlework, knitting and darning.

The standard of accommodation was far removed from the academic cloisters of higher learning. At Salisbury, where the college moved into a house on the Cathedral Close, there were just twelve small bedrooms for thirty-two pupils; since there was no infirmary, teenage diseases accounted for a high casualty rate. Whitelands consisted of two houses connected by a range of long, low buildings, which faced the Kings Road in Chelsea. The rooms were said to be 'ill-lighted and insufficiently ventilated' and the laundry and scullery were 'overrun with rats'. Another college refused to install baths on the grounds that it would not be a good idea to give teachers a taste of luxury which they would never again be able to afford.[25]

A solution was negotiated by Kay-Shuttleworth, who had long been occupied with plans for expanding the teaching force. He proposed a new set of grants to back up the training of pupil teachers within the schools. After a year of negotiations the approval of the National Society was won in return for assurances that there was no intention of diluting the 'two great principles' of education: 'that religion pervade the whole teaching of a school and that the main direction of education should be left in the care of those who would be prompted to approach and handle it from a care for the immortal souls of children.' The pupil-teacher scheme came into operation in 1846, and within two years Kay-Shuttleworth was able to report that over 2,000 apprentices were in training and that demand for places was such that standards of entry could be raised.

The development of the pupil-teacher system was accompanied by an expansion of training. By 1858 there were fifteen men's colleges catering for about 750 students, thirteen women's colleges with over 800 students and five mixed colleges with 500 students. At least 80 per cent were previously pupil-teachers who had qualified for Queen's scholarships, worth about £20 to £25, to enable them to attend a year at college.

The quality of teacher training was still problematic. There was little in the way of structure to the snippets of information learned by rote to satisfy examiners. Textbooks were an amalgam of disjointed facts and value judgements. Samuel Warren, who was apparently much distinguished in the Inner Temple, was persuaded to produce a text 'for the use of schools and young persons' based on *Select Extracts from Blackstone's Commentaries*, while James Cornwell, Principal of the Borough Road College, turned out a bestselling geography text containing such brain-teasing questions as, 'Describe England as compared with the rest of Great Britain.' The answer, which students were expected to repeat word for word, was, 'England is the largest, wealthiest, and in every way the most important part of Great Britain.' Critics asked what possible significance this could have for developing young minds. 'To what generation of labourers' children,' wrote a member of the Education Department, 'will it ever be expedient to discourse on the Schism of the Papacy, the Council of Basle, the Pragmatic Sanction, or the Wars of the Hussites?'

An acceptable standard of literacy was still a long way off. By mid-century about 25 per cent of the male population under twenty and 20 per cent of girls in the same age group were enrolled in elementary schools. But education occupied, on average, less than a single year of their lives. As Dean Hook observed, 'We have lighted a lanthorn which only makes us more sensible of the surrounding darkness.'

CHAPTER SEVEN

Protecting the Body

If the good parson was in part a teacher, he was just as likely to be something of a doctor. In the first half of the century, such doctors as there were favoured living in urban areas where they could build up a practice. Out in the country there were 'medical men' who gained a modicum of knowledge as assistants to apothecaries, but since they were notoriously deficient the parson was often the first call for medical aid. Edward Boys Ellman recalled,

> There was a parish doctor who very much neglected the people. One poor woman said, 'She would say this of the doctor, that he did not torment poor people, but left them to die.' My knowledge of drugs came in usefully, and I won my way in many cottages by doctoring and giving medicine. Soon after I went to Wartling there was a very bad epidemic of measles of a bad type; the average number of cases I visited in the day was over 80 for two or three weeks – adults as well as children. In one lonely cottage I found a father and four grown-up sons all ill with measles. The old man had lost his wife many years before and no woman ever entered the house.[1]

With the science of the body, let alone the mind, still in its infancy, a parson could hardly be expected to offer more than palliatives along with advice on isolating the sick and setting standards of general cleanliness. Fortunate were those who encountered a cleric with more than basic knowledge. George Crabbe, who was a better poet than parson, had been apprenticed to a doctor and had even set up his own medical practice in Aldeburgh in Suffolk before taking holy orders. Never afraid to give an opinion, Sydney Smith adopted the role of 'village doctor' after attending medical lectures at Oxford and clinical classes at Edinburgh's Royal Infirmary. When he moved from Foston to Combe Florey he dispensed medicines from the apothecary's shop set up in his rectory. After the outbreak of a fever, unidentified except that it was a 'very dangerous and infectious kind', Smith went from cottage to cottage with food and medicine. As the deaths multiplied, villagers refused to go into the infected cottages to nurse the sick or to carry out the corpses. By personal example, Smith shamed his flock into doing the right thing.[2]

Brandy and salt were traditional remedies for a variety of ailments. Their therapeutic qualities were supported by the occasional dramatic recovery, as followed treatment of a woman by the vicar of Ketteringham in Norfolk.

December 4, 1840 – The effect of my new medicine is astonishing! Thirling two years ago was at the brink of the grave and has had another attack of liver complaint. I began with brandy and salt, which at first produced a kind of intoxicated feeling, with increased headache and a warm glow through the whole frame. She persisted according to my prescribed plan, first rubbing the crown with about a tablespoonful and then the first thing in the morning taking internally the same quantity with double quantity of boiling water. She is much better. The cold fits are less, headache much relieved and pain between the shoulders almost gone and sickness quite cured. I could not but notice the improvement in her pulse from about 60 to 80. She is very grateful. May it be an open door for me to her soul. Lord, leave not her soul unhealed![3]

More dramatic, but no less effective, was the remedy for diphtheria applied by the Revd Thornton.

I kept four rammers, one for each patient, and I rammed myself first, and them afterwards, with sulphuric acid several times in the course of each day. That was our treatment. Sulphuric acid on rammers crammed down the throat, the burning effect being afterwards mitigated by copious libations of old port wine. All hail to the heroic treatment of those good old days! We eventually recovered, but a great hole was made in my cellar, and a baby died in the village. Poor little thing, it could not take the port, and succumbed in consequence.[4]

Publishers were quick to respond to the call for helpful hints. *Instructions for the Relief of the Sick Poor in Some Diseases of Frequent Occurrence* (1820) was addressed specifically to 'a parochial clergyman, residing at a distance from professional aid'. A manual of more general nature but one that was just as likely to be found on a vicarage bookshelf targeted the parson's wife. *The Female Instructor or Young Woman's Companion* (1824) is described as 'a guide to all the accomplishments which adorn the female character either as a useful member of society, a pleasing and instructive companion or a respectable mother of a family'. The author skips from social to domestic culinary to medical matters in a frenzy of encyclopaedic discourse, itemising such topics as 'Balsam, Bathing, useful remarks on; Boiling in general; Brewing, the art of; Cold, intense, to recover from; Cramp, cures for; Ducks, how to manage; Prayer for a family; Itch, cures for; Windows, how to clean; and Rules for conversation.'

The Female Instructor offers a wealth of advice on caring for the sick. There are cures for ague, cramp, stiffness of the joints ('submerge in the yoke of a new-laid egg'), dropsy, inflamed or sore eyes, bruises ('immediately apply treacle spread on brown paper; or electrify the part, which is the quickest cure of all'), coughs ('drink a pint of water lying down in bed'), the itch ('wash the parts affected with strong rum'), and rheumatism ('rub in warm treacle'). The pleasures and benefits of strong exercise had to be balanced against the dangers of over-exertion. Swimmers, for instance, are advised that if they 'overheat the body, especially in the hot days of summer, it may prove instantly fatal, by inducing a state of apoplexy'.

The antidotes for the calamities resulting from swimming were itemised under Drowning – Restoration of Life: 'On taking bodies out of rivers, ponds, etc., the following cautions are to be used; 1) Never to be held up by the heels. 2) Not to be rolled in casks, or other rough passage.' Instead, the body was to be 'gently rubbed with flannel, sprinkled with spirits, and a heated warming-pan lightly moved over the back and spine'. To restore breathing, 'introduce the pipe of a pair of billows into one nostril; close the mouth and the other nostril, then inflate the lungs ...' If all else failed, 'Tobacco smoke is to be thrown gently up the fundament,' but 'only with a proper instrument.'

Preventative medicine for childhood ailments consisted of 'plain food, simple clothing, regular hours and abundant exercise in open air'. But there was a continuing need to watch for advanced warnings of disability. 'Great care must be taken with breeding their teeth, as many die of that painful disease.'

The once fashionable practice of bleeding, using leeches to drain off infected blood, was regarded as harmful for pregnant women. Of practical help was the widespread lending out of bed linen from the parsonage for the months of confinement. It was expected to be clean on its return. A thick bar of soap and a bottle of castor oil might accompany the linen. The loan of a handbell for use in emergencies was also appreciated. For minor illnesses, a glass of port was a popular remedy, though many a parson had good reason to regulate access to his wine cellar.

The test of a parson's courage and conviction was at its toughest when he was caught up in an epidemic. Smallpox, typhus, scarlet fever, diarrhoea and measles were all virulent killers. But the most vicious and far-reaching disease was cholera. When it took hold in 1831, one of the worst-affected communities was Bilston (now part of Wolverhampton), a town of coal mines and iron foundries. Of a population of 15,000 there were over 3,500 reported cases of which nearly 750 were fatal.

The Revd William Leigh put himself at the head of the relief operation. He converted a former barracks into a cholera hospital, distributed lime for whitewashing houses, engaged cleaners to scrub out sickrooms and distributed handbills and posters warning of health risks. At neighbouring Sidgley, the Revd Charles Girdlestone recommended boiling drinking water and whitewashing pigsties. He then set up the Stourbridge Sanitary Association. Of the management committee of twenty-three worthies, six were parsons.

Leigh and Girdlestone were ahead of their time in recognising the likely origin of the contagion. The main water supply was from Bilston Brook. Though clean and clear at its limestone source it was heavily contaminated by washhouses and sewers by the time it reached the towns. But the hygienically enlightened had a hard time convincing others that water was a disease carrier. Common explanation ranged from pickled foods to an evil force floating in the air or, as Robert Hawker believed, 'Cholera spreads by atmospheric poison acting on the sick.' A variety of old wives' remedies included a belt of warm cloth round the stomach, pillows of hot bran and sulphur and doses of opium.

Leigh arranged for the dead to be removed from their homes at night when there would be nobody out on the streets. The victims were buried in mass graves. When the crisis had passed, he founded a school for orphans.

Death was never far away. When it hovered the good parson was on hand to offer Christian comfort and consolation. It could be a heart-rending experience. This is Francis Kilvert on taking the sacrament to a dying parishioner.

> What a scene it was, the one small room up in the roof of the hovel, almost dark, in which I could not stand upright, the shattered window, almost empty of glass, the squalid bed, the close horrid smell, the continual crying and wailing of the children below, the pattering of the rain on the tiles close overhead, the ceaseless moaning of the sick man with his face bound about with a napkin. 'Lord have mercy. Lord have mercy upon me,' he moaned. I was almost exhausted crouching down at the little dirty window to catch the light of the gloomy rainy afternoon.[5]

The routine task of attending a deathbed called for delicate handling. The Bible thumper demanding confession and remorse in return for salvation simply added another layer of misery. More was achieved by being there, listening more than talking and doing whatever was feasible to soften the grief and relieve the suffering. This was a skill of Augustus Hare, rector of Alton Barnes, 'perhaps the most primitive village in Wiltshire'.[6]

> When Prudence Tasker, who had been one of the first received into his newly-formed Sunday-school, was seized with violent illness, how tenderly did Mr Hare daily visit her dying-bed, obtaining for her the advice of an eminent physician in addition to that of the village doctor, often himself administering her medicines, applying her leeches himself, and trying to overcome the repugnance she felt to bleeding by telling her it was her 'pastor' who desired it; and how often since have her parents

dwelt upon the prayers which he offered up in that little chamber of death![7]

When cholera visited Alton Barnes, Hare's wife noted:

> We have had nothing but doctoring in the parish. The fever reached the house at the end of our lane, and on Sunday night a little girl, one of my best scholars, died of it. Her father lay dangerously ill and another child also. ... Augustus went into the infected house to read prayers to the sick man without much anxiety. ... The man is now, I hope, getting better; but they have it in another house next to Gideon's, and yesterday, as Augustus was passing in the afternoon, he happened to speak to the woman, saw she was crying, and, on inquiry, found that the girl who was so much better in the morning, was, they thought, dying. He came home for some brandy, and ran back with it in spite of the rain, and waited till the child had taken some, and by means of that and rubbing mustard on the throat began to revive; and to-day she is alive and certainly better. But it seems like a sort of miniature plague, attacking people so suddenly with swelling in the limbs, &c. Two more in the same house now have it. There is such a making of broth and gruel.[8]

Beyond the rectory there was little evidence of Christian charity in Alton Barnes. A rare instance was a farmer who allowed one of his workers time off to visit his dying mother. So overcome was the employee when he found that his wages had not been deducted that 'he still speaks of it with tears in his eyes'.[9] Hare converted a barn into a laundry and set up a non-profit shop where clothes and materials were sold.

Medical knowledge and training advanced with the century. With the opening of new hospitals and medical schools to supplement, if not rival, Edinburgh and Glasgow, more doctors were persuaded to broaden their professional horizons. One line of advancement was opened by the Poor Law, which required medical support for the workhouses. The logic was clear. Those who went into the workhouses were usually the halt and the lame. Their best chance of returning to ordinary life without further charge on public funds was for them to be restored to health.

The skill of the Poor Law doctors was not always apparent. The Aylesbury Union, one of the largest, had three changes of medical officer in three years, each one living far from the job in hand.[10] The guardians were accused of obeying the minimum terms of the law at the lowest possible cost. But elsewhere the Poor Law medical officer gradually assumed the role of general practitioner for the poor at large. From 1841 he was organising general vaccinations.

Edwin Chadwick, who had spent an unhappy period as secretary to the Poor Law Commissioners, had wider ambitions. He argued that measures to improve public health would cut down on the numbers of destitute and thus of the numbers at the gates of the workhouses. His chance to prove the point came in 1839 when he was asked to take on an inquiry 'into the sanitary conditions of the working class'.

Among his strongest supporters was Bishop Blomfield, who recommended house-to-house visiting, not only for spiritual reasons, but for detecting and removing sources of malignant disease. Charles Kingsley was another leader in the crusade against dirt and bad drainage, witnessing at first hand the horrors of slum life. As he wrote to his wife:

> I was yesterday ... over the cholera districts of Bermondsey; and, of God! what I saw! people having no water to drink – hundreds of them – but the water of the common sewer which stagnated full of ... dead fish, cats, and dogs under their window.

Parson and publisher, Charles Kegan Paul was with Kingsley when he visited a householder suffering from fever.

The atmosphere of the little ground floor bedroom was horrible, but before the Rector said a word he ran upstairs and, to the great astonishment of the inhabitants of the cottage, bored, with a large auger he had brought with him, several holes above the bed's head for ventilation.[11]

In Liverpool, more than 39,000 lived in cellars. For Manchester the figure was 15,000. In districts of East London families lived in wooden sheds or closed courts or tenements without lavatories, sometimes with an open sewer that was liable to overflow in wet weather. At Bethnal Green, a row of pigsties emptied their refuse into a pool of stagnant water.[12]

In his report on sanitary conditions, Chadwick argued the link between disease and environment. Moreover, he showed that social evils such as alcoholism, prostitution and delinquency were not the cause of poverty, as was widely assumed, but were caused by poverty. Published in 1842, Chadwick's report was an immediate best seller and was widely applauded, but the early results were disappointing. Intolerant of criticism, he was not the best advocate of his own proposals, which came up hard against economic reality. He was, for example, absolutely right in arguing for the piped disposal of sewage and for supplying urban areas with water for consumption and drainage. But the costs, not to mention the engineering challenges, were huge and it was easy for critics to point to apparently insurmountable obstacles. As a Leeds councillor commented, 'The people are more solicitous about draining rates from their pockets than draining the streets.'

Chadwick wanted a centralised, uniform administrative structure. What he got, in 1848, was a General Board of Health empowered to do no more than advise and supervise. Ten years later, 182 local boards had been set up but of these only thirteen had embarked on waterworks or sewage schemes. However, by then the case for reform had been made.

One of the most urgent improvements was in the provision of burial places, particularly in urban areas and most particularly in London. During epidemics of cholera or influenza the typical city churchyard was a veritable hellhole, with the ground like a ploughed field, queues of mourners miserably waiting their turn and gravediggers jumping on coffins to make more space. A commission appointed in 1842 urged new cemeteries outside urban boundaries but for ten years churchyards continued to deteriorate. Thereafter legislation made it possible to close overcrowded cemeteries, a move supported by the clergy even though they stood to lose their funeral fees. The opening of the Kensal Green cemetery cost the vicar of Paddington £200 a year.[13]

In the propaganda campaign that led to the raft of public health legislation towards the end of the century, it was the clergy who took the lead. Clerical memoirs and diaries of the period make frequent reference to the drive against dirt and infection. It was a rare board of health that did not have a parson chairing a committee and accepting a large part of the administrative load, including meeting parishioners in their own homes to note general cleanliness and any likely sources of infection. Pocket books such as *The Clergyman's Private Register* gave space for the sanitation details of each family visit.

Determined to cover the open sewer down the high street of Wheatley, Edward Elton petitioned the General Board of Health to set up a public inquiry to examine the state of sanitation in the village. In this way, Elton hoped to pave the way for the creation of a local board of health with power to borrow an advance on the rates. The opposition included at least one doctor who claimed that it was safer to leave the common brook open to the air. But after some astute political manoeuvring by Elton the counter petition failed, a local board came into being (Elton was chairman for many years), funds were raised and drains were installed.[14]

'Love and eloquence.'

Right: The self-important and pompous Mr Collins in Jane Austen's *Pride and Prejudice* was typical of the clergy as represented in popular fiction.

Below: A view of a Victorian workhouse.

A view of Victorian Oxford, which lent its name to the controversial Oxford Movement.

THE MODERN PURITAN

Hanging a Cat on a Monday   For killing a Mouse on a Sunday!!!

Above: A cartoon on puritanical excesses.

Left: Revd Robert Stephen Hawker.

The death of John Wesley, preacher and founder of the Methodists.

Left: Samuel Wilberforce, Bishop of Oxford. (Courtesy of the Wellcome Library, London)

Below: A Victorian blood-letting machine; bleeding was still widely believed to be a cure for certain afflictions. Parsons were often at least partly responsible for medical care in their parishes.

Above: A country parsonage in bad need of repair.

Right: Villagers setting off for church on a Sunday morning. (Courtesy of Seriykotik1970)

Above: The village choir, in a painting by Robert Webster. (Courtesy of Robert Cutts)

Left: The younger John Henry Newman.

Whitton vicarage. This large and appealing house is a long way from the miserable living conditions endured by many parsons. (Courtesy of David Wright)

Wells Vicarage. (Courtesy of Ad Meskens)

Truro Cathedral, built in the popular Gothic Revival style in the nineteenth century. The Nine Lessons, now familiar all over the world, were first read here. (Courtesy of Tim Green)

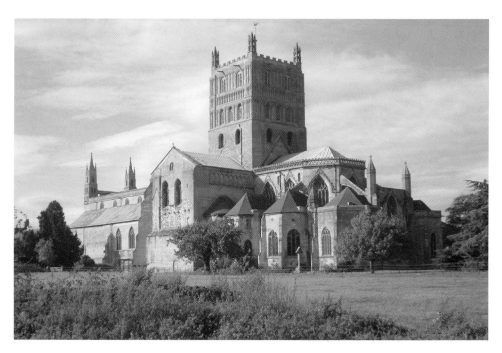

Tewkesbury Abbey, originally Norman and much restored during the Victorian era. (Courtesy of Paul Pichota)

Church of St Mary the Virgin, Bury. This church was completely rebuilt during the Victorian era, though a church has existed on the site since AD 971.

An artist's impression of an orderly Victorian schoolroom. The Church was heavily involved in running schools across the country. (Courtesy of the Wellcome Library, London)

Victorian schoolchildren gather for a photograph at Frenchay school in south Gloucestershire. (Courtesy of Paul Townsend)

Above: The Preacher, by Thomas Rowlandson. This shows a typical church interior in the early nineteenth century.

Right: Hawker's cliffside hut, built while he was rector of Morwenstow.

Left: Reverend Robert Allwood, who later emigrated to Australia. He was curate of Clifton from 1829 to 1839.

Below: Highgate Cemetery in north London. It was one of seven cemeteries opened in London during the Victorian era as a response to overcrowded graveyards, and is now a Grade 1 listed site. (Courtesy of Panyd)

Right: John Ruskin in 1882. (Courtesy of the Wellcome Library, London)

Below: The aftermath of a disaster at a colliery. This harsh industrial landscape required a new approach from parsons who struggled to relate to their congregations. In this particular disaster, the local preacher descended into a collapsed mineshaft to pray with trapped men below.

CATASTROPHE DE LA MINE D'HARTLEY (ANGLETERRE). — REMISE DES CORPS AUX PARENTS DES VICTIMES. Voir la page suivante).

Left: Charles Darwin, whose theory of evolution cut across traditional Church teaching.

Below: A depiction of the vice and poverty rife in London's streets.

In 1833, Richard Durnford was appointed rector of Middleton in Lancashire, a place where there were 'few resident gentry and no resident squire'. When the townspeople agreed on a local act to set up commissioners to manage roads, gas and drainage, Durnford saw it through into law and acted as chairman of commissioners from 1861 to 1870. He left on a wave of goodwill.

> The place in which for many years I lived in Lancashire was almost wholly undrained. In certain districts typhus periodically appeared, low fever was seldom absent, deaths too frequent from these causes, and the work of the clergy in consequence most perilous. The beginning of effectual drainage was made by a Board of which I was a constant member, consisting mainly of small traders and working men, elected annually by the parishioners. The owners of property were almost to a man hostile, and our difficulties in enforcing an imperfect law were considerable. In fact, we were driven to the Queen's Bench, and Middleton had the honour of obtaining a decision which rules the law on this subject. We were triumphant, and the result was beyond our expectations.[15]

William Butler was a member of the sanitation committee for Wantage. He was so distressed by what he found in one deprived part of the town that he bought the properties, had them demolished and rebuilt them as model homes. For audacity in the face of the establishment, though, the prize must go to Henry Moule, vicar of Fordington, who wrote eight letters of complaint to Prince Albert about the insanitary conditions of houses owned by the Duchy of Cornwall.[16]

A report from the medical officer of the Privy Council on the sanitary state of the country appeared in 1866. It showed that the battle against dirt and disease had a long way to go. There was only so much the parson could do until a system of state enforcement and administration was in place. Meanwhile, the medical acumen of the parson remained in strong demand.

> January 5, 1842 – Drew tooth for old Mrs Roberts. It was singular
> that I went to Ketteringham for the purpose of extracting it and
> I found her in great pain, upon which I drew from my pocket a
> pair of pincers which caused the poor old woman to shake and
> she begged I would use a piece of thread, I at last broke it off
> which perhaps was better than extracting the fangs.[17]

CHAPTER EIGHT

The New Breed

The last edition of the *Extraordinary Black Book*, still in circulation when Victoria was crowned, signed off with a blast at 'these rev'd gentlemen [who] pretend sickness in order to obtain a licence for non-residence, that they may bawl at the card table, frequent the play houses, tall-ho, shoot, play cricket, brandish the coachman's whip, and bully at fashionable watering places'.[1]

It was an extravagant, largely unsubstantiated flourish typical of the radical press, but it could not be ignored. For an institution that professed to be all-embracing it was disturbing for the Church to be reviled, even by a minority, or worse, treated as irrelevant. The problem for Church leaders was of not quite knowing what they were up against. The opposition spoke with a loud voice but who was listening? Anecdotal evidence suggested wide variations in respect for and loyalty to the clergy. But beyond the generalisations that the Church had formidable Nonconformist rivals, that it was strongest in rural communities where the squirearchy held sway and that churchgoers in town and country were predominantly middle class, not much was known about the strength or weakness of religious sentiment.

The opportunity to discover more came with the 1851 census, which allowed for a statistical inquiry into the religious health of the nation. It was masterminded by Horace Mann, a barrister who was assistant to the Registrar General. His analysis was published two years later. Mann's conclusions are to be treated with caution. In the days before reliable sampling, it was hard to produce valid baseline statistics. Mann did so by counting church attendances. Other possible criteria for estimating Christian allegiance were judged to be beyond accurate assessment. Even with a benchmark as clearly identifiable as church attendance, there was a question mark over the way the figures were compiled. To make the project manageable, Mann had to rely on returns on the number of church sittings, a method weighted in favour of the Evangelical tendency to show up at more than one Sunday service. Add to this the propensity of those responsible for the returns to round the figures up or down according to bias or level of commitment, and it is clear that the survey could offer no more than rough approximations.

The results were nonetheless revealing. Allowing for over 40 per cent of the population who were unable to get to church either because they were too young or incapacitated or had no church to go to, Mann reckoned that around 50 per cent of the rest were in church on the day of the census. Moreover, over half of all children aged five to fifteen, 2 million in all, went to Sunday schools. Allowing for an almost even split between the Church and the Nonconformist denominations, no other national body, then or later, could match this degree of allegiance. On the down side, Mann noted a fall in church attendance over half a century with only a modest recovery in the last decade, taking the round figure back roughly to what it was in 1801.

The grimmest news came from the towns. It was small comfort to the Church to know that Methodism was thriving in Liverpool, Manchester, Glasgow and London or that Irish immigration had sparked a Roman Catholic revival. The places where church attendance was lowest included all the cotton

towns, the great woollen towns, Leeds and Bradford, every large
coal town except Wolverhampton and the two great metal and
engineering centres of Birmingham and Sheffield where fewer
than one in ten attended church on census day.[2] The poorer
parts of London were in a class of their own. In Shoreditch in
East London, a fifth of the population had no church to go to.

Not surprisingly, the clergy found it hard to get to grips with
urban challenges. Raised in middle-class homes and educated in
the refined setting of Oxford or Cambridge, the typical parson
was out of his depth in the metropolitan melting pot. It was
asking a lot of a young ordinand to exchange 'the cool shadows,
the flowery meadows and the limpid streams where battle can
be done without diminishing the enjoyment of life'[3] for the hard
and often thankless service in the industrial heartland. 'I cannot
bear the thought of the black, black north,' wrote the son of
Samuel Wilberforce as he prepared to set off for Newcastle.
More than forty years earlier, Samuel had shown the same
reluctance to go to Leeds.[4]

Parts of London were equally unappealing. In 1858 the
rector of Bethnal Green resided in Cheshire, where he had
another living. The vicar of St Matthias's, Bethnal Green, a
zealous pastor, refused to accept the living if he was required to
live in the parish. He saw no reason why his children should be
exposed to the 'gin-drinking, fornicating rabble'.[5] The supply
of clergy willing to work in the least salubrious parts of the
country simply could not keep pace with the migration into the
already crowded tenements alongside the mills and factories.

Horace Mann was uncompromising. In his view, the
failure of the Christian mission in the new industrial centres
was explained by: 'the maintenance of social distinctions in
church' (the middle class commandeered the best pews); 'the
indifference of the Churches to the social condition of the
poor; the misconceptions of the motives of ministers' (the
educated voice proclaiming moral probity could come across as

unsympathetic and patronising); 'and the influences of poverty and overcrowded houses'.[6] He might have added that the model for the rural parish church was at odds with an urban setting where everything was on the move and there were no firm rules for social interplay. One of the most revealing statistics of the mid-century tells us that over half of the London population that was aged twenty or over had not been born in the city.

But the census and Mann's observations based on the figures told only part of the story. The Church had advanced since Victoria's childhood. Between 1801 and 1831, nearly 500 churches had been built; between 1831 and 1851, the number was 2,029, no less than 849 of them in industrial areas. Many more churches had been restored and enlarged. It was true that provision was not keeping pace with the increase of population (in London there were only 140,000 seats for a population of nearly 1.4 million), but the heavy emphasis on church attendance as the only indicator of Christian observance failed to take account of social realities.

Those without first-hand experience of factory conditions failed to appreciate that after six days of monotonous, often dangerous, labour, a Sunday outing to thank God for his benevolence was not the highest priority. Poverty was a deterrent to worship. If family income was too low to buy shoes and decent clothes, to appear in church was to invite contempt from the better-placed members of the congregation. Yet interest in religion was high, certainly higher than in the early part of the century. Press coverage of the religious census was as extensive as that for the 1851 Great Exhibition in Hyde Park. Daily prayers at home were commonplace, and even the poorest household was likely to possess a Bible and, often, a Book of Common Prayer. In 1850, a phonetic edition of the Bible was produced for the barely literate. Four years later, Holman Hunt unveiled his *Light of the World*, depicting the figure of Jesus, crowned with thorns, lamp in hand, knocking at a cottage door, neglected and overgrown. It was to become one of the most popular Christian images of all time, reproduced in cheap prints to adorn simple dwellings throughout the country. The original was given by the purchaser to the chapel of Keble College.

Christian writers enjoyed a wide circulation for tracts, sermons and other devotional works. In working-class households, Christianity was equated with honesty, generosity and loyalty. 'My first surprise about East London was its extreme respectability,' wrote Winnington-Ingram, later Bishop of London. 'In morality and sense of decency they are far ahead of dwellers in some other parts of London.' A contributing factor, though one that was much ridiculed by later generations, was the recruitment of middle-class ladies to spread the Christian message among the poor. House-to-house visiting was an Evangelical inspiration, first put into practice by Thomas Chalmers in the inner-city parish of St John's, Glasgow. In 1825 London Nonconformists founded the Christian Instruction Society, which soon had over a thousand members; each pledged to pay a Christian visit once a week.[7]

The practice was soon taken up by Anglicans, in several cases with startling success. When, in the 1850s, Charles Kemble took on the new South London parish of St Michael's, Stockwell, he was without a parochial structure or money to support one. Setting his mind to how he might make his presence felt, he appealed for help from the well-to-do minority. Such was the response that in 1859 he felt able to publish *Suggestive Hints on Parochial Machinery*, in which he heartedly commended the deployment of female visitors 'to diffuse Christian influence through all classes; to present Christianity under its practical aspect ... to effect a moral improvement in society and to edify God's church'. His ideal visitor was a married woman, 'one who knows the world and its trials'. It was the job of the person to assign the poor streets of his parish to these gentle folk who were to distribute tracts and books, invite children to Sunday school, persuade their parents to attend church, provide hospital letters for the ill and distribute 'meat, bread, coals, wine, beer, arrowroot, rice, tea or money'.[8]

Visiting became a major activity for thousands of suburban housewives with time on their hands and with few other opportunities for community involvement. With less than tactful handling, those on the receiving end could feel horribly patronised. But for all its defects, visiting was a genuine effort to keep the clergy in contact with non-churchgoers and to bridge the classes.

It was slow progress but, notwithstanding the severe strictures from Thomas Mann, a determined effort was being made to strengthen the Church in the industrial towns and cities. After the setting up in 1836 of the Church Pastoral Aid Society to raise funds in destitute areas, more than a dozen like-minded organisations were founded.[9] Between 1847 and 1861, the Church Commissioners distributed £400,000 to supplement poor livings. Over the same period close on 150 societies for social and moral improvement, nearly all with a Church connection, were founded in urban centres.[10]

In Whitechapel, the Evangelical W. W. Champneys made the brave decision to live among his people. His one church, which could hold 1,500, provided for a parish of 36,000. Only a handful of worshippers turned out on Sunday.

> When he walked in his parish he was shocked by the lack of sanitation or drainage, the sight of 40 people sleeping in one room, and being called to administer Holy Communion to a dying man in a room where 20 others were sleeping. He found hundreds of 'ragged boys' who slept in sugar hogs-heads, or wandered the streets all night, with no one concerned for their physical welfare, let alone their education.[11]

At the end of his twenty-three-year incumbency, Champneys had overseen the division of Whitechapel into four parishes, each with its church, vicarage and school. His savings bank, coal club, shoeblack brigade as a source of relief for vagrant boys, young men's institute and mothers' meetings were among the first in London. Champneys' congregation regularly exceeded 1,500.

The clergy who gave their lives to slum parishes were seen as missionaries in hostile territory, and not without reason. Violence was commonplace. After a mob attack, Wilson Carlile, an Evangelical parson whose work in the poorer parts of Kensington led to the founding of the Church Army, spent six months in hospital. His was not an isolated case.

The Church Parochial Mission Society gave support to overworked and underfunded incumbents. One such was Charles Lowder, a young Tractarian who, in 1856, threw himself into the social maelstrom that was London's docklands. St George-in-the-East was a large church with few worshippers. Rival attractions in the immediate neighbourhood included gin parlours, cheap eating houses and more than 150 brothels.

Lowder recorded first-hand knowledge of 'the narrow courts and alleys, as seen through the murky atmosphere of fog and dust, with all the horrors of sight and sound and smell ... scowling brutal faces of men, degraded monsters of women, poor little children half clad except with dirt, with naked feet and dishevelled hair, playing in the gutter, many of them stunted, half-witted and deformed.'[12]

Lowder was used to trouble, having already served his time as a curate in Pimlico, where services were frequently disrupted. But neither Lowder, nor his rector, Bryan King, had encountered anything like the tumult that erupted when an Evangelical colleague began preaching against the 'popish tendencies' of the services at St George's. Delinquency thrived under a veneer of religious conviction. Between June 1859 and May 1860, the parish thugs made each Sunday a day of open warfare. Wild dogs were set loose, missiles of rotten fruit exchanged, boys with pea shooters attacked from the gallery while soapbox orators screamed insults at each other across the chancel. The police refused to intervene in what was said to be a purely ecclesiastical matter and when volunteer bodyguards, including a famous amateur boxer, proved impotent, the church was closed. But Lowder, left alone after the Revd King suffered a breakdown, had his successes, including schools for 600 children, a home for reformed prostitutes and an active mission church.

Another High Church parson who had trouble with his Evangelical rivals was George Rundle Prynne of St Peter's in the poorest district of Plymouth. Urged on by the local press, the vicar of a neighbouring parish led a campaign of vituperation against the chanting of psalms, the wearing of the surplice in the pulpit and other ritual 'excesses'. This nonsense was interrupted by a cholera outbreak when Prynne set up a hospital and recruited as helpers the members of an Anglican sisterhood in Devonport. Their self sacrifice was extraordinary.

> I well remember on one occasion having been called to see a poor woman lying on a mattress on the floor in the agonies of cholera, and close on her confinement. It was a low, overcrowded room. I had to step over a dead body to get at her. Another dead body had just been put into its thin coffin and was being lowered through the window into the street below.[13]

On visiting another house and receiving no answer to his knock on the door 'he went in and found every inmate dead, and the house reeking with the most horrible stench. He and the curate between them removed the dead into the street'. When the epidemic subsided, the sisterhood started an orphanage for girls. Even so, sectarian warfare was soon resumed.

With the outbreak of cholera in 1849, the Revd James Gillman, vicar of Holy Trinity, Lambeth, did not go home for three weeks for fear of taking the disease with him. He slept on the sofa in the surgery of the parish doctor. Gillman achieved posthumous fame after his cheap life insurance scheme grew into the Prudential Assurance Company. When Bishop Blomfield urged his clergy to teach sanitation and personal cleanliness, they needed no prompting. They spoke out against polluted water, inadequate sewage, open sewers and disease-ridden hovels. Dozens of them spent the best part of their lives labouring, for little reward or thanks, in London's slums.

To the parish of Leeds came Walter Farquhar Hook, a forceful, witty and plain-speaking parson who modelled himself on Dr Johnson, with whom he enjoyed being compared. As we have seen, his great passion was education. In his previous life as the incumbent of Holy Trinity, Coventry, he had increased the school rolls ten-fold. He had also started a dispensary supported by penny subscriptions. The scheme was so successful that it eventually paid the salaries of three full-time doctors.[14]

As vicar of Leeds he had four town and nine suburban churches, with eighteen clergy serving a population that had spiralled from 53,000 in 1801 to 123,000 thirty years later. He found crowded streets and tenements, open sewers, ignorance and destitution. Church life was almost non-existent. With Methodism in the ascendancy, Hook's High Church principles were not easily accepted, not least by his own bishop. But energy and commitment paid off. 'His classes and lectures were endless, filling all his evenings, as visits, committees and interviews filled all his days.'[15] Twenty-two new churches were built in his time in Leeds, along with twenty-seven schools and twenty-three rectories. 'He had a tender, tender heart,' said one of his curates and, indeed, it was Hook himself who declaimed, 'Give me a person with a heart and let the heads take care of themselves.' He was at his best in mission room services when he met the poorest of his flock.

There would be shortened Evensong and perhaps the Litany. The vicar would then read a chapter from the Bible and expound it in a plain, practical manner. When this was done he would tell the congregation all the parish news, who had died, or who had got married lately, and familiar little items of gossip like that. Then the people paid their penny or twopenny subscription to the Religious Knowledge Library, the blessing was given, and they all went home. There was no theory of Christian fellowship at work, but just the simple practice of it.[16]

Mission rooms were the foundation for the churches and schools that came later.

In Sheffield, the Revd Samuel Earnshaw served as an assistant minister from 1847 until his death in 1888. He is remembered as a champion of the working class. In a famous sermon he condemned the oppression of the poor and the use of religion to keep the people quiet and submissive. Another radical voice was that of the Revd G. S. Bull, curate of Byerley near Bradford. He campaigned vigorously for temperance, education and shorter working hours.[17] From his vicarage window in Hey near Oldham, George Dooker Grundy could count 130 mill chimneys. Pollution killed off grass and trees. Apart from the local doctor, educated companionship was non-existent. Yet over sixty-two years, from 1840 to 1902, Grundy was absent from his parish for only three nights, when he was in London for his son's marriage.

Few, very few, men of his upbringing could have endured life at Hey as it was when he went there in 1840. But his mind was set on bringing men to God. It was the absorbing, the absolutely dominating influence of his whole life. ... When he went to Hey the mill-hands, who formed at least 90 per cent of the population, were to all intents and purposes heathens. I myself can remember that at a village three miles away, where practically the whole wage-earning population were employed in a cotton mill belonging to my other grandfather, not one of them ever went to church or chapel. The average congregation in the church was eight people all told. But at that time (1860–70) the church at Hey was crowded every Sunday, and it would hold nearly a thousand people. My grandfather had practically converted the mill-hands of his early years and their children of later years to Christianity ... at his death 'ard [old] Maister Grundy', as he was called locally, left Hey a very different place from what he had found it when he went there. The church at Hey, formerly ignored, had not only become the religious but the intellectual centre of the life of the parish and of the district.[18]

One thing nearly all these pioneering spirits had in common was their middle-class credentials. While Christianity in the broadest sense commanded respect, even devotion, at all levels of society, there was no escaping the fact that the Church was essentially a middle-class institution. Left-wing critics of a later generation, though they themselves were unlikely to have much social contact with the lower orders, condemned the Church for holding to its narrow base. But in offering leadership, education and social amenities far in excess of anything the state was willing to provide, the Church was committed to raising standards. It is hard to imagine that more could have been done by subscribing to the lowest common social denominator.

The good parson set an example. Class conscious he may have been, but he recognised that his responsibilities demanded more than a nodding acquaintance with the classics and an open invitation to dine with the squire. In 1850 Edward Munro, vicar of St John's, Leeds, from 1860, declared, 'The life of the clergyman should be a standing protest against the life around him.' An aloofness from worldly preoccupations was to be combined with sympathy for the tribulations of the people, whatever their social standing.

Advice on practising the good life was contained in a wide choice of reading materials. *The Clergyman's Obligations Considered, Practical Advice to the Young Parish Priest, The Clergyman's Instructor* and *The Duties of the Clerical Profession* were among the many enticing titles on offer. Throughout, the stress was on treating life seriously. There was no room for frivolity. Relaxation was equated with indolence. Sports were unclerical; so too were theatricals, boisterous music and all forms of dancing. 'We have no order of dancing dervishes in the English Church' declared Henry Jones in his widely adopted handbook, *Priest and Parish*.

Given the leading role of the Church in nearly all walks of life, it is no small wonder that the clergy also figured prominently in the kitbag of characters in popular fiction. Even less surprising was their frequent portrayal in less than sympathetic light. Since they presented themselves as the standard by which all other standards were judged, any slippage was open to attack or ridicule. And slippages there were bound to be. It was a matter of secret delight to readers of Trollope, Thackeray or Dickens to find that the self-appointed mighty could be brought low, that they might be no better than those they sought to edify. It was a form of guilty release, like the child's urge to scream aloud in church.

The elevated status the clergy awarded themselves also made them an obvious target for the popular press which, then as now, thrived on deflating pomposity. That there were small-minded, self-important clerics no one could deny, though whether they were representative is another matter. The same might be said of serial offenders against all the Church stood for. A tradition that lasted well into the twentieth century of headlining vicars caught with their pants down started with a coroner's report on a seventy-three-year-old clergyman who had died of an apoplectic fit in a brothel near Oxford Street.[19]

There were notable eccentrics who were less than assiduous

in their parochial duties but were often regarded with tolerant affection by their parishioners. John Lucy, rector of Hampton Lucy, near Warwick, had impeccable manners. As 'a most perfect gentleman of the old school [he would] sweep off his hat with punctilious politeness to an old woman picking up sticks'. But his lifestyle hardly accorded with Church conventions. Blessed with a private income and accommodated in some luxury, he favoured late dinners and was often in bed until four in the afternoon. A keen sportsman, he gave out hunting notices from his pulpit and when, aged eighty, he was too old to ride, attended hunt meetings on foot. Three years later, he fell ill with jaundice. A warning from his doctor that he had only weeks to live did not deter him going to London for a new set of false teeth. Until almost his last breath he enjoyed a daily bottle and a half of champagne laced with brandy. On his death in 1874, he had been rector for fifty-nine years.

In February 1856, the Revd Joseph Romilly made note in his diary of a 'queer man of the name of Beavor', who turned out to be the son of a 'fighting parson ... who was ... continually boxing with parishioners'. The man, 'wild and unclerical', followed in his father's footsteps. Romilly commented, 'In Norfolk there are three sorts of creatures – men, women and Beavors.'[20]

At Netteswell in Essex, the Revd Philip Johnson was a keen violinist, so keen that he spent most of his time in London where he could mix with fellow enthusiasts. In the thirty-eight years of his incumbency, he was rarely in his parish except for weekends. When he died, the elderly couple who looked after his rectory were surprised to be visited by a stranger who claimed to be the parson's widow. This was the first anyone in the parish knew that Johnson had been married.[21]

Also in Essex, Joseph Arkwright, grandson of the inventor of the spinning frame, used his inherited wealth from the Lancashire cotton mills to live the grand life as squire and parson of Latton. A curate was put in charge of the fifteenth-century church when

Arkwright was otherwise occupied, which was for most of the year. In fact, his only appearance in the pulpit was at Christmas, when he exhorted his tenant farmers and workers to goodwill and neighbourliness. After thirty years as vicar Joseph handed on the living to his son Julius.[22]

The West Country, with its predominance of isolated communities, where educated company or company of any sort was a prized rarity, was rich in oddball parsons. While researching his biography of Hawker, Piers Brendon collected a mixed assortment.

> One parson did not enter his church for 53 years and kennelled the local foxhounds in his vicarage. Another varied the colour of his communion wine, sometimes red, sometimes white. Another refused to take services but, 'clad in flowered dressing-gown and smoking a hookah', greeted his parishioners in the churchyard. Another drove away his congregation, replaced them by wooden and cardboard images in the pews and surrounded his vicarage with a barbed-wire fence behind which savage Alsatians patrolled. Another spent his life searching for the Number of the Beast. Yet another, the rector of Luffincott, to whom Hawker gave friendly advice on the subject, devoted his energies to calculating the date of the millennium.[23]

But then, the incumbent who 'equipped his stall in church with his own sanitary arrangements' was no less eccentric than a colleague who 'professed himself a neo-Platonist and sacrificed an ox to Jupiter.[24] The many who found solace in the bottle were models for the once ubiquitous Toby jug, suggesting that they were not entirely lacking the affection of their flock. One tippler who was praised for his sermon on brotherly love found himself before the magistrate later in the week for beating his wife.

A popular story retold over the years was of a parson in North Devon who was a connoisseur of wines.

He would taste, and unhesitatingly pronounce what vintage was in his glass. One evening [he was] tested, after a bout of drinking, with his eyes bandaged. He hit right almost invariably. Then, finally, he was given another glass. 'Now then, what do you say to that?' The parson tasted, made a wry face and said: 'Beastly stuff; never before had my mouth full of such rubbish!' It was water.[25]

The exceptions proved the rule. Those who transgressed and were found out achieved notoriety, while those who were a credit to their vocation had to struggle for recognition.

The good parson spent his days on poor relief and visiting the sick, giving medical care to the poor, organising thrift clubs, penny banks and friendly societies; planning, financing and managing day schools, Sunday schools and adult classes (by 1867, there were more than 4,000 adult schools, most of them organised by the Church), fundraising and speaking out against social evils. Conducting services was the least onerous part of his work. The parson's wife ran mothers' meetings and maternity societies.

Christopher Bird became vicar of Chollerton in Northumberland, where he succeeded his father in 1867, and remained for twenty-nine years until his death. He used his wealth to help the Central African Mission and the new and struggling diocese of Newcastle, built schools, restored the church and privately helped clergymen in distress or their widows. He was regarded affectionately as 'prophet, priest and king' among his people.

In 1851 George Martin accepted the almost inaccessible moorland Cornish parish of St Breward and remained there for thirty-one years. He arrived with a new wife at a village with no school, a tumbledown parsonage and leaking church which did not always have services. He left a flourishing school and a restored church.[26] Robert Elrington was vicar of Lower

Brixham in Devon for thirty-four years (1855–89). He rebuilt his church into one of the grandest on the coast, made a new vicarage and a school, was chairman of the local board, was said to have dealt almost single-handedly with a cholera epidemic in Brixham, and broke his health in a similar epidemic of scarlet fever.

It is one of the illusions of a passing acquaintance with the Church in action that a rural living promised an easy life for the parson. The charms of Burwash in East Sussex are, today, a magnet for London commuters. It is hard now to imagine that in the 1850s, the village was terrorised by smugglers and highway robbers. Extreme poverty was endemic while those who could afford it took to drink. The Burwash Wheel was said to be the roughest pub on the South Coast. As rector of Burwash, John Coker Egerton fought a battle that was not so much uphill as vertical.

Drunken abuse greeted him when he was out in the village. Typically 'a drunken man shouted to me that he always found beer more profitable to him than preaching; he also began to urinate and told me he was coming to church as soon as he had done'. Egerton could well take care of himself but, more surprisingly, he kept his humour. When he told a drunk that he was committing sin in the sight of God, back came the retort, 'What if I be; who made me sin; how did sin come into the world. Who made the devil.' 'Deep cogitation for a drunken man,' mused Egerton.[27]

Services often had an element of farce. Celebrating communion, 'somebody took the bottle of wine out of the vestry', while a few weeks later while conducting a wedding service, 'the man burst out laughing in trying to repeat the words after me'. Egerton soldiered on.

Edward Elton was another parson whose parish was anything but quiescent. In 1849 he accepted the living of Wheatley, on the London to Oxford road, described by his bishop as 'the most difficult village'. The ten pubs catered for the workers at the limestone quarries and for Oxford undergraduates who were out for a good time beyond the reach of the university proctors. Since there was no resident landowner, Elton was the only voice of authority. He was not welcomed. For his first Sunday service he had to be escorted to the church by a constable. After he planted an orchard by his newly built parsonage, the young trees were cut down one night by a vindictive parishioner. But Elton's perseverance won through. His 'turbulent and ill-conditioned' people were tamed by his energy and commitment. He raised money for new schools and a new church. He campaigned for better sanitation and for a village station on the new railway linking Thame and Oxford.

The country parson was as likely to encounter deprivation and suffering as his urban counterpart. When the railway ended the rural seclusion of East Dereham in Norfolk, the Revd Armstrong was almost overwhelmed by the misery that came with an expanding population.

A certain street in this parish has been unfortunate of late. The owner of No. 1, a lawyer, died miserably. At No. 2 was the sudden death of a woman with a large family and whose husband was a reprobate and separated from her. At No. 5 a young man, a painter, died wretchedly from drink. At No. 6 a baker went to bed in good health and in the morning his wife discovered that he was a corpse. Within the last few days the man at No. 8 fell down dead opposite the Vicarage gate. At No. 10 the man took to drink and made attempts on the lives of his relatives, so that they were obliged to send him away. To my horror I found him in the Reading Room, where he swore that he would see his wife and child, or kill them and himself too. I promised to see them. Their alarm was fearful. After hours of talk he promised to go away again if only he might see the child! I went to the house and brought the child in my arms. The poor wretched father and the child wept as if their hearts would break. At last I got the little girl away, and the man went off in a gig that I had provided.[28]

The parson who pushed hard against social conventions was liable to find himself in trouble. The Revd Sidney Godolphin Osborne was appointed to the living at Durweston in Dorset in 1841. He remained there for thirty-four turbulent years. Battle lines were drawn when Osborne started writing letters to *The Times* protesting at the low wages paid to agricultural workers. This brought an objection from the local MP, George Bankes, who claimed that by writing to a national newspaper naming him, Bankes, as a force for obstruction, Osborne had committed a breach of privilege.

The House of Commons rejected the motion, forcing Bankes into a humiliating withdrawal. He was soon back on the attack with complaints to the bishop about the disruptive behaviour of this 'popularity hunting parson'. But Osborne had too much to his credit as a parish priest for any action to be taken against him. It helped also that he had aristocratic connections, being the third son of Lord Godolphin. It was impossible to dismiss him as an ill-informed rabble rouser. Osborne was assiduous in gathering facts. If wages were poor, so too was the state of workers' cottages, which were little better than hovels. All this was faithfully reported in *The Times*, where Osborne had the freedom of the letters page. As he got into his stride, other social issues including education, sanitation, women's rights, free trade, prison reform and emigration were drawn to his spotlight. Identified in print by his initials – SGO – his Dorset supporters dubbed him 'Sincere, Good and Outspoken'.[29]

In mid-century, half the benefices of England were still in the hands of private patrons. Moreover, when Edward Batrum wrote his *Promotion of Merit Essential to the Progress of the Church* in 1866, he estimated that more than 50 per cent of the 6,245 livings in private patronage were 'obtained by purchase or given away from interested motives'. On the principle that charity starts at home, in at least 1,290 of those livings the names of patrons and incumbents were the same.

This was not always to the detriment of parishioners. With theological and pastoral training at a premium, it was an open question as to where true merit reposed, unless failure to be appointed to a suitable living was itself a qualification. Then again, self-appointment, particularly when it was linked to a private income, at least had the virtue of installing a parson who really wanted the job. By contrast, in the rare cases where parishioners had a voice in the selection of their parson, the contest could turn nasty, with the successful candidate being the one who handed out the most generous bribes.

The wealthy parson, though invariably self-appointed, could make a real difference to a deprived parish. Memories of Henry James Sperling, rector of Papworth St Agnes in Cambridgeshire, are entirely to his credit.

> He was rich, he was devout; his life was passed in a loftier region of thought and aspiration than common men wot of; but he was a philanthropist in advance of his time, who carried out into practice in a remote country village what other people were dreaming of. He owned every acre of land in the parish ... the whole rent of the estate was spent upon improvements: I think every cottage in the parish was rebuilt – many new ones added – roads were made – land was drained – schools were erected – the church rebuilt from the foundations; and in the meantime, if the people were not all they ought to have been, it was not because all was not done to make them so.[30]

Another parson of enviable reputation was Henry Addington Simcoe, rector of Penheale in Cornwall.

He lived in a beautiful old mansion with Elizabethan ceilings and panellings, that had come into the Simcoe family by purchase. He always wore Hessian boots with a tassel in front, and stood up over six feet, was of strong build and powerful muscles. Belonging to the Evangelical school ... he spent his energies and his money on all the organisations called into being by his party. He went about wherever invited to preach in pulpits and harangue on platforms. At home he had made his picturesque old manor-house into a store of everything necessary to daily life. The lads and girls of the parish of Egloskerry were taught trades under his eye – tailoring, bootmaking, basket-weaving and the manufacture of a thousand other commodities likely to be wanted in a region where there are no shops. He established a printing press in the house, from which issued tracts and a periodical, *The Light of the West*, printed on poor paper, with on the cover a representation of the Eddystone lighthouse.[31]

The composition of the league of patrons changed with investment by the religious lobbies. Charles Simeon, a leading Evangelical parson, raised money and used his own wealth to buy livings where reliable ordinands could be installed. By 1835 he had seventeen livings under his control. Within fifteen years some half a million people lived in parishes in the gift of the Simeon Trust.[32] When benefices came on the market it was often the bishops who were first to make an offer. At Oxford, Wilberforce built up the diocesan's patronage from fifteen livings to ninety-five, including most of the large towns.

The assessment of candidates for ordination became more rigorous. Those who appeared before Bishop Thomas Burgess at Salisbury had to demonstrate a close acquaintance with the Bible, ecclesiastical history and William Paley's *Evidences of Christianity* along with other standard works. He also demanded a knowledge of Hebrew and saw to it that a candidate's sense of vocation and personal piety were thoroughly tested.[33] Among other bishops who set higher standards, Henry Phillpotts of Exeter and Samuel Wilberforce of Oxford took a determined lead.

With the tightening up of royal patronage other wealthy patrons followed suit, though few were willing to match the terms stipulated by the Duke of Newcastle. Seeking an incumbent for Worksop, the qualities he sought ran to eleven pages. At minimum, the appointee had to be around forty years of age, and 'a gentleman, but not an unapproachable fine gentleman'. He must be:

> Remarkable in piety ... learning, good sense, judgement, justice and sound discretion. A good preacher with a good voice and agreeable and persuasive delivery ... His opinions should be *anchored*, not floating about on a voyage of discovery – not a Tractarian, or Evangelical or an anything else, but sound, orthodox ... the best of the old school of Church of England divines.[34]

While there was much to praise, the Church did itself no favours by holding to an outmoded system of administration. This showed most obviously in the treatment of curates.

John Smith had many disappointments to bear. A Cambridge graduate of acknowledged talent, he hoped for distinction as the first to transcribe the diaries of Samuel Pepys into plain English. Having spent three years in cracking the shorthand system adopted by Pepys, he then found that the blueprint was close at hand in the shelves of Pepys's library. A heavily expurgated edition was published under the name of Lord Braybrooke, who was later forced to admit that he had wielded the editorial blade rather too freely. Smith, meanwhile, had found employment as a curate in the Norfolk parish of Banham. From there, in 1835, he wrote bitterly of his ill-rewarded workload, proclaiming the

Church 'in danger' because the curates 'are not doing their work properly'. Why? 'Because they are not being paid properly.'

Thirty years on, the curate's lot had changed but not greatly improved. The change was the fall in absenteeism, from 50 per cent to 10 per cent, with the result that there were fewer stipendiary curates (down from over 3,000 to less than 1,000) representing parsons who rarely if ever visited their parishes. However, there were more curates acting as assistants to resident parsons. They were often younger ordinands serving a sort of apprenticeship, their lowly status and miserable income borne in the hope of eventually acquiring churches of their own. With up to 600 applicants for curacies coming forward each year (well over double the number in the mid-eighteenth century), expectations were often disappointed. There were simply not enough livings to go round.

Stuck in the master/servant groove, the parson, however admirable in other respects, could be a hard task master. The curate was landed with the drudgery of parish work while keeping to himself any opinions he might have on how Church affairs might be better managed. They could be patronised mercilessly. In Shropshire around 1840,

> The curates always came to luncheon at the (Stoke) Rectory on Sundays. They were always compelled to come in ignominiously at the back door, lest they should dirty the entrance: only Mr Egerton was allowed to come in at the front door, because he was 'a gentleman born'. How Grannie used to bully the curates! They were expected not to talk at luncheon, if they did they were soon put down. 'Tea-table Theology' was unknown in those days. As soon as the curates had swallowed a proper amount of cold veal, they were called upon to 'give an account to Mrs Leycester' of all that they had done in the week in the four quarters of the parish – and soundly rated if their actions did not correspond with her intentions.[35]

No wonder that curates had a reputation for heavy drinking. The dedicated curate was worth every penny of whatever modest sums came his way – rarely more than £100 per annum at a time when a butler, coachman or cook could earn £70 or £80 with all found, while an elementary schoolmaster could expect at least £150 with a rent-free schoolhouse.[36]

At Great Maplestead, Essex, Robert Hart kept a record of his manifold duties. These included regular services, classes for 'penitents', communion at the House of Mercy for fallen women in the village, teaching in the day school, confirmation classes, running a night school and visiting the sick. In the evening he worked on his sermons. His wife, Kate, ran the choir. A recurring diary entry is 'very weary all day' or just 'very weary'.[37] Since the curate had no security of tenure, he had to keep on the right side of his incumbent if he did not wish to be moved on.

Disaffected curates had the chance to air their grievances at the Church Congress, held at Wolverhampton in October 1867. The core complaint was the 'great gulf' between the curate and his vicar or rector, who 'thought of him not as a fellow priest, but as a humble dependant'.[38] But there were many voices raised against this despairing assessment. The consensus held that curates who had shown themselves fit for their work were given the respect and remuneration they deserved. Any blame for a sorry state of affairs was attached to curates who fell short of expectations. When Harvey Bloom secured a vacancy at Harwich he recorded his parson's recollections of curates past, including 'the fat and dumpling one who had thought of nothing but his food, and did practically nothing; the lean one who drank on the sly and had to leave because once he preached when intoxicated; the friend's son who had got the maid into trouble and in the end had bolted with a valued parishioner's wife'.[39]

Poverty among long-serving curates could be alleviated by grants from the Evangelical Church Pastoral Aid Society or the

High Church Additional Curates Society. By the late 1860s the two bodies were each funding some 500 curates. Also, there were occasional handouts from the Ecclesiastical Commissioners. In February 1873, the Revd Atkinson recorded an offer from the Commissioners to pay £120 a year to a second curate on condition that Atkinson paid for the first out of his own pocket.[40] The agreement was confirmed but, with his experience of curates, Atkinson was not hopeful of a successful outcome. Ten years earlier he had entered in his diary the first of numerous waspish comments on the quality of clerical assistants.

> My curate leaves me tomorrow, and I shall be alone. His reason for going is that he cannot live, he says, on £100 a year. I have never felt safe with him, and his ministrations are worth but little. He may not be able to live on £100 a year, but he is *not worth* that as a matter of value.[41]

Joseph Brunskill was a curate who did not easily submit to authority. The son of a small farmer and the product of St Bees Clerical College, which made him sensitive to the snobbery of Oxbridge colleagues, Brunskill held strong views and was not afraid to express them. He went through a rapid succession of curacies until in November 1853 he arrived at Mallerstrang, a remote parish in Cumbria, where the perpetual curate had been suspended for his over-fondness of the bottle. Brunskill entered a small, self-contained world.

> The weekly Monday market at Kirkby Stephen was the hub of the world. The annual routine of the small grazing farms was lambing time, clipping and sheep washing, haytime, mowing bedding, and cutting peat and 'flawes' (turves) for fuel. The routine was enlivened by four annual events, the first being Outhgill fair; the second the passing of the Scots drovers of sheep and cattle on their way to Yorkshire fairs; the third was Brough

Hill Fair, when a miscellaneous assortment of men and things defiled through the dale; and the fourth was the autumn Luke Fair at Kirkby Stephen when cattle and sheep were sold, mainly to pay the rents. Haverbread and blue-milk cheese were the staple diet, fustian and clogs their working attire, rushlights and farthing candles their lights. Their doctor was a long way off, so that much faith was placed in 'yerbs' and country remedies. The only two educated men in the dale were the schoolmaster and the parson.[42]

Brunskill took as his first priority the improvement of the school held in a loft at the back of the church with a schoolmaster who 'admits his ignorance of the art of teaching'.[43] But with little support from his bishop, Brunskill was powerless and when the suspension of his predecessor was lifted, he decided to move on. He was not paid for his period of notice.

In the family of the Church, the curates remained the poor relations.

CHAPTER NINE

Clerical Diversions

For the parson who savoured the quiet life, often to pursue intellectual interests in tandem with his clerical duties, there was always a contingent of more-or-less secluded rural parishes where the mood of churchgoers matched the calm and stability of the village community.

In mid-century, at Lydiard, to the west of Swindon, the parson in his pulpit 'looked out at the squire and his family in their allotted pew, the more prosperous farmers in black coats and, on benches, the labourers in their snow-white smocks, here and there a blue smock with a pattern in white thread on the breast, each male with a red pocket handkerchief; the women in scarlet flannel shawls.

> The men sat passive, not following in books, some unable to read, but silent with a stolid attentiveness, not liking to be absent because of the squire or the farmer or habit, but in no way sorry to be there, men without hostility and with quiet acceptance.[1]

Where better as a base for academic study with none of the distractions of a student body? If this was the idyll for an aspiring ordinand, he had to persuade a suitable patron that he was the man for the job. The Revd Octavius Pickard-Cambridge started with a huge advantage of being born in a rectory. His father was a squirson, both rector and squire of Bloxworth, a tiny tucked-away Dorset village 12 miles east of Dorchester. Set on becoming a naturalist, the young Octavius spent his early years collecting and cataloguing insects. He was tutored by William Barnes, another Dorsetman and parson scholar who taught himself eight languages and wrote poetry. A fellow poet, Coventry Patmore, wrote of Barnes, 'He has done a small thing well, while his contemporaries have mostly been engaged in doing big things ill'. One of the small things Barnes did well was to impart to his pupil a love of nature and the skill to record it in drawings and sketches.

After three miserable years training to be a lawyer, Pickard-Cambridge was allowed to study divinity at Durham with the aim of being appointed his father's curate at Bloxworth. Once installed he gave full vent to his passion for identifying and studying every British species of spider. Along with many hundreds of exotic specimens from other countries, he assembled the world's largest private collection of its kind. He was feted by learned societies and elected a fellow of the Royal Society and of the Zoological Society. But there was no question of him neglecting his parishioners. He was devoted to their interests and in a long life (he died just short of his ninetieth birthday) worked tirelessly on their behalf.[2]

Not all polymath parsons were quite so assiduous but few of those who pursued parallel careers could be accused of neglecting their duties. Keen clerical naturalists included William Kirby, rector of Barnham in Suffolk for sixty-eight years. Bees were his passion. Restricting himself to his own parish, he collected 153 species of wild bee and helped to found the study of entomology. Henry Ellacombe, who held the living of Clyst St George on the Devon coast for thirty years from 1855, was a genealogist, botanist and campanologist. His garden contained 5,000 different plants, many of them rarities. But he is best remembered for his book on the church bells of Devon in which he listed their sizes, tunes, quality, dates and legends. He lived to be ninety-four.

One of the country's highest authorities on roses was Reynolds Hole, who became rector of Caunton in Nottinghamshire in 1850. Eventually, he had some 5,000 rose trees in his garden and many more on his father's land. He wrote *A Book About Roses* and initiated the first National Rose Show in 1858.

For many parsons, studying nature had a religious significance, since it brought them closer to the glories of creation. As the Revd Francis Morris, author of a *History of British Butterflies*, concluded, God had given man 'an instinctive general love of nature'. The same could be said of those who explored the heavens. At Melplash in Dorset, Samuel Johnson built himself an observatory with his new vicarage. As a self-taught astronomer, he produced a handy guide to *Eclipses Past and Future with General Hints for Observing the Heavens*.

The great days of the parson-scientist came to an end after Darwin disrupted their gentle lives. It was not so much what Darwin said or what he represented that made for difficulties. The professional status claimed by scientists after evolutionary theory broke through into the intellectual mainstream counted against the amateur. In *English Men of Science: Their Nature and Nurture*, published in 1872, Francis Galton argued that 'the pursuit of science is uncongenial to the priestly character'.[3] Galton did not regard the Church with respect or affection. Indeed, he looked forward to the decline and fall of the clergy in favour of 'the establishment of a sort of scientific priesthood throughout the kingdom'.

Though the prospect sent a shiver down many an ecclesiastical spine, there was no denying the clerical withdrawal from the world of science. In 1849, nearly 10 per cent of the Royal Society members were Anglican clergymen. Fifty years on the figure was down to 3 per cent. The British Association showed the same trend. A run of nine parson presidents ended in 1862. After that, not a single clergyman served as president.

By contrast, the Church strengthened its connection with the humanities. Mandell Creighton spent what he described as the ten happiest years of his life (1875–1884) as parson of Embleton, a coastal parish in Northumberland, where he wrote most of his five-volume *History of the Papacy during the Reformation.* The son of a cabinet maker, Creighton's intellectual promise gained him a scholarship to Durham Grammar School and another to Merton College, Oxford. He was ordained in 1870. A sympathetic, broad-minded churchman, he wrote several history books for young people and was a passionate supporter of denominational education. Rising through the clerical and academic ranks he was appointed to the newly established chair of ecclesiastical history at Cambridge. In 1891 he was made Bishop of Peterborough and, five years later, Bishop of London. But for his early death in 1901 aged fifty-seven he would almost certainly have ended his career as Archbishop of Canterbury. Another parson historian was Creighton's near neighbour in Northumberland, the Revd Richard Dixon of Warkworth, who produced a Tractarian version of the *History of the Church of England* while serving his bleak, remote parish.

One of the most eminent historians of his time was William Stubbs, who doubled as rector of Chollerton in Wiltshire while holding the chair of Modern History at Oxford. In 1872 he founded Oxford University's School of Modern History, enabling post-classical history to be taught as a subject in its own right. His best known-work was a three-volume *Constitutional History of England,* which was quickly accepted as the standard authority. Stubbs was made Bishop of Chester in 1884. Five years later he became Bishop of Oxford. Among the more esoteric clerical accomplishments was a standard work on old musical instruments written by Francis Galpin of Hatfield Broad Oak. Clerical antiquaries were legion with county histories as a favourite study.

Other clergy of literary bent led anything but quiet lives. Though the son of a parson who was himself ordained in 1861, Charles Lutwidge Dodgson, aka Lewis Carroll, hardly counts, since he remained on the fringes of the Church. This left the field clear for Charles Kingsley, who became a favourite of young readers with his sturdily Protestant adventure story, *Westward Ho!*, and of readers of all ages with his novels of social protest, *The Water Babies* and *Alton Locke.*

There was much more to Kingsley than writing fiction. A frenetically energetic man, he served the Hampshire parish of Eversley as rector, occasional teacher and outspoken defender of the rights of the poorer villagers against rapacious landlords and vindictive magistrates. He kept a horse and frequently rode to hounds. He was also a keen gardener and anthropologist. But before all things, Kingsley was a family man, passionately in love with his wife, Fanny, and a devoted father. It was the irrepressible passion he brought to all his causes that made him such a powerful novelist and social reformer. The middle-class conscience was not so much touched as clobbered by the sufferings of Tom, the boy chimneysweep in *The Water Babies,* and of the eponymous tailor's apprentice in *Alton Locke.* Kingsley was one of the moving spirits of Christian Socialism.

If productivity alone was the measure of literary excellence, Sabine Baring-Gould would be one of the Victorian greats. His output ran to over 100 books, ranging from melodramatic novels to hagiographies, including sixteen volumes devoted to lives of the saints, an enterprise which helped to send his publisher into bankruptcy. Remembered chiefly for *Onward, Christian Soldiers* and for his collections of West Country folk songs (including *Widdecombe Fair*), many of which he sanitised with new lyrics, his non-fiction was stylish if somewhat lacking in substance. His two volumes of reminiscences, packed with anecdotage, still make for a good read.

Notwithstanding his extra-curricular activities, Baring-Gould was a conscientious parson. After serving his apprenticeship as a curate in the West Riding of Yorkshire and a spell as rector of Mersea in Essex, he inherited the family estate in Devon, which included the living at Lewtrenchard, held by his uncle. When he died in 1881, Baring-Gould made himself parson as well as squire. He gave his mornings to his 300 or so parishioners, reserving the afternoons for writing. He needed all the money he could earn. Lavish spending on restoring St Peter's church and hall (now a hotel) he built model cottages for his workers and gave generously to charitable causes. His family of fifteen was another drain on resources. There is a story, surely apocryphal, of his making conversation at a children's party when he approached a pretty little girl. 'And who is your father?'

The child burst into tears. 'You are, Papa.'

His marriage to a mill hand's daughter he had met in Yorkshire lasted until her death forty-eight years later.

Born in Geneva where his father was a protestant minister, Solomon Caesar Malan was an outstanding linguist and an authority on oriental languages who held the living of Broadwindsor in Dorset from 1845 to 1885, the year in which he presented his library of 4,000 volumes to Keble College, Oxford. When not in dispute with fellow translators or attending to his parishioners, Malan put together one of the finest collections of birds' eggs. The beneficiary was an Exeter museum.

A close rival for linguistic distinction was George Bayldon, vicar of Cowling in Yorkshire for over forty years, who taught himself nine languages and published an Icelandic dictionary along with a history of the Christian Church in verse. As a parson, his chief activity was to persuade his flock to forswear hard liquor. It was said that he had a hold over the boys of the village, who cheerfully signed the pledge in return for old newspapers, which they turned into kites. Bayldon was the only resident for miles around who took a daily paper.

Though he visited Spain only once, Edward Churton, parson at Crayke in North Yorkshire, was an authority on Spanish literature. His early career was in Hackney, where he was headmaster of the church school and where he married the daughter of the rector, John James Watson. He also got to know Joshua Watson, whose biography he was to write. It was Churton who encouraged his friend Francis Massingberd to write his *History of the Leaders of the Reformation*. This may well have acted as an antidote to the depression and self-doubt suffered by Massingberd as parson of the family living of South Ormsby in Lincolnshire.

Massingberd's afflictions are a reminder that rural backwaters were not to everybody's taste. Even those who found literary inspiration in the remote countryside could run up against acute personal problems. The Victorians are notorious for sublimating their sexual urges. For the most part we can only guess at the mental suffering of young single parsons who, stranded in far-flung outposts of the Church, had to cope with their frustration without help or advice. One who touched on the subject without, perhaps, realising the implications of his diary entries was Francis Kilvert, a curate until his mid-thirties who served parishes on the Welsh border. Kilvert was a true romantic. He wrote brilliantly of his attachment to the beauties of the countryside and of the pleasures of music and poetry. His dearest wish was to be married, but while he moved easily in society, his circumstances as an impecunious parson counted against him. He found relief, of a sort, in his relationship with girls who were some way short of puberty. Today's media, obsessed as it is with child abuse and other improper behaviour by celibate priests, would have pilloried Kilvert. Fortunately for him, his parishioners were more understanding.

Wednesday, 23 August, 1871

'It began with a lass and it will end with a lass.'

In the evening before sunset while the sun was yet warm and bright I went across the golden common and meadow to the Three Firs to call on Hannah Britton. I had not been long in the house when Hannah's beautiful seven year old child Carrie gradually stole up to me and nestled close in my arms. Then she laid her warm temples and soft round cheek lovingly to mine and stole first one arm then the other round my neck. Her arms tightened round my neck and she pressed her face closer and closer to mine, kissing me again and again. Then came the old, old story, the sweet confession as old as human hearts, 'I do love you so. Do you love me?'

'Yes,' said the child, lovingly clinging still closer with fresh caresses and endearments.

'You little bundle,' said her mother laughing and much amused.

'I wish I could take you with me.'

'You would soon grow tired of her,' said her mother.

'No,' said the child with the perfect trust and confidence of love, 'he said he wouldn't.' An hour flew like a few seconds. I was in heaven. A lodger came in and sat down, but I was lost to everything but love and the embrace and the sweet kisses and caresses of the child. It seemed as if we could not part we loved each other so. At last it grew dusk and with one long loving clasp and kiss I reluctantly rose to go. It was hard to leave the child. When I went away she brought me the best flower she could find in the garden. I am exhausted with emotion.

There is more of this in the sections of Kilvert's diary that survived the expurgating tendencies of his heirs. In August 1874 he wrote of a parishioner who was having trouble with her daughter 'who grieves her sadly by frequently lying and stealing. I told her she must correct the girl in time. "I do flog her," she said. "And the other morning she was a naughty girl and her brother Joseph brought her in to me in her shimmy while I was in bed. I held her hand while Joseph and Charlie whipped her on her naked bottom as hard as ever they were able to flog her."'

This troubled and frustrated man eventually found the love of his life. But he was married for just one month, dying, aged thirty-nine, of peritonitis.

If we go along with the Victorian conviction that fresh air and lots of exercise were the antidote to temptations of the body, the sporting clergy suffered none of the Kilvert tribulations. Combining respectability with the working off of excess energy, cricket became the favoured recreation, particularly for rural parsons. It was claimed for those who loved the bat and ball that they 'exercised an extensive and beneficial influence on the game and through the game on the whole spirit of the nation'.

On December 3rd (1917) died the Rev. Sir Emilius-Bayley-Laurie, Bart. His great score of 152 in the Eton and Harrow match of 1841 stood as a record for sixty-three years. At the time of his death, being in his ninety-fifth year, he was the oldest cricketer alive, having outlived all his contemporaries. It is startling to find that when he played for Kent in the side were Mynn, Felix, Pilch, Wenman and Hillyer. His life, like that of Jenner-Fust and Ponsonby-Fane, spanned, indeed, whole periods of cricket history. His father, Sir John Bayley, Bart., was President of M.C.C. in 1844. He himself lived near Lord's for many years, being Vicar of S. John's, Paddington, from 1867 to 1888.[4]

CHAPTER TEN

Church Building
and Rebuilding

The Victorians were enthusiastic church builders. In the half century up to 1876, over 2,500 Anglican places of worship were consecrated and many more older buildings adapted to contemporary needs. The favoured architecture was fourteenth-century Gothic, otherwise known as Middle Pointed.

There were several reasons why the Church was wedded to Gothic. Though the style preceded the Reformation, it was associated with piety and learning, while the period when it was out of favour concluded with clerical negligence and corruption.

There were also practical considerations. Classical design, though favoured for many public buildings, was expensive and ill-suited to the rural landscape where the Church was strongest. Another advantage was that architects could rely on masons whose knowledge of Gothic structures had been handed down over generations. But overriding all was comfort and reassurance of medievalism. The contrast to modernism with its brutalisation of work and vulgarisation of leisure was conscious and deliberate.

The Gothic revival was led by Augustus Pugin, a gifted and inspired architect who worked with Charles Barry on the reconstruction of the Houses of Parliament after the fire of

1834. The heavy emphasis on pageantry and patriotism that greets the visitor to Westminster can be largely credited to, or blamed on, Pugin. But it was religion more than politics that enthused Pugin. A romantic Gothic obsessive (he even produced a Gothic mould for his puddings), he dreamed of 'glamorous medieval cities, noble cathedrals with soaring spires ... and ... richly decorated interiors with choirs raising voices and hearts in praise of God'.

From the point of view of the Protestant establishment, there were two counts against Pugin. Unquestionably, he was an oddball whose wild outbursts against fools and charlatans (just about everyone who disagreed with him) tested the patience of his most devoted followers. But to make relations with the Church even more problematic, Pugin was a Catholic convert, one who raged against the Reformation as the destroyer of the only true religion. On the other hand, Pugin was out of step with his fellow Catholics, who were inclined to favour Italian Renaissance over Gothic architecture.

Then again, there were supporters of Gothic with impeccable Anglican credentials. One of these was John Ruskin, whose love affair with medievalism included all things Gothic, said by him to be man's nearest approach to the angels. With characteristic self-confidence, Ruskin told his followers, 'We want no new style of architecture, the forms already known are good enough for us.' But he kept his distance from Pugin.

So too did George Gilbert Scott, an architect who acknowledged Pugin's vision while claiming Gothic as the exclusive preserve of the Anglican Church. Best known today for the Grand Midland Hotel at St Pancras International, lately returned to glory after years of criminal neglect, and the Albert Memorial (described by Simon Jenkins as 'England's Taj Mahal'), Scott established Gothic as an architectural brand. He built 140 churches and restored many more, including eighteen of Britain's twenty-six medieval cathedrals. Of the counties of

England and Wales, only Cardiganshire is Scott free. His designs were adopted in Germany, Newfoundland, India, Australia and New Zealand.

It was an extraordinary achievement for the son of an Evangelical parson, raised in what was then a remote backwater of Buckinghamshire, where he had no formal education. Left to his own devices, he found his talent for sketching. Drawing what was to hand, his sketchbook was crowded with details of old churches. Starting out as an architect, Scott made his reputation building workhouses. He and his then partner produced fifty of them, 15 per cent of the total, mostly in Elizabethan style. But his career really took off when he discovered and fell in love with Gothic.

Scott was an early affiliate of the Cambridge Camden Society, named after a sixteenth-century antiquary by a group of radical theologians who wanted medieval colour and splendour to be restored to the Church. Their journal, the *Ecclesiologist*, given to dogmatic statements on what was or was not properly Gothic, favoured gargoyles, priests' doors, concealed frescoes, hammer beams and brasses. With the backing of the Camden Society, Scott was selected for the Martyrs' Memorial in Oxford and for the rebuilding of St Giles, Camberwell, after it was gutted by fire. A large version of a village church, it was said to be a fuller realisation of Pugin's ideal than anything Pugin himself created in his short life (he died, insane, aged forty in 1852). But the outstanding achievement of Scott's early career was the design for the rebuilding of the Nikolai Kirche in Hamburg. At once a religious and nationalistic symbol, its lofty tower and spire reaching up to a German political unity made in heaven, the church was, for many years, the tallest building in Europe. Only the spire survived Allied bombing.

The project put Scott at the head of the Gothic revival, though it led to a falling out with the *Ecclesiologist*, who disapproved of him exercising his talents on behalf of the Lutherans. It was the

least of his worries. Set on a high earning career, the workaholic
Scott was appointed surveyor of Ely Cathedral in 1847 and
of Westminster Abbey in 1849. Other notable architects such
as John Loughborough Pearson, George Edmund Street and
William Butterfield worked in the same style. In the textile
centres of the North, Leeds architect Thomas Taylor was active
in popularising Gothic. However, none of them could match
Scott's productivity.

The architects of the Gothic revival were energetic self-
promoters, but it was the clergy who had to pay their fees
and cover the substantial costs of building and restoration. A
diligent collection of the church rate helped to start the ball
rolling, until this bone of contention between the Church and
the Nonconformist sects was abolished by Gladstone in 1868.
The Ecclesiastical Commissioners and the Church Building
Society gave grants, but the burden of fund raising was carried
by the good parson, who put it high on his list of duties.

Emotional appeals played on the sensitivities of the Victorian
middle class. Here is the High Church Revd W. J. E. Bennett,
vicar of St Paul's Knightsbridge, speaking in 1843 shortly after
his inauguration.

> The existence of this poor population now immediately around
> you depends entirely upon *yourselves*. You are the indirect
> creators of it. It is you that have brought them here, from the
> magnificent dwellings in which you live, and the houses and
> carriages which you keep, and the many servants whom you
> require to minister to your wants. ... Come with me into the lanes
> and streets of this great city. Come with me and visit the dens
> of infamy, and the haunts of vice, ignorance, filth and atheism,
> with which it abounds. Come with me and read the story of
> Dives and Lazarus. Come with me and turn over the pages of the
> Holy Book, by whose precepts your lives are, at least, in theory,
> guided. Then look at your noble houses, and the trappings of

your equipages, the gold that glitters on your sideboards, and the jewels that gleam on your bosoms; then say within your secret conscience, as standing before the great and terrible God at the day of judgement, what shall I do if I give not of the one, to relieve the other?[1]

The response built the school and church of St Barnabas in Pimlico.

The campaigning bishop, James Lee, who presided over the newly constituted diocese of Manchester, used his contacts with wealthy industrialists to underwrite 130 churches during his twenty-one-year tenure. His successor, James Fraser, increased the score by 105. Bishop Wilberforce was responsible for 106 new churches in the Oxford diocese, while at Winchester, after Bishop Sumner was appointed in 1827, forty new churches were created and 400 restored or enlarged.

There were rich benefactors who needed no prompting. At Halifax, Edward Akroyd, the head of one of the country's largest worsted manufacturers, was a philanthropist on a grand scale. Having founded schools for child labourers, a pension scheme for his workforce and a working men's college, he created a model village known as Akroydon. As a devout Anglican, he wanted a grand church as the centrepiece of his community. Scott was called in to design All Souls with its spire of 72 metres, the dominant landmark of Halifax. With no expense spared, the richly decorated All Souls was regarded by Scott as one of his best churches. And so it proved, except that eventually the building fell victim to Scott's tendency to match different sorts of stone, in this case, magnesium limestone and local sandstone. Whenever it rained, the limestone turned water into a dilute acid which eroded the sandstone. With the decline of Halifax's industrial base, the congregation of All Souls dwindled to a point when the church had to be declared redundant. The threat of demolition was lifted when a trust was set up to preserve the structure. Now listed as Grade 1, it is used for concerts and exhibitions.

Less than a year after he was appointed Vicar of Leeds, Walter Hook decided that something had to be done about his 'nasty, dirty, ugly, old church'. It was certainly not fit for purpose.

> It was a cruciform building, with a square embattled tower rising from the centre. Some parts of the structure dated from 1089, and the whole had been roughly treated by the generations which came between. Every nook and corner of the nave was crowded with pews of incongruous shape and size. Long galleries projected from the west end, and from the north and south walls, and the clustered pillars of the fourteenth century were nearly cut through to give these support. So that the organ might be more conspicuous, and in order to increase the accommodation, the chancel arch had been almost entirely walled up and a gallery built against it. Because of this the choir was practically unusable for public worship, and during the monthly celebration of Holy Communion the congregation was quite shut off from the sight of the altar.[2]

Supported by a petition signed by several hundred parishioners, Hook embarked on a thorough restoration, but when the work started what was revealed behind the plaster was in such a poor state that a general collapse was feared. A new church was planned, the largest built in England since Wren's St Paul's.

Hook was shameless in exploiting the social aspirations of the nouveau riche, who were only too keen to boast a place of worship that put Leeds ahead of any other industrial city. One benefactor presented England's first ever peal of thirteen bells. A penny subscription among working people raised enough for a stained-glass window. Three years into the construction, Leeds Parish Church of St Peter was consecrated in 1841 with a sermon preached by an American, the Bishop of New Jersey.

The architect responsible for creating Hook's 'standing sermon' was Dennis Chantrell, whose practice in Leeds was best known for public buildings of classical design. But Chantrell was flexible. When Hook asked for Gothic, that is what he got. The church was Chantrell's crowning glory. Today, if he is remembered at all, it is for his marriage late in life to the artist Mary Elizabeth Dear, who was a third his age and for whom he had acted as guardian. The couple gained further notoriety when they were successfully prosecuted by the SPCA for starving their 200 cats and dogs. Hook, meanwhile, raised the money to build another twenty-one churches, twenty-seven schools and twenty-three vicarages.[3]

Demolishing a church to make way for another more in tune with the times was not unusual. At Wheatley in Oxfordshire, the Revd Edward Elton was given every encouragement by Bishop Wilberforce to do away with his parish church, which 'looked too much like a Nonconformist chapel'. The fact that it was barely sixty years old and more than adequate in size was not judged to be relevant, except by the villagers themselves, who protested at the waste of money and refused to contribute. Elton went with his begging bowl to Oxford, where he raised more than two-thirds of his budget.

The new Gothic church, thought by many to be far too grand for a rural parish, was consecrated by Wilberforce in 1857.[4] The architect was George Edmund Street, who also designed Cuddesdon Theological College and was diocesan architect of Oxford. Street was a religious man, who regarded the phases of Gothic architecture as reflections of the spiritual life of the Church. St Paul's Herne Hill, rebuilt by Street after a fire in 1858, was declared by Ruskin to be 'one of the loveliest churches of its kind in the country'. Having started his career in the office of Gilbert Scott, he was later to score over his former employer in competition for the Law Courts, 'a conscientious and dignified building'[5] in London's Strand.

At the peak of the church-building boom, Britain gained a cathedral – Gothic, of course. It was built in Truro to mark the creation or, rather, the revival of a diocese for Cornwall, hitherto lumped together with Devon. The inspiration came from Bishop Edward Benson, later Archbishop of Canterbury, who authorised the demolition of a sixteenth-century parish church to clear a site for the much grander edifice. All that was left of the original was the south aisle which the architect, John Loughborough Pearson, managed, not altogether successfully, to incorporate into his design. His model was Lincoln Cathedral, where he had worked on the restoration.

Benson was an active and creative bishop whose lasting achievement, the Service of Nine Lessons and Carols, remains one of the high points of Christmas celebrations. Superficially, his was a conventional clerical family, though beneath the veneer there was much to trouble Victorian sensibilities. After Benson's death in 1896, his wife, Mary, set up home and a close relationship with the daughter of her husband's predecessor as archbishop.[6] The Benson family of six, none of whom married, included E. F. Benson, author of the Mapp and Lucia novels, and A. C. Benson, who wrote the lyrics to Elgar's *Land of Hope and Glory*. Along with a third brother, Hugh, who died young, having converted to Rome, they shared a barely suppressed homosexuality.

For every three new churches built in Gothic style, at least one old church was given a Gothic facelift. At Kilndown in Kent, the wealthy philanthropist and co-founder of the Cambridge Camden Society, A. J. Beresford-Hope, transformed the church into a Gothic prototype with 'a glorious rood-screen, exquisitely designed and carved, and coloured and gilt to perfection ... stalls for the clergy, seats for the choir and a noble eagle on the chancel floor'.[7]

Beresford-Hope's architect, Anthony Salvin, applied the same principles in the redesign of the Church of St Lawrence at Castle Rising in Norfolk. The nave, 'fitted with goodly rows of open benches', was flanked by a reading desk with Gothic panelling while the pulpit, set into the north wall, was entered by a narrow staircase in a recess from the reading desk. It was, claims a modern critic, 'an exceptionally sensitive restoration for such an early date'.[8]

But this restructuring of church interiors was the cause of bitter disputes. Along with disagreements between high and low churchmen on what precisely constituted an authentic place of worship, there was open warfare between modernists and the first generation of conservationists, who believed that ancient buildings should be patched up but otherwise left alone.

Foremost among the purists was William Morris, the enemy of all things modern, aided by John Ruskin, the highly influential – if self-appointed – arbiter of artistic excellence. To promote conservation, Morris took the lead in founding the Society for the Protection of Ancient Buildings. Though given to wild and unsubstantiated claims of mass destruction, there were numerous examples of clerical insensitivity for SPAB to draw on. In the parish of Newland near Malvern, a fourteenth-century wooden church, said to be 'in a rickety state' was simply swept away to allow for a new building. The pre-Conquest tower of Whittingham Church, Northumberland, was rebuilt in 1840 in Gothic style. As late as 1882 it was seriously proposed to clear the great west window of Winchester Cathedral to make way for a memorial statue to Bishop Wilberforce. At Sixhills in Lincolnshire, the squire was so far from mindful of the church on his private property that he gave orders to pull down the tower for stones to repair local roads and the walls in his garden.[9]

What counted against the SPAB was its tendency to bossiness. Quick to judge, its representatives were liable to offend local sensitivities. When, in the summer of 1880, news got around of restoration work at the ancient church of St Nicholas, New

Romney, one of the five Cinque Ports, the attentions of the society were severely rebuffed, the incumbent accusing it of 'impertinent inquisitiveness'. Undeterred, an adverse report was circulated, which led to acrimonious correspondence in the *East Kent Times* where it was suggested that the SPAB should be renamed The Antiquated Society of Pryers. Tempers cooled after an architect appointed by the society was persuaded that no more than 'repairs necessary to keep the church in good order' was contemplated. Whether or not this represented a change of heart by the parson remains unknown.[10]

Gilbert Scott was a prime target for the SPAB. Scott was indeed guilty of some serious lapses, such as the removal of the pre-Conquest arch at Godalming to make room for an imitation thirteenth-century one, but he saw himself as a sensitive modifier. He set out his case in 1850 with his *Plea for the Faithful Restoration of our Ancient Churches*, in which he claimed that far more had been done to 'obliterate genuine examples of pointed architecture, by the tampering caprices of well-meant restorations, than had been effected by centuries of mutilation and neglect'.

The problem for Scott and for like-minded architects was the absence of consensus on what constituted a sympathetic restoration. The original style of many churches – probably the majority – was either Saxon or Norman. But to go back thus far was thought to be undesirable and, in any case, impractical. The very broad agreement was for recreating what had been around at the time of the Reformation. The aversion to anything later led to the disposal of seventeenth- and eighteenth-century embellishments, often with curious results such as the replacing of seventeenth-century pulpits with new pulpits in the style of the thirteenth century, when there were no pulpits. Likewise, altar rails of the same period were superseded by altar rails in the style of the Middle Ages, when there were none.[11] Many ancient fonts were consigned to rubble to make way for elaborate

Victorian versions, which looked to be more medieval. Much stained glass was lost to new memorial windows.

As one who felt strongly on these matters, Sabine Baring-Gould had his collection of horror stories.

On one occasion I went to Kenton [near Exeter], and was struck by the beauty of the pulpit. The body had been scooped out of one enormous tree. The sculpture, that was both bold and delicate, was applied. I spent a day making a working drawing. The pulpit was gilt and coloured, and I copied it in colours. In 1888 I revisited the church that had, in the meantime been 'restored' by Hayward, the Exeter architect. To my dismay the pulpit was gone, and a contemptible modern erection replaced it, of the type of those supplied by ecclesiastical tailors and furnishers. I went at once to the Vicarage to inquire what had become of the old pulpit, the carving of which was so superior to any I had seen in Devon, that I thought it must have been executed by Flemish workmen. The vicar replied that he did not know. The architect had condemned it, and it was swept away, but he believed that some scraps of carving were preserved in the school. So I went to the school-house, and there, in the cupboard among dusters, chalk, and broken slates was a considerable amount of carved, coloured and gilt oak that I at once recognised as having belonged to the massacred old pulpit.[12]

In 1896, it was reported that eighty-two altar screens had disappeared from churches in Devon 'during comparatively recent times'.

Ironically, it was the dedicated parson who was likely to do most damage. As the incumbent of St Breward, the otherwise estimable George Martin, determined to make his church relevant to contemporary needs, allowed his architect to set about a restoration in what has been described as 'an over-drastic way'.

It was the nave of the church and its furnishings which suffered most. The three arches of the north arcade were rebuilt and only the Norman pillars remain to remind us that the church was a Norman building. The barrel roof of the nave was taken down rather than restored though some of its timber may have been used to restore the barrel roof of the south aisle. At the west end of the latter a topsy-turvy font was installed. It was made up of a base (the capital of a Norman pier reversed) and a bowl (probably the base of the original Norman font which the fifteenth-century restorers decided not to replace). The fine bench-ends of the church were dismantled and only two (those incorporated into the parish priest's stall in the choir) remain in their original condition. Others were gaudily painted and eventually made into a tasteless reredos which was fortunately dismantled. These are now to be seen displayed in front of the pews.[13]

Tewkesbury Abbey was essentially Norman, although by 1864, when Scott was commissioned to make recommendations for restoration, it had undergone several radical makeovers. While Scott recognised the impossibility of reconstructing the Norman original, he proposed 'the removal of disfigurements such as the modern pews, galleries and whitewash and the bringing of the interior back to something like the state of propriety and to some approach to its original beauty'. When fundraising proved to be more of a challenge than anticipated, a Tewkesbury builder, Thomas Collins, who had collaborated with Scott on Gloucester, Worcester and Hereford Cathedrals, offered to start the work, including repairing much of the stone and removing the 'cumbrous galleries', at his own expense.

The incensed Morris joined battle with Scott, accusing him of an 'act of barbarism'. It is unlikely that Morris ever visited Tewkesbury to see for himself the damage that had been done by an earlier generation of restorers. It would have been interesting to discover what, for example, he would have suggested to overcome the damp caused by the accumulation of soil against the walls – 'streaming with moisture' – after centuries of grave digging.[14] Morris gave no credit to Scott for opening up the interior of the abbey to make it suitable for modern worship.

Scott made some controversial decisions, but they were nothing on the scale of the abrasive lawyer and architect, Lord Grimthorpe, who claimed the right to 'alter old buildings exactly as we feel like'. Scott he dismissed as 'timid, conservative and incompetent'. After Scott's death, he forced his dubious taste on St Alban's Cathedral, financing alterations out of his own pocket.

As the *Ecclesiologist* frequently reminded its readers, there were churches where restoration was a woefully inadequate description of what had to be done.

In the south chapel of Rippingale 'the scene of desolation on entering the interior is a disgrace to all parties who knowingly tolerate such an atrocious perversion of its use. The floor is torn up, uneven, and literally falling to pieces ... The east wall is falling outwards, and a most magnificent Early Decorated window of four lights has its tracery intercepted by the low roof, and filled up with mortar. The floor is of course strewed with filth, rubbish, deal forms, and unsightly and indescribable piles of deal woodwork.'

At Cliffe-at-Hoo 'the north aisle is used as a day-school, with all the accompanying juvenile nastiness; the west end of the same aisle is a rubbish hole, and is now filled with a store of brambles, coals, and cinders: the transepts are falling, and the tower is shored up with a gigantic buttress of brick'. A north chapel at Hingham was used as a gaol and as a dog-kennel.[15]

Required to do a lot on not very much, the parson of modest means, under pressure to restore or renovate his church or to start afresh with a new building, was tempted to cut corners by dispensing with an architect. But finance was not the only consideration. By the time the Gothic revival had taken hold, the concept of the priest architect who could bring spiritual value to his task was well established. The lay professional was suspect. 'The idea of someone designing a church one moment and a public house the next was anathema.'[16] However, while the *Ecclesiologist* was the first to admit that, say, the newly built St Bartholomew's Church (1844) and the restored St George's, both in the Cotswold village of Cam, reflected well on the incumbent and amateur architect, George Madan, such paragons were 'not likely to occur in sufficient abundance seriously to interfere with the calling of the professional architect'.

True enough. The best estimate is of around 150 clergy of the Victorian period who assumed the role of architect and craftsman, most of them engaged in revamping church interiors to suit contemporary taste. These so-called restorations were rarely successful. Over-confident of his abilities, William Lowder's clerical career left a trail of ill-begotten schemes, culminating in the tearing apart of St Leonard's in the Essex parish of Southminster, where he installed a screen and pulpit he had carved to his own specifications. *The Architect* was not impressed. On this level of achievement, wrote a critic, 'amateurs, or even ladies would be eligible to be accepted as architects for church buildings'.[17]

Of good reputation was the Revd John Hausen Sperling, author of *Church Walks in Middlesex*, who began the rebuilding of the church of Papworth St Agnes while he was still an undergraduate at Trinity, Cambridge, a commission that came via his father, who happened to be lord of the manor. But Ernest Geldart was the pre-eminent priest architect. Having trained with Waterhouse in his London office, he studied theology at King's before going on to design forty-three churches or church-related buildings. Compensating for a meagre income and ill health, he charged for his services.[18]

Another active parson architect was William Carus Wilson, who drew on a substantial private income to design and build two churches, one at Casterton, the other at Holme, both in Lincolnshire, not to mention a Clergy Daughters' School at Cowan Bridge, where his autocratic tendencies served as a model for hard-faced Mr Brocklehurst in Charlotte Brontë's *Jane Eyre*. However distorted his fictional portrait, Carus Wilson was certainly not lacking in confidence. Having fixed ideas on the 'English style of Architecture with lancet windows and buttresses as decidedly the most satisfactory for an ecclesiastical edifice', he published *Helps* [sic] *to the Building of Churches, Parsonage Houses and Schools*, which included model specifications. A more lasting venture into print was *The Children's Friend*, a monthly discourse on Evangelism and good works, founded by Carus Wilson in 1824. It ran until 1930.

A favourite of the *Ecclesiologist* was William Haslam, described as 'well known, practically as well as theoretically, as an experienced church builder' when that journal favourably assessed his designs for St George the Martyr in Truro. Though Haslam had professional help he was keen to promote his talents. After restoring the church in the Cornish parish of Perranzabuloe, where he was curate for four years from 1842, 'numbers of people came to see it, among them several clergymen, who asked me to come and restore their churches'. This he was very happy to do, 'riding about all over the county ... and was accounted the busiest man alive'.[19] Though, presumably, not quite so busy as the Revd William Jones or the Revd Thomas Thomas, who designed scores of chapels in Wales.

Of the rest, a commendation must go to Whitwell Elwin, rector of Booton in Norfolk, from 1849 until his death in 1900. His church, St Michael the Archangel, is popularly known as the Cathedral of the Fields, for that is precisely what it is, a noble but wildly extravagant edifice, built out of all proportion to the community it was intended to serve. Backed by a female admirer who made her money by selling land to a railway company, Elwin, who had no architectural training, took his inspiration from illustrations of great churches so that the west doorway is a reminder of Glastonbury Abbey, an opening above the chancel arch of Lichfield Cathedral, and the vivid stained glass in the west window of St Stephen's Chapel in the Palace of Westminster. The interior is distinguished by a hammerbeam roof decorated with angels, the work of craftsmen who carved ships' figureheads. The pinnacle turrets can be seen from miles around.

Elwin himself was as improbable as his place of worship. Mixing clerical duties with high Tory politics, for seven years he edited the *Quarterly Review* for the publisher John Murray, another Booton man. From his portraits, Elwin is distinguished by a jovial countenance, unusual among Victorian parsons, and he seems to have been popular, particularly with very young ladies, his 'blessed girls' as he called them. When this writer, as an impressionable teenager, discovered St Michael more than sixty years ago, there were still folk memories of wicked goings-on at the vicarage. The church then was already discarded and neglected. In this setting it was easy to imagine the repressed passions of Gothic melodrama. The truth is almost certainly more Lewis Carroll than Svengali. Now restored and in the care of the Churches Conservation Trust, St Michael the Archangel was described, appropriately, by Edwin Lutyens as 'very naughty but designed in the right spirit'.

The pace of restoration and reconstruction accelerated towards the end of the century. By around 1870, most churches could boast, or regret, at least one accommodation to contemporary taste. It was a triumph for Gothic but at the same time a victory for those who sought a more assertive and distinctive image for the Anglican faith. The new churches brought into their districts educated men and women ready to lead on schools and other social improvements.

If, early in Victoria's reign, there were many churches in urgent need of renewal, the same and more could be said of the clergy's living accommodation. A survey in 1835 found nearly 2,000 rectories unfit for habitation. In close on 3,000 parishes, the parson was without a residence of any kind. Multiple livings had allowed unoccupied rectories to fall into decay. After residency was re-established, it was not unusual for the newly appointed parson to begin by clearing his home of squatters.

When the vicar of Wantage took up his duties in 1846 he found himself moving into 'the coldest house' he had ever lived in; thatched, dilapidated, with walls so thin snails found their way into the drawing room. Writing in 1832, the vicar of Ingoldsby in Lincolnshire reported, 'There is no glebe house for the vicar, never was that I heard of one. There is a labourer's cottage but no apparent vestige of a parsonage.' He was mistaken; the labourer's cottage *was* the parsonage.[20]

Almost as unappealing was Kingsley's rectory at Eversley. It was on low ground, with the churchyard 6 feet above the living rooms. Every winter brought the threat of flooding. One wet January night found Kingsley hacking away at the walls to release the water that had come up through the floor. Taking on a rectory that suffered from damp, the parson was well advised to check the water supply, which could very easily be poisoned by graveyard drainage.

When Thomas Hayton was appointed vicar of Long Crendon in Buckinghamshire, he was moved to protest to his bishop at the conditions he was expected to endure.

The Glebe House for the Benefice of Long Crendon is perhaps one of the meanest edifices of the same nature in the whole range of your diocese. There is a kitchen & a parlour (about 8 feet by 10 each) with a small pantry below stairs; above there is the same number of rooms, such as I am sure your Lordship would scarcely deem suitable for your lowest menial. Indeed no clergyman within the memory of man, previous to myself ever resided in the village of Crendon, much less in the Glebe House.[21]

Hayton borrowed from friends to rebuild the cottage 'in the plainest style and at a most moderate cost'.[22]

As late as 1872, when Francis Kilvert visited the vicar of Llanbedr Paincastle, he found him living in a little grey hut built of rough dry stone.

There was a wild confusion of litter and rubbish almost choking and filling up all available space. The floor had once been of stone but was covered thick and deep with an accumulation of the dirt and peat dust of years. The furniture consisted of two wooden saddle-seated chairs polished smooth by the friction of continual sessions, and one of them without a back. A four-legged dressing table littered with broken bread and meat, crumbs, dirty knives and forks, glasses, plates, cups and saucers in squalid hugger-mugger confusion. No table cloth. No grate. The hearth foul with cold peat ashes, broken bricks and dust, under the great wide open chimney through which stole down a faint ghastly sickly light. In heaps and piles upon the floor were old books, large Bibles, commentaries, old-fashioned religious disputations, C.M.S. Reports and odd books of all sorts, Luther on the Galatians, etc. The floor was further encumbered with beams and logs of wood, flour pans covered over, and old chests. All the other articles of food were hung up on pot hooks some from the ceiling, some in the chimney out of the way of the rats. The squalor, the dirt, the dust, the foulness and wretchedness of the place were indescribable, almost inconceivable.[23]

The typical parsonage was no place to bring up a growing family. Even when it had been handed down in a reasonable state of repair, it was invariably too small for a brood of children, along with the usual complement of live-in servants. The vicar of St Mary Abbots, Kensington, held to the rule of 'another baby, another room'. An incumbent of Long Melford in Suffolk certainly took this advice to heart. Built in Tudor style in early Victorian days, the vicarage was enlarged in 1878 to become a rambling stately residence with five reception rooms, sixteen bedrooms and three dressing rooms. It was sold in 1946 to Dr Barnardo's Homes.

A parson fortunate enough to have a private income was expected to pay his own way. When Edward Boys Ellman accepted the living at Berwick in Sussex, he found the old rectory, 'in such a tumble-down state that it was necessary to rebuild it entirely'.[24] This he did in 'the style I considered suitable for the living' before going on to build a school and restore the church.[25] John Pridden, who rebuilt the vicarage at Cuddington, was said to have had a 'considerable knowledge and natural taste for architecture and engineering', a talent he extended to designing the Sea-Bathing Infirmary at Margate.

While at Foston, Sydney Smith raised £4,000 for a commodious parsonage. Unusual features of this residence included air tubes piercing the outer walls and opening into the grates, keeping fires burning cheerfully. A speaking trumpet near the front door allowed Smith to shout directions to labourers in the field who were kept under observation with the aid of a telescope.[26]

Idiosyncratic to the last, Robert Hawker created a Gothic home with a replica of his mother's tomb as a kitchen chimney. His model for a 'clergyman's house on a moderate scale' was taken from T.F. Hunt's DIY manual, *Designs for Parsonage Houses*, in which the author demonstrated how 'frugality may be exercised without the appearance of poverty'.

Towards the end of the eighteenth century, legislation had been put in place to enable incumbents to raise mortgages for building or rebuilding rectories. After 1836, the Ecclesiastical Commissioners were empowered to award grants in needy cases. The architect they favoured was William Railton, who built dozens of parsonages in a mix of styles, ranging from the 'ordinary nondescript' to the 'professedly Gothic'.[27] If Railton is remembered today, it is for his classical design for Nelson's column in Trafalgar Square.

In some cases it might have proved more useful to provide instruction in financial management. At Great Rollright, Oxfordshire, Joseph Heathcote Brooks decided to pull down the seventeenth-century rectory to make way for a residence that was far too grand for the living. Before long, he was so beset with creditors he could only leave his home via the back garden. One Sunday morning in 1851, having announced his text, 'Forgive us our debts as we forgive our debtors', he disappeared into the vestry and made haste to depart the parish and the country. Four years later he was in Prussia, where he fell through the trapdoor of an upper room and was killed 'upon the spot'. Another victim of this clerical building boom was the curate of Forest Hill, near Oxford, who went twice to prison for failing to meet his creditors and eventually died in the debtors' jail.

Religious fervour tended to outpace resources. Thomas Mozley, the parson journalist who married Newman's sister, resolved to build a church for his remote parish of Cholderton on Salisbury Plain. Probably under the impression that he was saving money, he acquired a ready-made oak roof he found abandoned on the Suffolk coast, transporting it to Cholderton by sea and canal. The size of the roof, which had ten bays, determined the size of the church, an impressive structure rather too large for the congregation it was intended to serve. When funds ran out, Mozley spent five thousand pounds of his own money but the project was still unrealised in 1847 when he left the parish to make his living in London as a *Times* leader writer.

On the principle that if the people would not come to the

church, the church had to go to the people, there were numerous examples of rebuilding to meet shifts of population. In 1884, Canon Walter Marcon, parson of Edgefield in Norfolk, had his thirteenth-century church dismantled brick by brick for re-erection at the centre of his congregation. Left behind was an octagonal tower and the old churchyard. Marcon was noted for getting around his parish on a bicycle, a mode of transport so unusual for the time, at least for the clergy, that it was recorded on his memorial window. It bears the legend, 'I have cycled every lane, high and low, on tyres wooden, solid and pneumatic.'

For wealthy parsons, all things were possible. Arthur Wagner, vicar of Brighton from 1824 to 1870, built three churches, including one that was below street level. The original idea was for a noble pile that towered over neighbouring buildings. But when wealthy residents objected to their view being obstructed, Wagner, nothing daunted, declared that a large part of his church would be underground. Consecrated in 1878, the Church of the Resurrection was in use until 1912, when it became a meat market. It was demolished in 1968.

The parson who fancied himself as an ecclesiastical designer was keen to be identified with his achievements, none more so than the Revd J. Edmond Long of White Roothing (now Roding) in Essex, who left his signature on the altar, a memorial to Queen Victoria (one of the first to be erected), a copper weather vane and on his own memorial tablet.[28]

Much of the criticism of Scott and other architects of the Gothic revival dates from the first half of the twentieth century, when respect for the Victorian legacy was at its lowest ebb. In its heyday, Gothic surroundings offered churchgoers comfort and reassurance, a reminder that whatever its current tribulations, Christianity spanned the ages with its all-embracing promise of salvation.

The Gothic architects were rightly criticised for failing to promote space and light or to recognise the potential for church buildings to be used for religious purposes other than formal worship. How much could have been learned from the great engineers who favoured clean lines and open vistas for their monuments to the Industrial Revolution? Ruskin came to regret his endorsement of Gothic after he realised his influence on cheap builders of villas, public houses and railways. Before long, the pendulum had swung towards modernism.

The reaction against Gothic architecture was savage and long lasting. Many of the finest buildings were demolished. The Albert Memorial went unloved for seventy years. When the doors closed on the Midland Grand, British Rail was keen to clear the site for the sort of miserable concrete block they put up at Euston. Today, Victoriana is back in fashion. A threat to a Gothic church or to any Gothic building is a call to arms for conservationists. Regard for Gilbert Scott has mounted with the restoration of the Albert Memorial and the Grand Midland.

At the other end of the architectural scale, the tiny St Mary the Virgin at Fretherne on the banks of the Severn, described as the 'worst type of village church' in the 1930s, is now credited with 'great beauty', while the heavily decorated Holy Innocents at Highnam on the outskirts of Gloucester survived years of critical abuse to be described by John Betjeman as 'the most complete Victorian church in the country'. Betjeman was equally enthused with the Gothic extravagance of William Butterfield, whose All Saints in Margaret Street, St Albans in Holborn and St Matthias in Stoke Newington are now accepted as national treasures.

CHAPTER ELEVEN

The Voice from the Pulpit

It was the duty of the parson to spread the word. At the peak of the Church revival, around 50,000 sermons a week were delivered from Anglican pulpits. The spiritual message with a social edge was paramount. Congregations were urged to lead upright lives of honest endeavour, forswearing idle pursuits and hard liquor. Morality was taught by cause and effect. God recognised and rewarded virtue while handing down punishment to those who lapsed.

Preaching on the 'deadly sin of stealing', John Keble recognised that restitution was not always possible but 'you can take patiently, nay, I will say thankfully, whatever pain, sorrow or disappointment God sends you for the punishment of those your old sins'.[1] It was a premise wide open to challenge. A simple observation of life showed that the innocent suffered just as much as the guilty. To which the good parson responded with a reminder of the life to come. 'Be sure your sin will find you out,' if not in this world, then in the next. By the same token, those who were afflicted without apparent cause were urged to delve deeper into their lives to find justification for suffering while looking towards redemption in an eternal paradise.

Though simplistic to modern eyes, the formula met with general acceptance, not least by those in good health and fortune who were able to tell themselves that, whatever the evidence to the contrary, they had to be doing something right. Variations on the theme can still be heard today.

It is easy to sneer at Victorian gullibility, but the Christian message was at the heart of a civilised society. Here is Keble preaching on Christmas day:

> Never let us quite take off our thoughts from ... His unspeakable love of which this day is the crown. It is such love as we never can fathom, never can come truly to understand ... To watch and study Christ in His cradle is the very mystery of humility; and if of humility, then of love, peace and joy. It is the very preparation, the beginning of eternal happiness ... Jesus himself is that little child, like whom we most especially become if we would ever be really fit for the Kingdom of Heaven.[2]

Who could not say Amen to that?

The parson who knew his business was well aware that to be effective his message was best kept simple. Augustus Hare urged the use of metaphors and anecdotes to drive home the essential points in clear, idiomatic English.[3] In country churches, the experience of working the land offered handy analogies. Charles Kingsley was a master of this technique. 'The tree draws nourishment from the earth beneath and from the heavens above; and so must our souls, my friends.'[4]

The trouble or, maybe, the advantage with this form of address was that it could mean anything or nothing. The actor W. G. Elliot, a regular churchgoer, collected examples of fatuous advice from the pulpit.

> This I heard in Kent. The parson, preaching, said: 'Now are we to understand by this passage that His character was capable of improvement?' I leaned forward, interested to hear the solution of such a strange problem. 'The answer to that,' he went on, 'is Yes and No.' I fell back.

On one occasion, the Vicar was in the pulpit and spoke the following winged words: 'In the present day, dear brethren, there is much controversy as to whether we should rely on the Old or the New Testament. For my part, I am of opinion that you should read both together. Otherwise, it is like a Seidlitz powder. If you take the contents of the white paper and omit the blue, nothing happens. On the other hand, if you swallow the blue particles and leave out the white – the same result! So it is with the two Testaments.'[5]

A parson who was keen to parade his learning could easily leave his congregation behind as he meandered off into the theological thicket. Worst of all was the dull, monotonous tone 'which expressed no anxious interest in the heart of the preacher and suppressed it in others'. It was the style of Dean Andrew, Rector of St James, Westminster. 'He used to preach with his spectacles on and his head down, and never raised his head from his book till he came to some marked passage, when he would raise his head, take off his spectacles and, looking round at his congregation, would repeat the passage with emphasis.'[6]

Frequent complaints were heard of dull and drowsy preachers who 'do immense harm to the cause of religion which they utterly fail in bringing home to a man's conscience'.[7] As Anthony Trollope commented, 'There is, perhaps, no greater hardship at present inflicted on mankind in civilized and free countries, than the necessity of listening to sermons.'[8]

A common intellectual objection to the clergy was that they were ill-versed in theology. But at parish level it was more often said that the parson knew too much. There were exceptions. Saved by his eloquence and respect for his learning, the Revd John Coleridge, father of the poet, who presided at Ottery St Mary in Devon, was given to introducing lengthy Hebrew quotations into his sermons. The villagers were less taken by his successor, who was apparently unable to receive messages in the original language.[9] However, Coleridge had a broad grasp of his duties as a parish priest; it was the obsessive pedant who failed in his pastoral work. At a village in Shropshire the sermon was beyond endurance.

> He would wrangle at great length and with inspired vigour with an unseen antagonist, while his people lolled unconcerned in the pews in front of him, thinking, no doubt, of their Sunday dinner in the pot at home, or of their flocks on the hills. One dark winter afternoon this old man had a more than usually difficult point of theology on his mind. Candles were lit on the pulpit, great volumes were placed in a pile at his elbow, and his brain was in fine fettle for the occasion. Time went on and there seemed no likelihood of an early decision. Gradually the farmers and their wives slunk out, unnoticed by the parson in the darkness of the church and the bright illumination of his own mind. At last only the faithful clerk was left. He bore it as long as he could, but the thought of his own fireside became too much for him, so he crept up to the parson. 'Sir,' he said respectfully, 'when you've done, p'r'aps you'll blow out them candles, lock the door, and put key under th' mat.'[10]

Intelligent churchgoers were easily and rightly offended by the fantastical assertions heard from the pulpit. Thomas Giordani Wright, a Newcastle doctor, could barely contain himself when he was advised that

> Christ's expressions towards his Mother were always harsh and not in his usual mild style of discourse – from which the lecturer concluded that our saviour had a foreknowledge of and wish to obviate as much as possible the idolatrous worship paid to her by the Romish church(!!) This clergyman gave us tolerable discourse upon the necessity of constant attention to religious duties but in speaking of the importance of the above duties they

were contrasted with worldly enjoyments – one antithesis was 'the pursuits of literature and science which bring only pleasure but not profit'!!!! This coming from an enlightened minister of the Church of England certainly made me lift up my eyes in amazement.[11]

Ringing the changes from Sunday to Sunday was a formidable challenge for those who were not born orators. But there could be no excuse for the rambling, inconsequential delivery of Parson Thomas of Disserth.

> Ha, yes, here we are. And it is a fine day. I congratulate you on the fine day, and glad to see so many of you here. Yes indeed. Ha, yes, very well. Now then I shall take for my text so and so. Yes. Let me see. You are all sinners and so am I. Yes indeed.[12]

Many a sermon was lost to the nervous mannerisms of the preacher. A Norfolk parson was notorious for the 'curious and irritating cough' which only manifested itself when he rose to speak. Then there was the vicar who whistled with every 's' and deluged the front pews when he announced 'Songs of Praise the Angels Sang'.

Along with guides to effective speaking came the pulpit anthologies advertised in the religious press, for those 'whose avocations afford but little time for composition'. Arthur Roberts, rector of Woodrising in Norfolk, published seventeen volumes of village sermons. Newman's *Parochial and Plain Sermons* filled eight volumes. With its alphabetical list of popular themes, the massive, frequently revised *Dictionary of Illustrations Adapted to Christian Teaching* ran to nine editions. Other popular helpmates included *Sermons to a Country Congregation*, *Pulpit Aids* and *The Spiritual Garland*.

Copycat sermons were satirised by Church critics, who accused the perpetuators of being lazy and unimaginative.

Parsons who knew their business were also quick to criticise their less than effective colleagues. For 'many among our country clergy,' wrote the Revd Francis Witt, 'the composition of original sermons is far too much neglected; disuse begets distrust of one's own powers, and a disinclination to the labour'.[13] But as a contributor to *Fraser's Magazine* pointed out, 'what can be more absurd or unreasonable than to expect each and every one of 18,000 men, of average ability and education and with no special training either in oratory or composition, to write year after year two sermons a week and a few over, even if they had nothing else to do?'[14] For those who wrote their own sermons, careful preparation was urged, though few went so far as John Gott, Dean of Worcester, who recommended composition while kneeling.

The manner of delivering a sermon was a favourite talking point among clergy. Should it be read or spoken from the heart, with or without notes, or acted from a memorised script? Improvisation was suspect, in that it encouraged the speaker to indulge in the instincts of the moment and, probably, to say things that he would later regret. Certainly, young parsons were advised to begin their ministries 'with written sermons, whatever they might think right to do after two or three years' experience'.[15] But a recitation from a prepared script could be deadly dull. The remedy, according to the *Church Quarterly Review*, was for the parson who relied on a written sermon to take pains to know it well, 'and not to keep his eyes upon the manuscript, but look his people in the face'.[16]

The parson had to work hard to hold the attention of his congregation. There were many distractions.

No sooner is [the farmer] seated in church than there obtrudes upon him the defenceless condition of his yard and his stock; the idleness of the boys, the wandering propensities of this animal and the vicious nature of that. Such thoughts may be dispelled one minute, but it is to return the next; and, not to speak of the prayers, the sermon had need be very impressive, or very interesting, to exclude those sublunary cares which are, indeed, the life of the agriculturist, and his duty too.[17]

A frequent error in preaching was for the parson to assume that a long sermon was more effective than a short one. Sermons of an hour or more were common in the early years of Victoria's reign. As the century progressed, sermons became shorter and snappier, lasting typically for twenty minutes or, at most, half an hour.

The content too changed perceptibly. Gradually, Hell lost its power to frighten. An increasingly literate society was less inclined to take tales of fire and brimstone seriously. With the coming of the railways, even remote parts of the country were opened up to scepticism. While few parsons were ready to challenge the Old Testament, that which could not safely be denied could be curtailed or ignored. Even the devout Edward Pusey was drawing back from promoting Hell as a place of indescribable torment ('Woe unutterable, woe unimaginable, woe interminable!'). Instead, he emphasised the pain to be endured by the loss of God. Whenever Christians gave way to temptation, it was this agonising loss that they risked. 'Hell, my brethren, is full of Christians who, when on earth, never thought of it.'[18]

In 1866, Bishop Tait slapped down one of his clergy who had told his congregation that 'at every ticking of the clock in every four-and-twenty hours, God sends a heathen soul straight to never-ending misery'.[19] Unfortunately, nothing could be done to stop the distribution of *Books for Children* by the Revd Joseph Furniss, whose depiction of Hell suggested a sadistic nature at odds with his calling. A seventeenth-century tract, 'Hell Opened to Christians to caution them from entering into it' along with horrific woodcuts was reprinted in 1807 and was around for most of the century.[20]

Then there were Bible-thumping preachers like Charles Haddon Spurgeon, whose pulling power was as much a tribute to his entertainment value as to his sharing eternal truths. At a time when there were few rival attractions, a preacher who could play on the emotions of his congregation was the equal of a great actor. Short and round, Spurgeon was no matinee idol. 'He has high shoulders and low forehead and none of the beauty of holiness; his voice is not harmonious and his appearance ungraceful.'[21] But what Spurgeon lacked in physical presence was more than compensated for by strength of personality and oratorical skills. With his phenomenal memory (he claimed to be able to identify by name up to 5,000 of his followers), he had a talent for convincing whoever he met that they were somehow unique in his eyes.

A Baptist minister whose popularity crossed denominational boundaries, Spurgeon made an early start as the teenage pastor of the chapel at Waterbeach near Cambridge. By the age of twenty, he attracted a Sunday congregation that rarely fell below 400. What the incumbent of the established church of St John made of that is not recorded. In 1853 the 'boy preacher' was invited to be the guest speaker at New Park Street Baptist Chapel, the largest of its kind in London. So successful was he that he soon took up permanent residence. Here again his popularity outgrew the capacity of the church, even when it was enlarged by knocking out the back wall.

At this point the elders decided to go for broke with a new 5,000-seat auditorium, the Metropolitan Tabernacle, to be built at the Elephant and Castle. The site was donated by the Fishmongers Company. Miraculously, this tribute to Victorian religious enthusiasm has survived in a district that has suffered more than its share of demolition and brutalist rebuilding. Less fortunate was the Exeter Hall on the Strand, which held 5,000, and the Royal Surrey Gardens Music Hall (accommodating 10,000), where Spurgeon preached to capacity audiences while the Tabernacle was under construction. The Exeter Hall was demolished in 1907 to make way for the Strand Palace Hotel, while the Surrey Gardens Music Hall, once the largest venue in London, burned down in 1861. It was at Surrey Gardens that one of Spurgeon's meetings ended in tragedy. A false claim of fire caused a panic rush to the doors. Seven died and many more were badly injured. His largest gathering was either at the Crystal Palace in 1857 or, a decade later, at the Agricultural Hall in Islington. At both events, there were audiences of up to 25,000.

Apart from a powerful voice (yet how many actually heard what he had to say?) we are left with a few hints to explain Spurgeon's appeal. He spoke a language ordinary people could understand. In keeping his message simple, he gave an interpretation of the Bible which left no room for doubt. The Bible was divinely inspired; the essence of faith was trust. This could get dangerously close to tautology; to believe, you had to believe. 'Those who do not believe are like the condemned man in his cell. He that believeth not is condemned already.'[22] His emotional power was soul-stirring. As an eyewitness recorded, 'While he was preaching, I felt as if I was the only one in that great audience he was speaking to ... I was never so touched by a sermon in my life ... In fact, I could not restrain my tears, so exactly did he specify me.'[23]

Spurgeon caught on to the Victorian love of melodrama. On facing death, 'It may come to us on a sudden ... What think ye? What think ye? Could you gather up your feet in the bed and look into eternity without feeling the cold sweat of fear stand upon your brow?'[24] As he spoke he roamed the platform, pausing often to direct comments at someone who had caught his attention. He had no need for notes and though he must have prepared what to say, at least in outline, his sermons had to be recorded in shorthand. When published, they sold in millions.

For a humble pastor, Spurgeon lived quite grandly in a large house in Upper Norwood staffed by a butler, cook, maids, gardeners and a coachman, but no one seemed to resent his wealth. It was said that he worked himself into premature old age. When he died, in 1892, he was only fifty-seven. Some 6,000 mourners filed by his coffin.

Not everyone was captivated by Spurgeon. Clergy who were accustomed to more conventional forms of preaching found it hard to appreciate what he had to offer. Visiting London from his Norfolk parish, Benjamin Armstrong was not impressed by his evening at the Tabernacle. 'I never heard anything more dull and commonplace ... There was nothing extraordinary in the address and the only clue I could discover to the unbounded popularity of the man was his wonderful assurance.'[25]

The extensive press coverage that helped to spread Spurgeon's fame was not limited to the 'prince of preachers'. Indeed, much to his surprise, the Revd Armstrong was taken up by the *Norfolk News*, 'an able but very radical Norwich paper'. He feared the worst. In the event, all was well.

> Four columns in large type are devoted to us, when, lo! greatly to the amusement of all, the result was highly favourable. The reporter visited the church in the afternoon, which is our poorest service, and many regretted that he had not chosen the morning or evening. 'The sermon was exceedingly good, the singing and chanting fine, and the congregation joined in all the responses with spirit, and sang with vigour.'[26]

The hostility of the clergy to Spurgeon and his kind was prompted less by distaste for the superficiality of the sermons than by envy of their ability to draw a crowd. On the principle that if you can't beat them, you should join them, there were parsons who were ready to follow the Evangelical example – particularly after 1855, when Lord Shaftesbury persuaded

Parliament to modify the law prohibiting out-of-church religious meetings of over twenty people. Open-air preaching became quite fashionable. Archibald Tait, successor to Blomfield as Bishop of London and subsequently Archbishop of Canterbury, shocked some of his colleagues by taking direct action.

> His diary shows him going off from the House of Lords to speak to a shipload of emigrants in the docks, from the Convocation discussions on Church Discipline to address the Ragged School children in Golden Lane, or the omnibus drivers in their great yard at Islington. He preached to the costermongers in Covent Garden Market; to railway porters from the platform of a locomotive; to a colony of gipsies upon the common at Shepherd's Bush.[27]

On Tait's initiative, a Diocesan House Mission was set up 'for distinctly evangelistic or aggressive work in crowded districts'.

Some of the most effective sermons were intended to prick the middle-class conscience. When Thomas Rowsell, Curate at St Peter's Stepney, preached in Cambridge, he left an indelible image of inner-city misery.

> He had seen a whole family living in a single room & at the time he visited it the husband was laid on the bed of sickness & the dead wife had been lying there for 10 days! – It was a heart rending sermon ... we must go into the dens of misery, we must spread Christianity by works of mercy (like all our Saviours miracles), we must relieve these densely-peopled, unwholesome, immoral herdings together in one close room ...[28]

It is impossible to judge the overall impact of Victorian preachers beyond saying that it had to be to the benefit of the community that so many voices were raised in defence of generosity, good neighbourliness and common decency. The pulpit accommodated bigots and reactionaries but, much to their dismay, they rarely went unchallenged. When the Revd Thomas Best, the parson at St James, Sheffield, chose to acknowledge the Shakespeare Tercentenary by denouncing the plays as 'an abomination in the sight of God' (it was idolatrous, he declared, to honour 'the memory of a man who wrote so much that would not be tolerated in any decent domestic or social circle') it was another Sheffield parson, Samuel Earnshaw, who made an effective counter-attack. Nothing but harm would be caused, he said, if the Church insisted on 'multiplying moral and religious restraints', pointing out 'certain things that one stigmatised as irreligious and ungodly about which Scripture is silent'. With undisguised delight, a Sheffield theatre quoted Earnshaw on its hoardings.

CHAPTER TWELVE

Family Values

The family was central to Church teaching. The Church itself, with God the Father as its head, played on the family image while at the domestic level each family was seen as an essential part of the Church foundation. However imperfect, the family gave life its structure and meaning.

It was the duty of the parson to do all that he could to strengthen family bonds. Often he was starting from a low base. The veneer of responsibility favoured by the governing classes covered a host of sins. But the greater challenge was to instil family values where there was abject poverty and a deficit of social sentiment. At the heart of Church teaching was the role of wives and mothers as the conscience of the nation. Seen today, the concept was excruciatingly patronising, but it made sense at the time.

Prudish and often myopic they may have been, but the clergy had few illusions as to the male capacity for piggish behaviour. They were well aware of commercial sharp practice, of the casualties of industrial expansion and the evils of alcoholism and prostitution which thrived on mass poverty. Limited in their capacity to provide material remedies, they promoted standards to which all classes might aspire. Feminine virtues were central to their aims.

Tennyson may have been quoting the 'hard old king', but the sentiments of *The Princess* found their way into many a sermon.

> Man for the field and woman for the hearth:
> Man for the sword and for the needle she:
> Man with the head and woman with the heart:
> Man to command and woman to obey:
> All else confusion.

Self-help books, so beloved by the Victorians, were strong in praise of the feminine ideal. The female, wrote the Revd William Thayer, 'is qualified by nature for ministrations of love and kindness to the unfortunate and suffering members of the human family. The female sex are universally acknowledged to be better suited to perform errands of mercy than males. Their tenderness, sensibility, and fervent sympathies and affection, adapt them to such merciful errands.'

And again, 'Women do not hesitate, like men, to perform a hospitable or generous action; not haughty, nor arrogant, nor supercilious, but full of courtesy, and fond of society; ... I never addressed myself in the language of decency and friendship to a woman, whether civilized or savage, without receiving a friendly answer. With man, it has often been otherwise.'[1]

'Be good, sweet child,' advised Charles Kingsley, 'and let those who will be clever.' In the short time they were at school, working-class girls heard a lot about their future role in the home. Respectability was inculcated at an early age. Education and Church teaching were not the sole drivers. Credit must also go to rising living standards. Nonetheless, the clergy undoubtedly had a strong influence on moral behaviour. The illegitimacy rate, having increased from 5 per cent in 1845, fell to 4 per cent in 1900. Even in East London, the poorest sector of the capital, illegitimacy was under 3 per cent at the turn of the century.

Middle-class women, with time on their hands, were urged

to reflect and act upon their social duties. 'From her very constitution and nature,' wrote the Revd John Todd, 'from her peculiar sensibilities and tenderness, it seems to me that the great mission of women is to take the world ... and lay the foundations of human character ... she can make it, shape it, mould it and stamp it just as she pleases.'

Parents and parsons joined forces to urge each generation of daughters to 'resist the little temptations, to do the little duties, to overcome the little difficulties of everyday life',[2] so that they might grow up to exercise a civilising influence on society in general and men in particular.

> To us women and girls is allotted the rule and government of the homes of the land. We are the companions of fathers, brothers and husbands, and it is our privilege to influence them, often to work with and for them, and not rarely to comfort and sustain them. If we keep these homes of ours pure, refined and virtuous, we wage war against decay, and occupy the proud place of helping to build up the country, and strengthen the hands of the State. Loving, moral and religious, must be the character of the women and girls of the country if the homes over which they preside are to be pure, restful, attractive and refined. Wherever the homes of the land fall below this standard, statistics prove that the strength, life and progress of that country is sapped, notwithstanding its armies, its laws and its institutions.[3]

To prepare for this solemn task, girls were to be protected from any influence that might blight their faith before it could reach full bloom. 'Would that I could induce you to abjure fiction of the present mode altogether,' wrote a clerical contributor to a girls' magazine,

> ... But if be vain asking on my part, at least let me implore – yes, girls, *implore* of you this much wise self-restriction – 1st, that

you will never touch a novel before luncheon, and secondly that
you will only read such as your mother, or motherly elder sister,
approves and permits![4]

Books receiving the seal of moral approval included *The Home
Naturalist, The Girls Indoor and Outdoor Books,* the *History of
Bible Plants* and *Restful Work for Youthful Hands.* The precise
nature of the moral risk encountered by literary pleasure-seekers
was spelt out by the Revd Thomas Gisborne at the beginning of
the century when he published his *Enquiry into the Duties of the
Female Sex.* Novels, he said, 'commonly turn on the vicissitudes
and effects of a passion the most powerful of all those which
agitate the human heart. Hence the study of them frequently
creates a susceptibility of impression, and a premature warmth
of tender emotions, which ... have been known to betray young
women into a sudden attachment to persons unworthy of their
affection, and thus to hurry them into marriage terminating in
unhappiness.'[5]

While the married woman was, foremost, a support and
comfort for her husband, her virtues were not reserved
exclusively for the home. By the 1830s what Florence
Nightingale described as 'poor peopling' was heavily promoted
by the Church. The practicalities were spelt out by Mrs Reaney
in *English Girls, Their Place and Power.*

In one cottage she finds Mrs B in great trouble. Work has been
slack of late, and the reduced wages brought home on Saturday
have not lasted out the week. An empty cupboard, the children
hungry, the good man expected home to dine as usual. Mrs B is
overcome with the sadness of her lot, and hugs her babe in silence
to her heart while forcing back the too readily flowing tears.

Now this is an occasion when tact and judgement are in great
use. The English girl might be lavish in her sympathy; might open
her purse and pour out its contents upon the cottage table ... but

the good thus accomplished would be doubtful. Mrs B's sorrow might be lessened for the moment, but her resources for self-help and self-reliance would be impoverished for the future, and that despondency which is the poor's greatest bane to happiness would be fostered and strengthened. The English girl is equal to the occasion. With a cheerful word and sunny smile she slips off her walking attire, turns up her sleeves, and forthwith proceeds to make a tasty dinner out of such supply as the cupboard affords in its extreme poverty. A little flour, a few small onions, a pinch of salt and pepper, and in five minutes an onion dumpling, costing from 1¾d to 2½d is boiling steadily in the saucepan, and the poor wife is pouring out her gratitude.[6]

A brief reading from the Bible and an offer to escort the older children to Sunday school rounds off the visit. If the Church idea saw the woman as 'the teacher, the natural and therefore divine guide, purifier, inspirer of the man', as Kingsley put it, the role of the man, though more commanding, was no less plied with encouragement to aspire to saintly virtues.

Thomas Arnold set the Gothic tone at Rugby with his emphasis on the chivalric virtues of courage, loyalty, integrity and service. The idea was acclaimed in schoolboy stories led by Tom Brown and Eric, who risked his life to save a friend, in Dean Farrar's *Eric or Little by Little*. The public school ethic gained popular currency with organisations like the Boys' Brigade and the Scouts ('Young Knights of the Empire'). The *Boys' Own Paper* was launched in 1878, followed two years later by the *Girls' Own Paper* with its clarion calls to young ladies to do their duty come what may.

> Never give in, girls,
> Though oft you are fain,
> When hopes fade before you
> And labour seems vain;

Strive onward, keep doing –
Somewhat they must win
Who keep the straight pathway,
And never give in.[7]

But the ethical model of first choice for the Church was provided by the novelist Charlotte Mary Yonge. Born into the squirearchy at Otterbourne near Winchester, Miss Yonge, an only child, 'fell headlong in love with religion' when she came under the influence of John Keble who occupied the neighbouring vicarage. All her High Church standards of perfection were embodied in *The Heir of Redclyffe*, published in 1853. It is the story of a young aristocrat, Sir Guy Morville, who, having anonymously settled the debts of his wayward uncle, is the victim of rumours spread by his disreputable cousin and heir that he is a reckless gambler.

The melodramatic result is that his planned marriage to his guardian's daughter is called off and he is disowned. All this he bears with Christian fortitude, never once tempted to reveal what he knows to save his reputation. When eventually his good name is restored, he marries his beloved Amy. On their Italian honeymoon, he finds his wicked cousin dying of a fever. Forgiving all, Guy nurses his persecutor back to health while himself succumbing to the disease.

The Heir of Redclyffe was given a rapturous reception and not just in High Church circles. As a confession of faith and exemplar of an ideal life the book had massive appeal. At Oxford, William Morris and Edward Burne-Jones, seeing in Guy the spirit of the modern Crusader, decided to adopt his chivalric principles for their Pre-Raphaelite Brotherhood. Among officers in hospital during the Crimea War, *The Heir of Redclyffe* was the book in greatest demand. Sir Guy became the prototype for favoured young men everywhere. The substantial royalties that came to Charlotte Yonge she handed on to overseas missions.

Towards the end of her life (she died in 1901) she devoted her energies to organising Sunday schools and girls' societies.

The post-Victorians rejected *The Heir of Redclyffe* as an exercise in mawkish sentimentality, though 'if the daily life of manor house and parsonage came to be thought tame and uninteresting or their occupants too, too good, that may be due perhaps as much to a general lowering of ideas and loss of home interest as to an excess of virtue'.[8]

While it is easy to sneer at the ethical aspirations of the Victorian Church, what came after was hardly meritorious. The debasing of Thomas Arnold's standards of public and grammar school excellence is a case in point. Arnold was not a games enthusiast but his successors were. Muscular Christianity was incorporated into philistine athleticism. It was a short step to believing that war was a game fought on the rules of the playing field. It is unlikely that the Victorian Church would have made that cardinal error.

CHAPTER THIRTEEN

Rites of Passage

The promotion of the family gave added significance to services that marked the stages in the life cycle. These occasions were guaranteed to attract a strong congregation. Even those who rarely attended church responded to the pull of tradition when it came to a baptism, confirmation, wedding or funeral. Though rarely conceded, the ceremonies had pagan origins, which the Church adopted then modified to meet civilised standards. In the early years of the Church revival, success was judged by the degree to which the parson could stem the flow of alcohol.

One can easily sympathise with the parson who objected to the 'profamation of a solemn rite' when the young people he had just confirmed went straight from the church to the public houses, where the attractions included 'lewd women and dancing'.[1] But confirmation was equated with the coming of age and thus a legitimate excuse for a party. Teenagers could be forgiven if the religious significance of the ritual was secondary to having a good time. Drunken brawls may have been the exception, but every confirmation was accompanied by tea and treats. It was not unknown for youngsters to be confirmed two or three times as they changed parishes for 'the lark of the thing'.[2] When parsons tried to crack down on the festivities, there was a sharp drop in the number coming forward as candidates. More successful were those clergy who took the lead in making confirmation a happy experience, if less dependent on stimulants.

Persuading communicants to keep up their attendance at church was more of a challenge, one that was exacerbated by class divisions. For those not used to approaching the communion rail it could be a perplexing experience. Francis Kilvert tells of a countryman who, given the cup for the first time, touched his forelock to the parson, adding 'Here's to your good health, Sir'. Not to be outdone his friend added, 'Here's to the health of our Lord Jesus Christ'.

Weddings and hard liquor were seemingly inseparable. A Liverpool parson pointed out that the sign of a cross in a marriage register was not necessarily an indication of illiteracy. In his experience, in one case out of five, either the bride or the groom was too drunk to sign their full name. Benjamin Armstrong refused to go ahead with a wedding when he found that the bridegroom and the best man could barely stand. It was a bad day for Armstrong. Later, he visited a cottage to baptise a child 'where screams, while in its cradle, caused the mother to undress it; a rat had been feeding on its little arm'.[3]

Baptism or 'naming' rituals were deep rooted in folklore that predated Christianity. For this reason, perhaps, the ceremony was often performed at home, with the parson putting in a brief appearance to formalise the occasion before the festivities began. There were those who relished the opportunity for joining in a happy event. Sabine Baring-Gould recalled a clerical neighbour in Yorkshire, 'a bachelor in a very large house in a park – made over to the Church as a rectory', who delighted in domestic baptisms.

If the happy father was a labourer he would invite the farmer for whom he worked to come, bring a bottle of gin and sit over the fire with the parson, so soon as the ceremony was over. At a farmhouse, the table was laid with spirits, tumblers, pipes, and a pack of cards, and so soon as the child was baptized the farmer with two friends and the rector sat down and made a night of it.

The parson's housekeeper was sure to leave his study window unlocked so that he might let himself in by throwing up the sash and climbing over the sill. Below the window was a flower bed, much trampled on and 'with the parson one night having slept in it, unable to get the sash up or throw his leg over the sill'.[4]

The more serious minded were offended by the sacrilege implied by parents who neglected to bring their infants to church. In an early incumbency, in the 1840s, Dean Hole faced the task of refurbishing his church, one of 'the dirtiest and most desolate' buildings in the parish. 'The font, never used for its sacred purpose, the babes being baptized at home in a yellow basin, generally associated with porridge or the pudding, was filled with broad ropes, by which coffins are let down into the grave, with an assortment of candle ends.'[5]

Canon law ruled that the font should be of stone and generally placed by the church door, 'to signify entrance into God's church by baptism'. But if baptisms were held at morning or evening services, the congregation could see little of what was going on. At St George's, Hanover Square, London, the problem was solved by using a marble wine cooler kept under the altar which could be wheeled out on castors.[6] Where no font existed, a basin on the altar was made to serve.

It was time to reassert the sacred nature of baptism, but the campaign to bestow clerical dignity brought its own problems. While Sunday baptism became increasingly popular, many churchgoers resented longer services to accommodate a line-up of squalling infants. In city churches, the crush of newborns could be overwhelming. At St Mary's, in the London parish of Newington in 1869, the parson baptised fifty children on an Easter afternoon followed by thirty adults in the evening. In

Leeds at around the same time a vicar and two curates baptised twice a day to bring their combined total for the year to nearly 2,000.

Proud parents, along with their nearest and dearest, were keen to be involved, even if their enthusiasm was not always matched by their ability to abide by the script. In the legion of recorded howlers is that of a hard-of-hearing godmother who, when asked if she renounced the devil and all his works, responded enthusiastically, 'I heartily recommend them all.' A parson who was understandably irritated by the list of exotic names he was supposed to repeat over the newborn settled for plain 'John'. Only later did he discover that he had christened a girl.

It was the job of the parson to keep a record of the parish baptisms, nuptials and deaths, a duty that was taken more seriously after 1812 when Parliament ordered churches to store their registers in an iron chest. The state expected parsons to act as agents who could be held to account if they fell short in their administrative chores. This continued after 1836, when Nonconformists were permitted to marry in their own place of worship. As designated registrars, the clergy had to send copies of documents to a central office. This was not always done efficiently. Returns were often delayed or forgotten entirely. When they were dispatched, they were at the mercy of the Post Office, where officials were unhelpful if the packages were wrongly addressed. The London post office caused havoc when a large number of registers were declared not deliverable and burned. At a parish in Northamptonshire, the daughter of the parish clerk was found to have used the old registers as lace parchments.[7]

In many rural parishes, the parson had no choice but to match the church service with local customs. Invariably, it was the service that took second place. John Atkinson, vicar of Danby in the Yorkshire Dales, recalled having to preside over four weddings, held simultaneously.

The couples, with their attendants, came up to the church in one cavalcade. First, there were no less than seven horsemen, each with a pillion-borne female behind him. Three of these were brides; the others attendants. Of other attendants, male and female, there must have been at least as many more; and then came those who had gathered to see the weddings. But besides, there were from a dozen to a score men, mostly young, who carried guns, and who, as the weddingers passed down the little slope leading to the churchyard gate, fired a salvo. As may be supposed, more than one or two of the horses, being neither sobered by age and hard work, not yet trained to stand fire, were startled and began to plunge and rear. I fully expected a disaster. However, with the exception of one of the pillion ladies, who slid gently – though not without raising her voice – backwards down over the crupper of her steed, no casualty occurred. After the ceremony was over, great was the scramble among the small boys for the coppers, which it was and is customary for the newly married man, or his best man, to scatter the moment the chancel door is left. And then an adjournment to the field adjoining the churchyard was made, and there were a series of races, all on foot, to be run for the ribbons which were the gift of the several brides.[8]

It was all harmless fun, and Atkinson took it in his stride, as he did when the father of a bride,

A personage who, in the very large percentage of cases, is just the one 'person or party' who does *not* 'give away the bride', being indeed very rarely present at the ceremony at all – made ready answer, 'Ah dia'; and then ignoring, as usual, the positive direction of the rubric, addressing himself to the bridegroom he added, 'Tak her. She's a guid an'!'[9]

Every parson could draw on anecdotes of bizarre weddings. On Christmas Day 1867, Benjamin Armstrong had to struggle with a tongue twister.

Married a young parishioner of the name of Mahershallalsahbaz
Tuck. He accounted for the possession of so extraordinary a
name thus: his father wished to call him by the shortest name
in the Bible, and for that purpose selected Uz. But the clergyman
making some demur, the father said in pique, 'Well, if he cannot
have the shortest he shall have the longest.'[10]

In the days when, for reasons never satisfactorily explained,
weddings had to take place in the morning, with noon as the
deadline, punctuality was a virtue. It was not much in evidence
for W. H. Thornton when he rode 10 miles to stand in for a
colleague. At the appointed time he found himself locked out of
the church with just one elderly citizen for company.

> I took up my position in the churchyard where I could see all the
> church path down below to the village. When my watch informed me
> that it was after half-past eleven, I went to the old man and told him
> that the law did not permit me to marry after noon, that there was
> no sign from below, and that I was going home; if the bridegroom
> should come, he was to present him with my compliments and
> recommend him in future to practise the virtue of punctuality.
>
> While we were speaking, however, the wedding party emerged
> from the houses and came slowly up the hill. By the time they
> arrived at the church, it wanted only ten minutes to twelve, and
> the law was imperative. I went straight to the bridegroom and
> scolded him well, bidding him at the same time to be quick, and
> to get the church opened.
>
> 'Now see, sir for yourself,' said he, 'what jealousy is capable
> of. The clerk of this parish wants to marry this young woman
> himself, and as she prefers me to him, he has gone away and
> taken the keys with him.

To gain entry, the groom had to climb in through a window,
falling head first into a pew.

I can almost see his forked legs at this moment as he went down. The bride turned to me with a smile and said, 'This, sir, is what I do call a regular jolly lark.'

'Silence, you scandalous woman,' I cried, 'or I will see you at Jericho before I marry you.'

Then the bolt of the little belfry door was slidden back and we entered, the whole party in a titter of amusement. I hurried on my surplice, and entering the altar rails knelt down in order to steady them, but dared not remain upon my knees, as it was just upon twelve o'clock. When I reached the ring portion of the service, I bade Mr Jones put the ring upon the third finger of the woman's left hand, and say, etc. He seized the second finger and the ring would not pass.

'You stupid jackass,' said she, 'what are you up to now?'

I hurried over the service, declined to take a fee, and 'discoursed' them, as the Irish say, in the churchyard as roundly as ever newly married couple were discoursed since the world began. I blew them up sky-high, and rode off, declaring that Parracombe people might in future marry each other with whatever horrid rites they thought proper, but that I would never again be party to 'burgling' a church to oblige the best of them.[11]

The typical wedding that fell well short of the ideal was one forced on a young couple when the bride carried the 'offspring of unhallowed lust beneath her bosom'.[12] The good parson with an understanding of human nature bit his lip and carried on, but there were those of his calling who suffered agonies at the thought of giving holy sanction to such a grievous lapse in moral behaviour. Yet what was the alternative? While there were cases where the parson refused to cooperate, in the eyes of the Church, living in sin and illegitimacy were even greater breaches of convention.

In remote districts, all manner of improper relationships were liable to surface.

Near Cholderton, but outside my parish boundary, were two cottages not visible from our direction. I called now and then and found the people very outlandish. Their church and vicarage were on the Avon, four or five miles off. The clergyman had to publish banns, and in due time perform a marriage. He had never seen or heard of the couple.

After the ceremony the man put the usual 7s.6d. into the hands of the clerk, who handed 5s. out of it to the clergyman. The instant the newly-married couple had disappeared under the porch, the clerk turned round to the clergyman, who was still holding his fee in his hand, and exclaimed, 'Why, she's his niece.' It was the fact. The uncle and niece had lived all their life in that solitude, and this was the result.

The poor clergyman was aghast. What was he to do? I am sure I could not say what was the best to be done, or what could be done, indeed. As the law then stood they were legally married, till the marriage could be set aside by an ecclesiastical suit. Practically the deed was done, and was irrevocable.[13]

In July 1853, the Revd Joseph Romilly reported a curious incident at a wedding in Ely Cathedral.

Towards the end of the service 2 ladies rushed up to the communion table looked the bride anxiously in the face & exclaimed 'it's not she': – they then rushed out again. It turned out that the runaway whom they sought had been married in that same Church an hour before.[14]

In town and country, the number of church marriages continued to rise throughout the century. In 1851, 85 per cent of all marriages were conducted by the Church of England but, with the steady increase in the number of civil ceremonies, the balance shifted. By 1900, church marriages were down to 642 in every 1,000, from 907 in 1844. The corresponding figure for civil marriages was 179 against twenty-six. Still, this was a respectable showing for a Church that was supposedly under devastating attack from secular forces.

Death was never far away. The good parson was always on hand. On 9 May 1870, John Egerton was visiting in his East Sussex parish of Burwash when he was 'suddenly sent for to see a woman who was lying dead by the roadside at Willenden Hill'. The following day,

> Old Park the butcher at 82 committed suicide this morning, about 6 o'Clock by hanging. He had been suffering a great pain in his head for some time. I called to say that I thought it better not to toll the church bell in such a case, I saw the body. It is feared that the woman who was found dead last night had been killed & knocked about. She was not a woman of good character if I am rightly informed & had a husband living at Hightown.

Less than a week later he was officiating at the funeral of 'Nancy Gibbs ye woman who was killed by Harry Hazelgrove who is committed on charges of manslaughter'. [15]

A reminder of the final reckoning and an aid to coping with bereavement, the Victorian funeral was also a symbol of respectability and status. For the wealthy departed, only the best would do. When Francis Kilvert attended his aunt's funeral at Worcester Cathedral, he was shocked at the expense. 'Everyone had hatbands down to the Choristers who wore them round their college caps. And there was a heavy fee to the choir for the Choral service.' The high cost was no guarantee that all would go well.

> So the clergy and choir came to meet us at the door, then turned and moved up the Cathedral nave chanting in solemn procession, 'I am the Resurrection and the Life saith the Lord'. But meanwhile

there was a dreadful struggle at the steps leading up from the Cloisters to the door. The bearers were quite unequal to the task and the coffin seemed crushingly heavy. There was a stamping and scuffling, a mass of struggling men swaying to and fro, pushing and writhing and wrestling while the coffin sank and rose and sank again. Once or twice I thought the whole mass of men must have been down together with the coffin atop of them and some one killed or maimed at least. But now came the time of the fat chief mourner. Seizing his opportunity he rushed into the strife by an opening large and the rescued coffin rose. At last by a wild effort and tremendous heave the ponderous coffin was borne up the steps and through the door into the Cathedral where the choristers, quite unconscious of the scene and the fearful struggle going on behind, were singing up the nave like a company of angels. In the Choir there was another dreadful struggle to let the coffin down. The bearers were completely overweighted, they bowed and bent and nearly fell and threw the coffin down on the floor. When it was safely deposited we all retired to seats right and left and a verger or beadle, in a black gown and holding a mace, took up his position at the head of the coffin, standing. The Psalm was sung nicely to a very beautiful chant.[16]

Funerals and hymns went together. 'Lead, kindly light' and 'Abide with me' were among the favourites, along with Ellerton's 'Now the labourer's task is o'er' and Newman's 'Praise to the holiest in the height'. After Gladstone's funeral, 'Our God, our help in ages past' entered the list of suitable hymns for a grand send off. It was also sung at the queen's funeral. Gospel songs were favoured by Evangelicals. As the hearse carrying the Earl of Shaftesbury left Westminster Abbey, the band of the Costermongers' Temperance Society struck up 'Safe in the arms of Jesus'.[17]

A tidy churchyard was not complete without floral decorations, though it was not until the last decade of the century that artificial flowers in glass cases made their appearance. Kilvert favoured primrose crosses at Easter and was keen for parishioners to 'adopt some little design in the disposition of flowers ... instead of sticking sprigs into the turf aimlessly anywhere, anyhow and with no meaning at all', adding that he did 'not like to interfere too much with their artless, natural way of showing their respect and love for the dead'.[18]

As the century progressed, funeral ritual and the accompanying symbols of mourning took on ever more ostentation. The economy founded on death extended, from monumental masons pandering to social rank with bigger and more elaborate grave stones to undertakers with their gilded coffins, professional pall bearers and plumed horses to draw the hearse and from drapers specialising in uniform black to florists with their ornate wreaths, mingling 'fragrance with the memory of the dear one who has gone'. Reminders of the departed were kept for years. Special mourning cards, lined in black, gave biographical details and even the cause of death along with a biblical or other religious text.

Wealthy families could go to extraordinary lengths to soften the blow of the grim reaper. In Highgate Cemetery, one of several large burial grounds created to make up for the lack of space at inner city parishes, the grave of a senior army officer had seats ranged on each side so that his family could join him for Sunday tea. To add to the bizarre nature of the occasion, a glass panel showed the head of the embalmed corpse. Victorian epitaphs were strong on bad poetry and mawkish sentiment.

> Here lies a son, whose tender life
> To a mother's heart most dear,
> Bereft of life through wicked strife
> Who once was all her care.
>
> By pugilism, a shameful sight,
> To every mother's eyes,

That dimmed the heavenly orbs of light,
Which forc'd convulsive cries.

But still my hope shall ever be,
Though folly closed his life,
That he's in heaven, from troubles free,
From vanity and strife.

Then let all youths a warning take
At his untimely fate,
And call on God for mercy's sake,
Before it is too late.

This was the dedication to Thomas Pyle who died in 1853. He was aged fifteen.

Quality usually accorded with brevity. On a tomb in Islington, Elizabeth Emma Thomas, aged twenty-seven, was said to have

No fault save what travellers give the moon:
Her light was lovely, but she died too soon.

Faith in the afterlife was much on display.

There's a beautiful land beyond the skies,
And I long to reach its shore.
For I know I shall find my darling there
The beautiful eyes and amber hair
Of the loved one gone before.

Unconscious humour was not unknown. In Woolwich,

Sacred to the memory of Major James Brush, Royal Artillery, who was killed by the accidental discharge of a pistol by his orderly, 14th April, 1831. Well done, good and faithful servant.

And this for a man who had hanged himself:

> So very suddenly fell
> My neighbours wonder'd at my Knell,
> Surprised that I should be no more
> The Many they'd seen the day before.[19]

There is a risk of overdoing the epitaphs. Wonderful collections published early in the last century, but now rarely seen, offer a wealth of oddities which are hard to resist.

Working-class funerals were, at best, prosaic, with the mourners parading in their Sunday best. Basic costs were liable to be covered by one of the many funeral clubs set up to collect subscriptions against the day of judgement. But the event often fell short of expectations. Shoddy coffins could be ill-shaped or liable to fall apart during the service.

The Revd Egerton, who presided at the funeral of a local farmer on an August Monday in 1857, recorded the 'smell very offensive; ought to have been buried on Saturday'.[20] A few years later, 'when old Master Fellowes was being carried to be buried, the cart upset at the corner by Mr Buss's and the coffin and the mourners were all thrown out'. A Mrs Clear complained that her late husband 'bursted' as he was being carried into church.[21] The funerals of workhouse inmates, said Egerton, 'were hardly decent'.

Parsons recorded bizarre experiences at the graveside. At East Dereham there were two occasions when Benjamin Armstrong was almost defeated in his ministrations by the sheer weight of the corpse. In February 1855, he buried a parishioner 'whose weight, with the coffin was 60 stone'. A large crowd gathered in expectation of a grisly disaster but after a struggle to get the coffin into the church the event passed off without incident.[22] In August 1874, Armstrong buried the wife of a Dereham solicitor. 'She was a woman of enormous size and it took 12 men to carry the coffin from the cemetery chapel to the grave ... stopping every ten yards to take breath.'[23]

When infectious illnesses struck funerals were conducted in great haste and with minimum ceremony. It was not unusual for victims of smallpox or cholera to be buried at night. Even so, there were serious risks for the participants.

> *23 Jan 1882* ... Mr Taylor ... says ye man who caught ye small pox by acting as bearer at Mr Munn's funeral at Robertsbridge, can't live 48 hours. Half Robertsbridge is getting re-vaccinated.'[24]

In remote areas, funeral rites were governed more by custom than by clerical convention. In his Yorkshire parish, the Revd Atkinson found that no funeral was complete without lengthy choral accompaniment.

> The custom used to be to sing a hymn, or part of one of the old version of the psalms, when the body was brought forth from the death-room, and set on the chairs arranged for its reception in front of the house. Singing was continued or repeated on 'lifting the body', and again once or oftener on the road to the church – that is, in the days preceding the acquisition and use of the hearse ... There were, indeed, in some places regular stations at which the body was rested and a hymn or psalm sung. ... When the funeral procession began to move down the grassy slope by which the churchyard was approached, a hymn was raised, and the singing continued until the churchyard gate was reached. ... The practice was such that the rubric prescribing the meeting of the corpse by the priest and clerks at the churchyard entrance, and their singing or saying the prescribed sentences as they preceded the body into the church, was not only practically but completely ignored. The singing was persevered in to the very entrance of the church. The singers were supreme, and 'the priest and clerks' nowhere. This I stopped by remaining steadfast in the

entrance to the churchyard until the loudest and longest-winded
of the singing men had sung themselves out.[25]

At the beginning of the century it was accepted that all except
suicides had the right to be buried in their parish churchyard.
But until 1880, the law gave the parson the power of decision
as to who might qualify for internment. With the sharpening of
divisions between the Church and the Nonconformists, some
clergy imposed their own rules of entry to the grave. In 1857,
George Corham of Walkeringham felt justified in refusing to
allow a Methodist-baptised person to be buried. As a result, he
was beset with requests for adult baptisms, for it turned out
that dissenters were keen for their arrival on earth and their
departure to be acknowledged by the Church.[26] As an old
countryman told the Revd Armstrong, 'I allus say, begin and
end with the Church whatever you do between-whiles.'[27] For
those of stronger Nonconformist convictions, the municipal
cemeteries introduced in 1852 provided an alternative final
resting place, at least in urban areas.

The parson was always on hand to give support to a family
suffering bereavement, though he was not always able to satisfy
the calls on his benevolence.

Tom Hagley (Rector of Brightling) gave me the following
specimen of what a Sussex clergyman is expected to do for his
parishioners. 'Please Sir, my husband died just upon six months
ago, & he always said he wd. will all he'd got to me, but he never
made no will at all. So please Sir, wd. you make a will for him, &
my son says he'll sign it directly!'[28]

Rural churches often had residents who were some way short of
demise. At Luxborough there was a squatter who had made a
one-room cottage in an angle of the church wall. He had a wife
'dirty, taciturn and as old as her husband'.

They did not mix at all with their few neighbours. One day the carpenter at Dunster said to the doctor, 'I have had an odd order today, sir. A living man, an old fellow from Luxborough, has been to my place and has ordered his coffin. I told him to lie down on the floor that I might take his measure, and then I chalked around him. 'A little more room for the shoulders, sir,' he said, 'if you please, I might grow a bit stouter before I die.'

Shortly afterwards the old man came with a donkey and took the coffin away, and when Mr Abraham next called at his house he discovered that some of the stones had been shifted from the wall, the earth (which was higher inside than out) had been removed, and the aperture lined with slabs. There the coffin was thrust in, and was used as a drawer to contain bacon, old nails, twine, mouse-traps, and other sweetmeats.[29]

CHAPTER FOURTEEN

The Genesis of Doubt

The greatest challenge for the Victorian parson was to come to terms with uncertainty. Charles Darwin is generally credited with introducing doubt into the theological debate, but long before the publication of *On the Origin of the Species* intelligent churchmen had questioned the literal truth of the Bible stories. The Old Testament was, for them, a set of morality tales, true in spirit if not in substance. Thomas Macaulay told the newly ordained Samuel Wilberforce that 'not two hundred men in London believed in the Bible in its entirety'. As for the average citizen, he had neither time nor inclination to ask if the world was really 6,000 years old, whether there had been a universal flood or if Jonah had been literally swallowed by a whale.

An entry in the diary of Charles Greville gives a convincing reading of the public mood.

> Religious feuds are rife ... Everybody says it is all very alarming, and God knows what will happen, and everybody goes on just the same, and nobody cares except those who can't get bread to eat.

But within the Church, there were more disorientating forces at work. The thoughtful parson who had first-hand experience of the hardships and anxieties of his flock must often have given pause to wonder at the state of the world as ultimately governed by a wise, benign and loving God. The contradiction was too obvious to ignore. What did He think he was up to? Then, but only to be wondered fearfully in the still of the night, did He really exist?

From those who were firm of conviction and purpose, the stock response was to give absolute trust to Christ and the Gospels while bearing the daily tribulations as, in some way, a preparation for the life to come. For proof that God was real, the unquiet mind was exposed to the work of parson, philosopher and naturalist William Paley, whose *Natural Theology or Evidences of the Existence and Attributes of the Deity* was published in 1802 and was still to be found on students' recommended reading lists until well into the twentieth century. It was a wide-ranging book with many hostages to fortune, not least Paley's assumption that the benign nature of the Almighty could be seen in the general happiness and well-being that marked the order of things. Harder to refute was Paley's argument for a divine intelligence as the source of creation. He was not the first to use the watchmaker analogy but circumstances gave it popular currency.

In crossing a heath, suppose I pitched my foot against a stone, and were asked how the stone came to be there; I might possibly answer, that, for anything I knew to the contrary, it had lain there forever: nor would it perhaps be very easy to show the absurdity of the answer. But suppose I found a watch upon the ground and it should be inquired how the watch happened to be in that place; I should hardly think of the answer which I had before given, that for anything I knew the watch had always been there ... The watch must have had a maker: there must have existed ... an artificer ... who formed it for the purpose which we find it actually to answer; who comprehended its construction and designed its use ... Every indication of contrivance, every manifestation of design, which existed in the watch, exists in the works of nature; with the difference, on the side of nature, of being greater or more, and that in a degree which exceeds all computation.

Paley concluded, 'The marks of design are too strong to be got over. Design must have a designer. The designer must have been a person. That person is God.' Recognising that the finished product had imperfections he added, reasonably enough, 'It is not necessary that a machine be perfect in order to show with what design it was made'.

The young Charles Darwin was much taken with Paley, whose exposition, 'beautiful in its simplicity and force gave me as much delight as Euclid'. Only when he hit on natural selection was Darwin able to take Paley to task for his easy assumption that complex organisms were put on earth readymade. But this left untouched the core of Paley's argument that the wonders of nature, however they were created, pointed to a higher intelligence. The problem, as Newman pointed out, was that this essentially theistic approach bore no greater relationship to Christianity than to other religions. Newman dismissed the very idea of seeking a proof for Christianity that went beyond conscience and revelation. In terms of theological corroboration, science and philosophy had nothing to offer.

This was not how the scientists and philosophers saw it. Verifiable evidence and arguments grounded in logic were their stock in trade. It was the Enlightenment thinkers who led the storm troops. While David Hume warned against conclusions based on analogies, it was Voltaire who famously defended scepticism with the crisp aside, 'Doubt is not a pleasant condition but certainty is absurd.' The scientists were soon to prove his point.

When Victoria was crowned, Darwin had recently returned from a six-year, 40,000-mile voyage round the world. He had yet to make up his mind whether species were mutable. Within a year he had formulated his theory of evolution, though his conclusions were not to be made public for twenty years. While his first-hand research played a dominant role in Darwin's reasoning, he was undoubtedly influenced by the work of other scientists, starting with that of his grandfather, Erasmus Darwin, who had put forward his own theory of evolution at the end of the last century.

Darwin also benefited from his friendship with Charles Lyell, whose *Principles of Geology* argued that the earth had been shaped by slow-moving forces acting over a very long period of time. Though he dismissed evolution, Lyell was passionate in his belief that the story of man was to be found in the laws of nature. There was no room for miraculous intervention. The discovery of the remains of ancient man along with the animals they had hunted made nonsense of the belief that life was perfect and without death before the Fall.

The debate on first causes escalated with the publication of *Vestiges of the Natural History of Creation*. The book had all the makings of a cause celebre. In plain language it challenged the common assumption that the diversity of life was God-made. This was not to deny a creator, but 'it being admitted that the system of the Universe is one under the dominion of natural law, it follows that the introduction of species into the world must have been brought about in the manner of law also'. This full-frontal attack on the Church was made all the more sensational by the author's anonymity. At various times, Thackeray, Dickens and even Prince Albert were given unsought credit for *Vestiges*. Eventually it came out that the writer was a Scottish polymath, Robert Chambers, who gave his name to *Chambers's Encyclopaedia*.

While Chambers may be said to have pre-empted Darwin with his theory of evolution, he relied more on reasoned supposition than on hard facts. As a result he was attacked on two sides

– by scientists, who demanded evidence in place of what they saw as fanciful speculation, and by conservative theologians who feared the crumbling of the central pillars of the Church. Among the eminent scientists who regarded Chambers as a fraud and, because he wrote for a general readership, a menace to good order, was Adam Sedgwick, Professor of Geology at Cambridge and, variously, President of the Geological Society and a Fellow of the Royal Society and President of the British Association. He wrote of Chambers that in attempting to destroy the distinction between moral and physical he made sin a 'mere organic misfortune'. If his claims were true, 'Religion is a lie; human law is a mass of folly,' and, 'morality is moonshine.' But Sedgwick set himself apart from those who insisted on a literal reading of Genesis.

The attack on rigid orthodoxy intensified with the publication in English of the work of biblical scholars in Germany. Benefiting from a more liberal environment for theological inquiry, David Strauss, who wrote a revisionist life of Jesus, and Ludwig Feuerbach, in his *Essence of Christianity*, struck out at beliefs that failed rational assessment. Strauss declared bluntly that 'all miracles, prophecies, narratives of angels and demons' are 'simply impossible and irreconcilable with the known and universal laws which govern the course of events' while for Feuerbach a belief in revelation not only undermines moral sense but also 'poisons, nay destroys, the dominant feeling in man, the sense of truth'. It was not the historical but the mythical Jesus that gave us eternal truths. As the literary midwife for Strauss and Feuerbach, George Eliot was sufficiently won over to their views as to lose what remained of her faith, though she held tight to Christianity as a moral code.

Predictably, the new thinking brought a mixed response from Church elders. Reacting to geological findings, John Keble took his stand 'on the conceivability and indeed certainty of the Almighty having created all the fossils and other apparent outcomes of former existence in the six days of the Creation'. A more flexible approach was to try to reconcile geology and the Old Testament by, for example, extending the six days of Creation to periods of indefinite length. But the loudest voices proclaimed orthodoxy as the only foundation for peace of mind and the only defence against social chaos.

'Consider the miseries of wives and mothers losing their faith in Scripture', said Newman from his elitist and paternalistic standpoint. It was the duty of the priest to suppress his own doubts and suppress doubts in others. Bishop Wilberforce judged religious doubt to be a moral sickness. It was presumptuous of man to question the revelation God had given him. Said the Evangelical J. C. Ryle, 'We hold that nothing whatever is needed between the soul of man the sinner and Christ the Saviour, but simple, childlike faith.'[1]

The critically minded were not impressed. Of several embarrassing encounters between clergy and sceptics, one of the more shameful was initiated by William Cockburn, Dean of York. Cockburn was a controversial figure who had been summoned before the archbishop's court for selling the lead off the Minster roof and pocketing the proceeds. Had he not been well connected (his first wife was the sister of Sir Robert Peel) he would almost certainly have lost his deanery. As it was, when the British Association met in York in 1844, it felt bound to allow Cockburn to read a paper denouncing all those who questioned the biblical account of the creation. Moreover, he argued, the findings of geology confirmed Genesis word for word. Adam Sedgwick was put up to respond. His counter-attack was devastating. Yet so immune to contradiction was Cockburn that he managed to persuade himself that he had emerged the victor.

Cockburn was not alone. When Sabine Baring-Gould was ordained in 1864, his bishop assured him 'that all scripture, including, of course, the sensuous Song of Solomon, was absolutely true and every word inspired by the spirit of God, and that every statement in scripture was sure, whatever science might say to the contrary'.[2]

What was later claimed as a defining moment in the clash between science and religion took place at Oxford in 1860. Having already taken Darwin to task for the speculative element in evolutionary theory, Bishop Wilberforce cheerfully agreed to participate in a British Association debate on the impact of Darwin on intellectual development. Deploying all the oratorical weaponry at his command, Wilberforce gave a knockabout performance, ridiculing the fanciful notion (and many did find it fanciful) that mankind in all his glory was born of the hairy ape.

To the delight of the largely clerical audience, Wilberforce wound up by asking 'if anyone were willing to trace his descent through an ape as his grandfather, would he be willing to trace his descent similarly on the side of his grandmother?' This brought Thomas Huxley to his feet. He saw no reason to be ashamed of having an ape as an ancestor. 'If there were an ancestor whom I should feel shame in recalling, it would rather be a man – a man of restless and versatile intellect – who, not content with success in his own sphere of activity, plunges into scientific questions with which he has no real acquaintance, only to obscure them by an aimless rhetoric'. He was rewarded by a round of applause.

It should be said that Wilberforce had powerful supporters, They included Sir David Brewster, inventor of the kaleidoscope and a founder of the British Association and, most damningly for Huxley and friends, Admiral Robert Fitzroy, captain of the *Beagle* and voyage companion of Charles Darwin, who was a devout Christian. As a participant in the Oxford debate he held the Bible aloft and implored the audience to believe God rather than man. Fitzroy was no dilettante; rather he was a scholar, scientist and pioneering meteorologist. The evolutionists did not have all the best brains.

Moreover, those such as Huxley, who was the first to describe himself as 'agnostic', took pains to emphasise an open-minded approach to religion. 'It is wrong for a man to say that he is certain of the objective truth of any proposition unless he can produce evidence which logically justifies that certainty.'[3] In other words, argued Huxley, on the available evidence, it was impossible to affirm or deny the existence of God. It was certainly the case that Darwin had not delivered the last word. The quest for the origins of life remained, and still remain, elusive. Images of creatures emerging from the primeval slime are the stuff of science fiction but remain unsupported by geological study.

Two months after the publication of *On the Origin of the Species*, Christian orthodoxy suffered another setback, this time from within the Church. As its title suggests, *Essays and Reviews* was a ragtag of articles by a group of authors who shared a wish to open up the theological debate to free inquiry. They were led by Benjamin Jarrett, Professor of Greek at Oxford and soon to be Master of Balliol, who famously demanded that the Bible be read 'like any other book'. His aim was to break through the barricades piled high by the dogmatists to reveal the core of the Bible as the essential guide to the good life.

Other contributors to *Essays and Reviews* argued for taking Old Testament prophecies with a grain of salt, the impossibility of miracles and the incongruity of eternal damnation with a loving God. While there was nothing new in any of this, it came as a shock to the Church establishment to find those in their own ranks who were prepared to go public with their revisionist opinions. Moreover, it was the first time that advocates of what was loosely described as the Broad Church had come together to present their case, if not in entirely unified form, at least in a sequence of arguments suggesting that a programme for change to rival the High and Low Church parties was not far off.

How did the incessant controversy affect the front-line

parson? Charles Kingsley, himself troubled by doubts, was emphatic in warning younger clergy not to tie themselves in intellectual knots trying to prove the improvable. 'You may think too much,' he told a curate, 'Use your senses much and your mind little.' He urged his fellow clergy to serve God in the everyday business of running a parish rather than by 'weary voyaging on the ocean of intellect'. The Church was a force for good. Was that not sufficient justification for taking holy orders? If more was needed, there was comfort in the extension of Paley, that the wonders of scientific discovery were just another way of exploring the wonders of God.

The problem for the parson who took the broad view was that he had made a solemn promise on ordination to teach the scriptures as written, not as he would like them to be interpreted. In 1864, 11,000 Anglican clergymen signed a solemn declaration that the Church 'maintains without reserve or qualification, the Inspiration and Divine Authority of the whole Canonical Scriptures, as not only containing but being the word of God'.

It was a brave parson who refused to sign. Those who voiced their doubts openly were pilloried for spreading seeds of discontent. Fundamentalists were quick to take action against those who strayed too far from their party line. Of those on the cast list of *Essays and Reviews*, the two beneficed parsons, Rowland Williams and Henry Wilson, were both successfully charged with the heresy of suggesting that the Bible was not the incontrovertible Word of God. The verdict was reversed on appeal to the Judicial Committee of the Privy Council but not before the two miscreants had spent a lengthy period of suspension from their livings.

By then, another high-profile case, this time involving the Anglican Church overseas, had taken over the headlines. Prompted by questions put to him at his Zulu mission station, John William Colenso, first Bishop of Natal, advocated a reinterpretation of the Old Testament to accommodate the latest geological evidence. Dismayed at the prospect of having to revise their teaching, Colenso's fellow bishops deprived him of his office. Once again, the Privy Council intervened on the side of liberalism and common sense. Colenso was reinstated, but not before every parson in the land was made aware of the trembling theological foundation.

The public appetite for religious discord was fed by the publication of some 400 books and pamphlets in just four years up to 1864.[4] These included a translation of Ernest Renan's *Vie de Jésus,* which portrayed the founder of Christianity as the hero of a historical romance, the proponent of an essentially humanist doctrine. The reaction of the zealots was to become yet more diehard, taking their line from J. W. Burgeon, fellow of New College Oxford, who declared from the university pulpit that the books, sentences, words, syllables – 'aye, and the very letters' – of the sacred text were absolutely infallible.[5]

Where was the good parson to turn? The agony of those who lost their faith was encapsulated in one of the most popular novels of the nineteenth century. *Robert Elsmere* is the story of a young and earnest parson and his equally devoted wife who find total contentment in parish work until Robert comes under the influence of an outspoken unbeliever. His faith ebbs until he can no longer justify his living. With his heartbroken but devoted wife he retreats to a poor London parish where, until an untimely death, he gives himself to the deprived and destitute.

'I wanted to show,' wrote Mrs Humphry Ward, 'how a man of sensitive and noble character, born for religion, comes to throw off the orthodoxies of his day and moment, and to go out into the wilderness where all is experiment, and spiritual life begins again. And with him I wished to contrast a type no less fine of the traditional and guided mind – and to imagine the clash of two such tendencies of thought, as it might affect all practical life, and especially the life of two people who loved each other.'[6]

Interest in the book was enhanced by the social and intellectual standing of the author. Mrs Humphry Ward was the niece of Matthew Arnold and daughter of an Oxford don. Having married a noted academic, she became a pioneer of women's education. Such was the notoriety of *Robert Elsmere* that William Gladstone favoured the book with a lengthy if censorious review in *Nineteenth Century*.

Few parsons followed hard in Elsmere's footsteps, though many took refuge from scepticism by devoting themselves to good works that required neither doctorial justification nor a closer examination of motive beyond humanitarian sympathy. In his *Short Studies on Great Subjects*, the polemical historian James Anthony Froude (the younger brother of Hurrell Froude, with whom he had little in common) compared the quiet life of the eighteenth-century clergyman with the feverish activity of the contemporary parson. Wrestling with uncertainties, he 'conceals his misgivings with which he flings himself into his work ... building and restoring churches, writing books and tracts; persuading themselves and others with spasmodic energy that the thing they love is not dead, but sleeping'.[7] Froude was writing from his first-hand knowledge, having, as a young ordinand, despaired of the Church at war with itself. He was said to be the model for *Robert Elsmere*.

Those besieged parsons of more cheery disposition, who were also firmer of purpose, gained solace from the will to believe, a powerful force in Victorian society and one which still retains its potency to this day. They recognised the lasting power of the Bible stories. It was not their job, they reasoned, to rock the theological boat. In any case, it was not at all clear that ordinary parishioners wanted to be part of the debate. For all the fuss over the reinterpretation of the Bible, the antidote was Frederick William Farrar's *Life of Christ*, 'written by a man of faith for men of faith', by far the best-selling biography of the Victorian age.[8]

It was Samuel Taylor Coleridge who gave intellectual strength to the will to believe. Coleridge was convinced of the reality of an invisible world, upon which the visible world, the world of nature, was dependent. There was a big difference, he argued, between 'reason' and 'understanding'. While understanding brings logic to bear on objects, reason enables man to respond to what is real in his whole being. 'It is one thing,' said Coleridge, 'to apprehend and another to comprehend.' He argued that we can apprehend God but only with a very limited comprehension, adding, 'In the Bible there is more that finds me than in all the other books I have read.'[9]

Or, more broadly, gazing upon Mont Blanc, 'Who would, who could be an atheist in such a valley of wonders?'

This is where the romantic movement overlapped with the Broad Church. John Ruskin spoke for both when he glorified a creating Spirit as the source of all beauty and a governing Spirit as the founder and maintainer of all moral law.[10] It was a sentiment that brought great comfort in an age of 'unrest and paradox', as Matthew Arnold called it. Time was needed, said John Stuart Mill, to marshal the great stock of new ideas. 'This has not yet been done, or has been done only by a very few: and hence the multitude of thoughts only breeds increase of uncertainty. Those who should be the guides of the rest, see too many sides to every question. They hear so much said, or find that so much can be said, about everything, that they feel no assurance of the truth of anything.'[11]

The rationalists or agnostics may have doubted the existence of God, but they conceded a whole realm of thought outside the parameters of science. At the same time, much of what was assumed to be proved beyond doubt, such as the 'survival of the fittest' dimensions tacked on to evolution, were acknowledged to be no more than subjective speculations. For intellectuals who wanted to remain in the Church, there dawned the realisation that science could clarify without harming core religious beliefs, and that scepticism was essential to progress. We owe to scepticism, said the historian Henry Buckle, 'that spirit of inquiry which, during the last two centuries, has gradually encroached on every possible subject, has reformed every department of practical and speculative knowledge; has weakened the authority of the privileged classes; has chastised the despotism of princes; has restrained the arrogance of nobles; and has even diminished the prejudice of the clergy'.

As trust in the Church as the only one foundation began to fade, the void was filled by a faith in human advancement. Looking about them at the huge advances made by their technological and industrial superpower, how could the Victorians not believe that all things were possible?

> Disease will be extirpated [wrote Winwood Reade], the causes of decay will be removed, immortality will be invented. And then, the earth being small, mankind will migrate into space, and will cross the airless Saharas which separate planet from planet, and sun from sun. The earth will become a Holy Land which will be visited by pilgrims from all the quarters of the universe. Finally, men will master the forces of Nature; they will become themselves architects of systems, manufacturers of worlds. Man then will be perfect; he will then be a Creator; he will therefore be what the vulgar worship as a God.[12]

But progress, though purely secular in this instance, could just as easily have a religious dimension. When Kingsley visited the Great Exhibition he was moved to tears. To him, 'it was like going into a sacred place'. A few days later he was in his pulpit, rhapsodising his experience.

> If these forefathers of ours could rise from their graves this day they would be inclined to see in our hospitals, in our railroads, in the achievements of our physical science, confirmation of that old

superstition of theirs, proofs of the kingdom of God, realizations of the gifts which Christ received for men, vaster than any of which they had dreamed.

The Romantics detected a divine spirit in what Carlyle called 'the progress of man towards higher and nobler developments', while those under the Broad Church banner saw the Creator as one who established general fixed laws, leaving mankind to work out its own salvation. 'I believe that the *Divinae particula aurae* is independent of evolution and deals only with it as a medium and mode of action,' wrote Tom Mozley. 'I believe that the vast human conflict around us is the work of free wills, operated on by a Higher Will, and in communion therewith.'[13]

The Church establishment moved slowly to accommodate the new thinking. The once popular image of Christian orthodoxy – angels on fluffy clouds – passed into folklore, while a literal interpretation of the Old Testament was reserved for the fundamentalist minority. At the end of the century, Bishop Stubbs of Oxford was one of several senior clergy who felt free to tell ordination candidates that large parts of the Bible were not to be seen as integral to God's revelation. Educated theology embraced doubt as integral to faith. 'There lives more faith in honest doubt', wrote Tennyson, 'believe me, than in half the creeds.' Liberal thinkers moved into the clerical mainstream, where they argued for an open-ended search for truth.

In his summing up to his classic *The Varieties of Religious Experience*, William James had this to say. 'The universe ... [is] ... a more many-sided affair than any sect, even the scientific sect, allows for. What in the end, are all our verifications but experiences that agree with more-or-less isolated systems of ideas ... that our minds have framed. But why in the name of common sense need we assume that only one such system of ideas can be true?' He concluded, 'The obvious outcome of our total experience is that the world can be handled according to many systems of ideas.'[14]

James knew that mankind thrives on diversity, that theology based on certainty is a contradiction; it makes no sense. If somehow we knew beyond doubt that God exists – if he had proved his presence and his purpose – mankind would lose its reason for being. For after certainty, what then?

But an open discussion on those lines was all but impossible for the parson to initiate. His congregation wanted reassurance, not controversy. When they entered their church it was to find comfort that was denied to them in their daily lives. The clerical tendency was to take what lessons could be learned from the old Bible stories, without delving too closely into the contradictions or absurdities that come as part of the theological package.

Though serving its purpose in the short run, it was a strategy that began to fail in the wake of the First World War when cynicism fed a universal grief. Why had the Church, a supposedly civilising influence, not done more to stop the slaughter?

Except for those blinded by patriotism, there was no answer. Thereafter, the Church was under pressure to update its message. The tragedy was that it took so long to adapt.

reason to be proud of its
built, churches restored and
institutions created. Church
celebratory, with a closer
congregation. Support was
church charities led the way in
self help. A strengthening
moral and social behaviour.
and non-residence had all
actively engaged parsons had
increased from 16,194 in 1851 to 23,670 in 1901. Of the latter,
over half were under the age of forty-five. If the patronage
system was still in place, the manner in which it was conducted
was changing. The Benefices Act of 1898 abolished resignation
bonds used to compel an incumbent to stand down in favour of
one more congenial to the patron, usually a close relative. The
Act also banned the sale of next presentations and the public
auction of right of appointment unless attached to an estate of
more than 100 acres – a sop to the propertied classes. The great
majority of appointments were in the hands of the bishops
or Church-connected institutions. Even so, where private
patronage still ruled, patrons were liable to put their personal

preferences ahead of any concern for the views of the parish. As late as 1934 this sort of advertisement could appear in *The Times*.

> Patron of vacant living in East Anglia invites recommendations. Net value about £530, large rectory and grounds. Primary qualification, capacity to be guide, philosopher and friend to agricultural people, for which in this case gentle birth essential. Open mind towards Bishop Barnes [the controversial Bishop of Birmingham], birth control and psychic research secondary but helpful.[1]

It was not until 1986, when the Patronage (Benefices) Act strengthened the role of the parochial church councils, that parish representatives were given the power of veto over a patron's choice of candidate.

Having remained steady for over forty years, the parson's income came under pressure in the late 1870s when the prices of wheat, oats and barley, and thus the value of the tithe, fell under competition from the American prairies. By 1901, a tithe that had been worth £100 in 1835 was down by a third.[2] The disparity pointed up the failure of the Church to introduce a national pay structure. Moreover, while other professions could count on a pensionable retirement, the parson not blessed with a private income had to work until he dropped.

Part of the difficulty was the reluctance of the Church to get to grips with the concept of professionalism that embraced vocational training. Throughout Victoria's reign, the favoured route to ordination was via a classical education at Oxford or Cambridge. There were no special classes for ordinands and it was not until 1843 that a voluntary exam was introduced at Cambridge. Even then, a similar course at Oxford failed for want of episcopal support. At neither university was theology a regular degree subject until the 1870s. And it was not until the 1920s that ordinands had to spend a minimum of a year's residence at theological college.

But well before the end of the century it was clear that the days of the gentleman parson who relied on his social standing to see him through his pastoral duties were severely numbered. While there were still rural parishes that made few demands, the urban centres required something more from their clergy than a working knowledge of Greek. This was where the newly established theological colleges, often in proximity to a cathedral, came into their own. Durham, Chichester, Wells, Lichfield, Canterbury, Salisbury, Gloucester, Lincoln and Ely – all diverted their wealth into clerical education. The colleges drew on the sons of farmers and tradesmen, the core of the aspiring lower middle class, who could not afford university but could afford the modest fees for two years of theological immersion.

Even if there was no degree at the end of it – though Durham, Lampeter and King's College London were soon to gain university status – the college diploma was a much sought-after badge of higher education. By 1879, one in six parsons had no letters after his name. While Oxford and Cambridge still accounted for two-thirds of the practising clergy, their dominance over the Church was ended by medicine, the civil service and the law competing for the brightest graduates. In 1841, Oxbridge provided 86 per cent of candidates for holy orders, Trinity Dublin and Durham 7 per cent between them and the theological colleges only 7 per cent. Twenty years on, the corresponding figures were 65 per cent for Oxbridge, 9 per cent for Dublin and Durham and 26 per cent for the colleges.[3]

Parsons of the old school were inclined to look down on their non-graduate colleagues, who were said to be half educated. A more constructive reading of the times recognised that theological colleges gave more attention to commitment and zeal than to academic distinction. In this context, St Aidan's in

Birkenhead, founded by Joseph Baylee, an Irish Evangelical, set the pace.[4] Locked into fundamentalism, Baylee was distrusted by those of more liberal persuasion, but there was no denying the value of the pastoral training provided by St Aidan's. Dubbed 'parochial assistants', his students were sent out into the parishes of Birkenhead and Liverpool to work with the local incumbents. Each week they had to report back on their house-to-house visiting and exchange views on the challenges they encountered. The ordinand of more conventional education, lacking supervision, had to 'learn by experience, costly to others and painful to himself'.[5]

Success depended on strength of personality and commitment. Fortunately for the Church, in the ranks of the clergy there was no shortage of either. Critics of the elaborate fussiness of the Gothic style saw buildings that were dusty and old fashioned, with the clergy to match as they peered through the cobwebs to a long-lost golden age of received religion. This was unfair. Whatever his background, the typical parson was conscious of his duties and did his best to meet them. Yes, of course, there were black spots. When the Revd A. C. Davies arrived at his rural outpost in 1889, he was told that Communion had not been held in living memory and that the Communion plate had disappeared. Eventually, it was found, along with other church effects, stored away in a nearby cellar. The altar was a small semi-circle table on which the old men of the village put their hats.[6] Davies soon had that little matter in hand.

The point here was that, once discovered, failures in provision were corrected. Far more damaging to the reputation of the Church and to its ability to serve its people was the persistent rivalry between High and Low Church parties, fed by the ludicrous fear that the forces of Rome were about to overthrow the Reformation. Attempts to impose a distinctive Protestant uniformity on church services culminated in the 1874 Public Worship Regulation Act, which forbade those practices, such as the mixing of wine and water in the chalice and wearing of Eucharistic vestments, deemed to be opening the back door to the papacy. That Disraeli allowed the legislation to slip through under his watch can only be explained by his lack of interest in religious disputes.

Five parsons were imprisoned for failing to comply with the law. One of these, Richard Enraght of Bordesley in Bedfordshire, offended the Low Church by publishing his justification for confession, prayers for the dead, the adoration of the Blessed Sacrament and the eastward position. Sentenced in 1880 to forty-nine days in Warwick Gaol, Enraght was released early on a technicality. He then returned to Bordesley, where he resumed his old ways until the Bishop of Worcester forbade him to serve.

With justification, Broad Churchmen also felt persecuted by those who happened not to agree with their views. The Revd John MacNaught, vicar of St Chrysostom's in Liverpool, was forced to resign his living after voicing his opinion that not all parts of the Bible were divinely inspired. In 1860, Dunbar Isidore Heath, vicar of Brading on the Isle of Wight, was hauled up before an ecclesiastical court, accused of unorthodox views. Heath was something of an eccentric, given to fantasising about the life hereafter, but he was no more of an oddity than numerous Evangelical parsons who traded in grotesque prophecies. The only difference was that Heath was deprived of his living. And so it went on.

Weakened by dissension, the Church was in no position to resist the encroachment of the secular state into areas of its traditional authority. The power of the vestry, once the chief managing body for local government, presided over by the parson, was gradually lost to elected councils and to statutory bodies. The trend started with the transfer of responsibility for the poor to elected Guardians, but devolution to elected councils and to statutory committees soon covered everything from road maintenance to the provision of parish cemeteries. The number of clerical magistrates – 1,043 in 1873 – was down to under forty by 1906.

The greatest impact was made by the 1870 Education Act, which threatened what until then had been virtually a Church monopoly of elementary education. Locally based school boards were empowered to set up schools for five- to twelve-year-olds. In principle, the Church could hardly object to the state taking up a challenge that the clergy had borne for so long. In any case, some accommodation had to be made with the Nonconformists, who objected to their taxes being used to support the Church.

The sting in the legislation was the limiting of religious teaching to non-denominational instruction. Even in church schools, parents had the right to withdraw their children from religious education. Secular politicians spoke darkly of the insidious propaganda that the clergy were liable to spread, though they failed to come up with a convincing alternative to the Christian message. The Church feared the rise of a secular teaching force opposed to all that the clergy stood for, including a strong moral code.

The fear was misplaced. The Anglican version of Christianity continued to be taught in schools, usually with the tacit approval of Nonconformist parents, who rarely exercised their right to withdraw their children from morning assembly or scripture classes. There was indeed vociferous Nonconformist opposition to the 1902 Education Act, which put the elementary schools on a firmer administrative footing and extended financial support for the voluntary schools, but broad-based religious instruction remained in place. Its firm hold on the curriculum was confirmed by numerous inquiries into standards of teaching, typical of which was a Board of Education report on the *Education of the Adolescent*, published in 1926.

The teaching of religious knowledge, like that of English, cannot be confined to a separate period or number of periods.

It will affect the teaching of other subjects, such as history and literature, and the wise teacher will be anxious, in the various departments of school activity, to bring home to the pupils, as far as their capacity allows, the fundamental truths of religion and their bearing on human life and thought.

In other respects, the Church set education standards which the state felt bound to follow. In 1876 the National Society declared that in new schools each child should have a minimum of 7 square feet of floor space, that lavatories should be provided and that the classroom height should allow for proper ventilation. And there were plenty of new church schools where the regulations applied. In 1870 the count was of 6,382 Anglican schools. By 1886 the number had increased to 12,000. They catered for over 2 million pupils.

In country parishes, the parson remained the dominant figure on the management committee to run the school and appoint teachers. The school itself was invariably an adjunct to the church, with the parson taking an active role in teaching the three Rs as well as giving religious instruction. There were many parishes, however, where battle lines were drawn between parson and teacher, each assuming entitlement to set the style and content of instruction. The pressure to keep up was all the greater after 1880, when schooling was made compulsory for all children between the ages of five and ten.

Rising standards in general education were a spur to the Sunday schools to sharpen their act. Until the 1870s, Sunday school teachers were generally untrained and often ill disciplined, presiding over what a curate in Salford called a 'disorderly bear-garden'. This changed with greater professionalism in the state and voluntary elementary schools. It was not unusual for day school teachers to give model classes for the benefit of Sunday teachers or participate directly in Sunday classes.

The trends in education were replicated in health and welfare, where the doctors and lawyers were asserting their expertise at the expense of the 'amateur' clergy. One result of all this was that the Church found it increasingly hard to straddle the political fence. For most of the century the Church had acted chiefly as an arbiter between the classes, holding to the basic precepts of free capitalism while prompting the better-off to mitigate the hardships of those who lost out by the system. While there were Tory and Liberal parsons, the Church as a corporate body tried to remain above the political fray.

The difficulty for the parson who wanted to do more, while fighting shy of open involvement in party politics, was underlined by the early history of Christian Socialism. In its original form, Christian Socialism had little to do with Christianity and nothing at all to do with Socialism. Cooperation was the guiding principle – employers and workers as a happy band of brothers. The inspiration was an idealised version of the medieval guilds. It came in response to the Chartist agitation, which reached its peak in April 1848 with the presentation to Parliament of the Six Points, a petition headed by a demand for manhood suffrage.

Revolutionary outbreaks across Europe were taken as a sure sign that Britain was next in line for insurrection. Middle-class panic brought the troops into London, the Duke of Wellington at their head. Thousands of special constables were enrolled, the artillery lined up outside the Bank of England and the royal family decamped to the Isle of Wight. When, in the event, the Chartists turned out not to be revolutionaries and an uneasy peace was restored, the ruling consensus held that nothing further need be done.

There were those in the Church who disagreed. One of them was Frederick Maurice, chaplain of Lincoln's Inn and one-time professor at King's College, London, a shy intellectual made nervous by a pronounced stutter, who was most at home in academia. Despite his sheltered and privileged life, or maybe because of it, Maurice, who held advanced theological views, was deeply sensitive to the less fortunate and wanted to do something for them. But his radicalism was tempered by a respect for order and discipline, which precluded an extension of the franchise to the untutored masses. Only educated men were worthy of the vote. The rest had to wait until they had learned to understand their responsibilities and to take them seriously. Meanwhile, it was the duty of the middle class to encourage and support their lower brethren by financing schools and colleges.

The paternalistic approach was much favoured by Charles Kingsley, who joined with Maurice in publishing a penny journal called *Politics for the People*. Its aim was to make the working class aware that it could not be free until it was 'fit to be free'. On course to enlightenment, cooperation was to take precedent over the competitive spirit and class conflict. As a political programme it was hopelessly naïve, as Maurice and Kingsley, both highly intelligent men, should have realised. But in pursuit of his ideal it is to Maurice's credit that he founded the Working Men's College in London's Red Lion Square, which served as the model for similar ventures across the country. By contrast, his Society for Promoting Working Men's Associations to establish cooperative workshops had a short and disappointing life, as one enterprise after another fell to commercial reality.

A harder-nosed version of Christian Socialism emerged later in the century. Like their predecessors, the leaders were not so much socialists as radical liberals, but they spoke out for state intervention to curb social evils, while stressing the overriding need for class cooperation. Representative of the movement, if not wholly typical, was Stewart Headlam, a colourful if erratic social reformer who combined a curacy at St Matthew's, Bethnal Green, with active membership of the Fabian Society. In 1888 he was elected to the London County Council. He campaigned for the redistribution of wealth and, at the 1887 Church Congress, called for legislation to 'put a stop to the robbery of the poor that has been going on for so long'. There was a strong element of self-sacrifice in this, since Headlam enjoyed a substantial private income and was a friend of the rich and famous.

The Guild of St Matthew, founded by Headlam in 1877 to campaign for land nationalisation, a progressive income tax and universal suffrage, helped to make socialism a talking point in the higher reaches of the Church. Like its sister organisation, the Christian Social Union, set up to reconcile intellectual freedom with received religion, it was financed and directed by upper-class clergy. At the head of the CSU was J. R. Illingworth, rector of Longworth from 1883; Henry Scott Holland, a canon of St Paul's who went to Eton; Charles Gore, a Harrow man and ice-principal of Cuddesdon Theological College until 1884 when he was appointed principal of Pusey House; and Brook Foss Westcott, headmaster at Harrow and, from 1890, Bishop of Durham. They could talk happily for hours about goodwill and social harmony. But they had lasting influence.

There still remained those clergy who took refuge in vague hopes of better things to come. The Bishop of Peterborough, William Connor Magee, who became Archbishop of York in 1891, looked to making 'labour just towards capital and capital towards labour and yet not to attempt to define what in every particular case was the precise amount of justice due on one hand or the other'.[7] The case for not taking sides in industrial disputes was put revealingly by Frederick Temple when he was Bishop of London. 'My heart is with the dockers, but my head is with the directors.'

Others were freer with their convictions. In *The Christian Church and the Problem of Poverty*, published in 1894, H. C. Shuttleworth, rector of St Nicholas, Cole Abbey, argued that it was no longer enough for the Church to support the relief of the poor. 'She must go on to inquire what influences have combined to make men poor, and how these influences should be dealt with.' When *The 1897 Lambeth Conference Report on*

Industrial Problems advocated old-age pensions, the delegates were doing no more than following up on the initiative of good parsons across the country. Twenty years earlier, the Revd Lowery Blackley at King's Somborne in Hampshire, a keen supporter of friendly societies, had launched a crusade for compulsory national insurance for sickness benefit and old age. The Bishop of Winchester was among the clergy who were enthusiastic supporters.

As Bishop of London, Mandell Creighton was applauded by the Webbs and other leading Fabians for siding with 'good and even progressive government in all local concerns'.[8] They might well have extended their praise for the foot-soldiers of the Church such as Alexander Mackonochie, vicar of St Albans, Holborn, who ran a choir school, an orphanage, an infant nursery, a youth club, a Sunday breakfast for destitute boys and a soup kitchen.

Rural clergy were generally sympathetic to the needs of farm labourers, who were poorly paid and miserably housed. At Halberton in North Devon, Edward Girdlestone led a campaign against low wages. Indigent farmers who shouted him down at a vestry meeting threatened to take themselves off to the Wesleyan chapel until they found that the minister there was in full agreement with Girdlestone. There was support too from James Fraser, Bishop of Manchester, who defended the right of farm workers to form a union with a vigorous letter to *The Times*, asking, 'Are the farmers of England going mad?'[9]

However, the newly created Agricultural Labourers' Union was not universally admired by the clergy. There were those who feared that the use of the strike would lead to yet further social disruption, which could only bring harm to the countryside. Then again, the rural parson was heavily dependent on the farmers and labourers for financial and moral support. When the vicar of Stockton in Warwickshire spoke out for better conditions he suffered social ostracism, the cutting of his wife and daughters at dances and parties, the emptying of his church and the drying up of subscriptions.[10]

Girdlestone himself warned the Union against political agitation that went beyond the aim of benefiting farm workers and criticised those who blamed the church for the failings of the landowners. While admitting that the clergy had not done all they should have done to make a better life for their humbler parishioners, he went on,

> It is equally true that, were it not for the kindness of the clergy in the rural districts; for the sacrifices which they have made to build and endow schools; for the many meals which they have sent from the parsonage to the cottage, when the breadwinner is ill, the wife confined, the children poorly fed; the many comforts which they have denied to themselves and their families in order to clothe and feed the naked and hungry among their flock; not to mention the prayers by the sick-bed, and their loving words of comfort to the widow and fatherless in their sorrow, the conditions of the agricultural labourer would have been very much worse than it is.[11]

That there was still vigour in the concept of self help was proved by the wife of the rector of Old Alresford in Hampshire. Mary Sumner was a single-minded lady whose cause it was to make the mothers of England care more about their children, 'instead of leaving them to the nurse if they were rich and to the street if they were poor'.[12] To this end, she founded the Mothers' Union, initially as a diocesan organisation. In less than ten years it gained a nationwide following and a membership of well over a quarter of a million. It was all about empowerment. As Mary Sumner put it so memorably, 'Those who rock the cradle, rule the world.'

Despite the advance of the secular state, in the closing years of Victoria's reign, the parson was likely to serve on a wide variety of committees and agencies concerned with social matters. 'It sometimes takes my breath away,' declared the Bishop of Liverpool, 'to hear the programme of weekly work ... announced upon a Sunday as the parochial bill of fare for the next six days.'

Philanthropy thrived. In London alone in 1885, there were more than 1,000 charities, the great majority of them Church led. Of a sample of 446 wills totalling bequests of £76 million, £20 million went to charity. In an attempt to introduce some sort of order to charitable work by defining areas of competence and to encourage recipients of charity to become independent self-respecting citizens, the Charity Organization Society was set up in 1869. The founders were Samuel Barnett, a curate in the Whitechapel parish of St Judes, 'the worst parish, inhabited mainly by criminals', and the social housing pioneer, Octavia Hill. In the attempt to make best use of resources, soup kitchens were discouraged on the grounds that food was distributed without enquiry into the needs of the recipients. But the charitable impulse of the middle class, or rather, perhaps, its desire to assuage guilt, was not easily redirected. The vicar of St Mark's, Kennington, complained that the soup kitchen had been 'far and away the most popular object of yearly subscription'. After it was discontinued, the charitable offering from the big houses in the parish dropped by two-thirds. Many parsons were inclined to resist the efficiency rulings of the COS. 'I am one who can't naturally refuse,' a Brixton vicar confessed while a neighbouring incumbent proudly announced that in his parish, 'no request for help from the poor was ever turned down'.[13]

Much was achieved in supporting medical care. In London, district dispensaries and nursing associations were closely associated with the churches. In 1899, Lambeth's parishes were sponsoring sixteen nurses.[14]

From the pulpit, exhortations to be good were blended with praise for doing good. 'Congregations these days,' commented an inner-city parson, 'are judged not only by what they teach about God, but what they do for God. All philanthropic work, and all social work, ought to be religious work.'[15] A later generation of social critics, addicted to state planning, scoffed at the self-help facet of COS activity. But today, with the welfare state in retreat, most of what the COS was trying to achieve makes sound, practical sense.

The middle-class conscience prompted private schools and colleges to start their own city missions. Samuel Barnett and his wife, Henrietta, were the moving spirits of the first, Toynbee Hall, which opened its doors in 1884. By 1887, sixteen schools and colleges were responsible for missions in working-class parts of London. Bristol was favoured by Clifton College and Manchester by Rossall. Senior boys from Winchester came to Portsmouth to help Robert Dolling, who set up a mission as part of a parish that hitherto had had just one church to serve a population of 27,000. These worthy enterprises were soon to be swept up, and almost submerged, in the wake of the welfare state. But their example, as with so many other Church ventures, prepared the way for far-reaching reforms.

As the Church entered the new century, opposing – or perhaps it would be more accurate to say negative – forces were making an ever greater impact. The evidence was in the declining attendance at church services. The numbers had held up well until the last fifteen years of Victoria's reign, but with the completion of the railway network and the dawning of the first age of mass travel, Sunday observance came in for heavy competition. It is unlikely that Thomas Cook, an earnest young Baptist, knew what he was starting when, in 1841, he organised the first railway excursion. Before long, a refrain heard often from the pulpit was of the regrettable modern tendency for parishioners to desert their church in favour of spending Sunday as a holiday. And it was not only the railways that were at fault. 'That innocent machine, the bicycle,' said a parson in

1898, 'is doing more to abolish church-going and to undermine Christianity than other social force.'

But the reach of the Church was not to be judged by slide rule calculations of Sunday observance. Church attendance was shrinking but, as the Bishop of Rochester warned his clergy in 1903, it was unwise to dismiss 'diffusive Christianity'.[16] It was often capricious and shallow; nonetheless, much of what might be thought antagonistic was Christian in its own way. Indifference to the Church did not necessarily imply unbelief or hostility. Raw and uncompromising atheism was rarely encountered. 'Diffusive Christianity' comprised a general belief in God, a conviction that God was just and benevolent though remote from everyday concerns, a confidence that the good would be rewarded in the life to come and a belief that the Bible was a uniquely worthwhile book – though not to be taken literally in every detail.

That said, for the decline of formal worship the clergy must share the blame. Dismally routine services, irrelevant to anything except middle-class conventions, were rejected by a generation caught up on a social revolution. Quasi-religious movements – Marxism, Fascism – became the preferred options because they looked to be certain of their ground. Often the Church was caught out, circling topical issues before retreating to its medieval defences. Only when the alternatives proved to be monstrous delusions did the Church begin to regain its credibility, as an 'antidote to every kind of utopian thinking'.[17] It turned out that there were no easy, one is tempted to say, scientific answers to the big question.

The Victorian Church is still with us. We see it in the buildings, many now lovingly protected by the Ancient Monuments Society, the very organisation set up to repel the Gothic revival, and by such as the Friends of Friendless Churches and the Norfolk Churches Trust. We see it in the carefully orchestrated services to celebrate the seasons and to mark the rites of passage. We see it in the special pleading for the underclass, a preoccupation for every parson whatever his and, post Victorian, her place in the hierarchy. And we see it in the few remaining doctrinal debates, though it is hard to imagine the Victorians in combat for long over gay marriage.

For the dwindling number who attend Sunday services, for those who instinctively think C of E when asked to name their religious denomination, as much as for those who sense a will to believe, the Church is a reassurance, a comfort zone, a residue of hope that there is more to life than life itself. For this, if for no other reason, the claim that the Church is fading away is mistaken. Roger Scruton calls it a 'creative muddle ... a genial mixture of belief and scepticism, of Christian devotion and ironical self-doubt'. Above all, a 'symbol of the English genius for compromise'.[18]

Put like this, the Church may seem not to amount to much. But humility, toleration and sympathy are great virtues and a welcome alternative to the secular asceticism of militant atheism. With credit to his Victorian heritage, the good parson still has much to offer.

Acknowledgements

My greatest debt is to the legion of local historians who gather together documentary material on their churches. They provide a magnificent service. Of the major libraries, all praise goes to the courteous and ever helpful staff of the London Library and Lambeth Palace Library. I have had constructive advice from lay and professional members of the Church too numerous to name, but I must thank Richard Chartres, Bishop of London, who agreed not only to find time in an overloaded timetable to read the manuscript but also to provide a foreword.

Jill Fenner, my assistant until her blissful retirement to the Scottish Highlands, agreed to help translate my scrawl into comprehensible English. My agent, Michael Alcock, has exercised his twin virtues of patience and perseverance to good effect, supported by my editor, Sarah Kendall, who knows precisely how to manage a curmudgeonly author. This book would never have got started had it not been for the encouragement of my wife, Mary, who shares my passion for exploring old churches.

Notes

Chapter 1

1. Anthony Russell, *The Clerical Profession*, 1980; pp. 55–6
2. C. Kegan Paul, *Memories*, 1891; p.14
3. P. H. Ditchfield, *The Old-Time Parson*, 1908; pp. 143–4
4. Washington Irving, *Old Christmas at Bracebridge Hall*, 1822; pp. 48–9
5. Sabine Baring-Gould, *The Church Revival*, 1914; pp. 118–19
6. Peter Virgin, *The Church in an Age of Negligence*, 1989; p. 138
7. A. Tindal Hart, *The Curate's Lot*, 1970; p. 169
8. Sabine Baring-Gould, *The Church Revival*, 1914; p. 131
9. Richard Yates, *Patronage of the Church of England*, 1823; pp. 60–1
10. From 6 November, 1813 to 11 March, 1814. Quoted in Sabine Baring-Gould, *The Church Revival*, 1914; pp. 116–17
11. Letter to the Revd John Crow from his brother, James Crow, 1837. Quoted in C. K. Francis Brown, *A History of the English Clergy 1800–1900*, 1953; p. 40
12. A. Tindal Hart, *The Curate's Lot*, 1970; p. 106
13. *Ibid.*; p. 107
14. *Ibid.*; p. 127

15. Augustus Hare, *The Story of My Life*, 1896, Vol. VI; p. 177
16. A. Tindal Hart, *The Curate's Lot*, 1970; p. 130
17. *The Blecheley Diary of the Rev. William Cole*, 1931; p. 175
18. Nigel Yates, *Buildings, Faith and Worship: The Liturgical Arrangement of the Anglican Churches 1600–1900*, 1991; pp. 47–55

Chapter 2

1. Timothy Maxwell Gouldstone, *The Rise and Decline of Anglican Idealism in the Nineteenth Century*, 2005; p. 11
2. Richard Yates, *The Basis of National Welfare; Considered in Reference Chiefly to the Prosperity of Britain and the Safety of the Church of England*, 1817
3. C. P. Fendall and E. A. Crutchley (eds), *The Diary of Benjamin Newton: Rector of Wath, 1816–18*, 1933; pp. 57–87
4. Peter Virgin, *The Church in an Age of Negligence*, 1989; pp. 196–7
5. Sabine Baring-Gould, *The Church Revival*, 1914; p. 140
6. M. H. Port, *Six Hundred New Churches: A Study of the Church Building Commission 1818–1856 and its Church Building Activities*, 1961; p. 67
7. Frances Knight, *The Nineteenth Century Church and English Society*, 1995; p. 65
8. *Ibid.*; p. 66
9. Anthony Russell, *The Clerical Profession*, 1980; p. 58
10. David Verey (ed.), *The Diary of a Cotswold Parson*, 1979; p. 48
11. *Ibid.*; p. 34 (entry for 12 October 1827)
12. James Jerram, *Memoirs of Charles Jerram*, 1855; pp. 275–9

13. C. P. Fendall and E. A. Crutchley (eds), *The Diary of Benjamin Newton: Rector of Wath, 1816–18*, 1933

14. Peter Virgin, *The Church in an Age of Negligence*, 1989; p. 82

15. The full story can be found in Owen Chadwick, *Victorian Miniature*, 1960

16. *Ibid.*; p. 87

17. James Obelkevich, *Religion and Rural Society: South Lindsey 1825–1875*, 1976; p. 38

18. Alan Bell, *Sydney Smith*, 1982; p. 28

19. *Ibid.*; p. 107

20. Mary C. Church (ed.), *Life and Letters of Dean Church*, 1895; p. 138

21. *Ibid.*; p. 203

22. Thomas Mozley, *Reminiscences Chiefly of Towns, Villages and Schools*, Vol. 2, 1885; p. 12

23. John Skinner, *Journal of a Somerset Rector*, 1984; p. 30

24. *Ibid.*; p. 30

25. Piers Brendon, *Hawker of Morenstow: Portrait of a Victorian Eccentric*, 1975; p. 38

26. *Ibid.*; p. 61

27. *Ibid.*; p. 122

28. Alfred Blomfield (ed.), *A Memoir of Charles James Blomfield*, Vol. 1, 1863; p. 76

29. G. C. B. Davies, *Henry Phillpotts, Bishop of Exeter*, 1954; p. 152

30. William Addison, *The English Country Parson*, 1947; p. 218

31. *Ibid.*; p. 143

32. Owen Chadwick, *The Victorian Church*, Part 2, 1970; p. 177

33. G. C. B. Davies, *Henry Phillpotts, Bishop of Exeter*, 1954; p. 89

34. *Ibid.*; p. 68

35. Alfred Blomfield (ed.), *A Memoir of Charles James*

Blomfield, Vol. 1, 1863; pp. 53–4

36. Standish Meacham, *Lord Bishop: The Life of Samuel Wilberforce*, 1970

37. Frances Knight, *The Nineteenth Century Church and English Society*, 1995; p. 164

Chapter 3

1. A. B. Webster, *Joshua Watson, The Story of a Layman 1771–1855*, 1954; p. 85

2. Established Church Act 1836

3. John Skinner, *Journal of a Somerset Rector*, 1984; p. 198

4. Pluralities Act 1838

5. Registration Act 1836

6. Municipal Corporation Act 1835

7. Church rates were abolished in 1868

8. *Apologia pro Vita sua*, 1876; p. 43

9. John Steegman, *Victorian Taste*, 1970

10. Robert Southey, *Colloquies on the Progress and Prospects of Society*, 1819

11. William Cobbett, *History of the Protestant Reformation*, 1826

12. Sabine Baring-Gould, *Early Reminiscences 1834–1864*, 1922; p. 275

13. Piers Brendon, *Hurrell Froude and the Oxford Movement*, 1974; p. 27

14. John Henry Newman, *The Arians of the Fourth Century*; p. 47

15. John Henry Newman, *Thoughts on the Ministerial Commission, Respectfully Addressed to the Clergy*, 1833; pp. 1–2

16. David Newsome, *Newman and the Oxford Movement in the Victorian Crisis of Faith*, 1970; p. 50

17. Piers Brendon, *Hurrell Froude and the Oxford Movement*, 1974; pp. 185–6
18. Kenneth Ingram, *John Keble*, 1933; p. 33
19. Timothy Maxwell Gouldstone, *The Rise and Decline of Anglican Idealism in the Nineteenth Century*, 2005; p. 5
20. Thomas Arnold, *Principles of Church Reform*
21. John Julius Norwich, *The Popes*, 2011; p. 382

Chapter 4

1. Edward Boys Ellman, *Recollections of a Sussex Parson*, 1912; p. 191
2. P. H. Ditchfield, *The Old Time Parson*, 1908; p. 66
3. Herbert B. J. Armstrong (ed.), *A Norfolk Diary. Passages from the diary of the Rev. Benjamin John Armstrong*, 1949; entry for 9 October 1870; p. 156
4. Michael Johnson, *Holy Trinity Church in Ages Past*, 2005; p. 14
5. Thomas Mozley, *Reminiscences, Chiefly of Towns, Villages and Schools*, Vol. 2, 1885; p. 68
6. K. S. Inglis, *Churches and the Working Classes in Victorian England*, 1963; p. 50
7. *Christian Observer*, May 1965. Quoted in K. S. Inglis, *Churches and the Working Classes in Victorian England*, 1963; p. 51
8. *Rank and Degree in Church*, 1887. Quoted in K. S. Inglis, *Churches and the Working Classes in Victorian England*, 1963; p. 51
9. Washington Irving, *Old Christmas at Bracebridge Hall*, 1822; p. 49
10. *Ibid.*; pp. 50–1
11. Herbert B. J. Armstrong (ed.) *A Norfolk Diary. Passages from the diary of the Rev. Benjamin John Armstrong*, 1949; entry for 4 January 1855

12. *Ibid.*; entry for 31 March, 1861
13. William Plomer (ed.), *Kilvert's Diary, 1870–1879*, Readers Union 1944; entry for 29 October 1874
14. Sabine Baring-Gould, *Early Reminiscences 1834–1864*; 1922; p. 148
15. Edward Boys Ellman, *Recollections of a Sussex Parson*, 1912; p. 196
16. Ian Bradley, *Abide With Me. The World of Victorian Hymns*, 1997; p. xii
17. *Ibid.*; p. 53
18. *Ibid.*; p. 123
19. *Ibid.*; p. 145
20. Revd John Breay, *A Fell-Side Parson*, 1995; p. 64
21. David Verey (ed.), *The Diary of a Cotswold Parson*, 1979; p. 31
22. Herbert B. J. Armstrong (ed.), *A Norfolk Diary. Passages from the diary of the Rev. Benjamin John Armstrong*, 1949; entry for 22 January 1865
23. *Ibid.*; entry for 20 February, 1867
24. *Ibid.*; entry for 17 September, 1883
25. William Plomer (ed.), *Kilvert's Diary, 1870–1879*, Readers Union 1944; pp. 66–7

Chapter 5

1. William Wilberforce, *A Practical View of the Prevailing Religious System of Professed Christians*, 1829
2. Stephen Tomkins, *The Clapham Sect: How Wilberforce Transformed Britain*, 2010; p. 1
3. Sir Richard Coupland, *Wilberforce: A Narrative*, 1923
4. William Wilberforce, *A Practical View of the Prevailing Religious System of Professed Christians*, 1829
5. Thomas Mozley, *Reminiscences, Chiefly of Towns, Villages and Schools, Vol. 2*, 1885; pp. 62–4

6. Hansard, 24 July 1834

7. Piers Brendon, *Hawker of Morwenstow: Portrait of a Victorian Eccentric*, 1975; p. 80

8. Frances Knight, *The Nineteenth Century Church and English Society*, 1995; p. 74

9. Parliamentary Papers 1834. Quoted in G. Kitson Clark, *Churchmen and the Condition of England, 1832–1885*, 1973; p. 170

10. Revd Leonard Jenyns, *Memoir of the Rev. John Stevens Henslow*, 1862; p, 88

11. Samuel Best, *Parochial Ministrations*, 1839

12. G. Kitson Clark, *Churchmen and the Condition of England, 1832–1885*, 1973; pp. 183–5

13. D. W. Bebbington, *Evangelicalism in Modern Britain*, 1989; p. 106

14. Jeffrey Cox, *The English Churches in a Secular Society*, 1982; p. 41

15. Elie Halévy, *History of the English People in the Nineteenth Century*, 1923; p. 165

16. D. W. Bebbington, *Evangelicalism in Modern Britain*, 1989; p. 131

17. James Obelkevich, *Religion and Rural Society: South Lindsey, 1825–1875*, 1976; p. 85

18. Herbert B. J. Armstrong (ed.), *A Norfolk Diary. Passages from the diary of the Rev. Benjamin John Armstrong*, 1949; entry for 8 July 1855

Chapter 6

1. F. D. Maurice, *Has the Church or the State the Power to Educate the Nation?*, 1939; p. 129

2. J. M. Goldstrom, *Elementary Education 1780–1900*, 1972; p. 25

3. Thomas Cooper, *The Life of Thomas Cooper*, 1872

4. Frances Knight, *The Nineteenth Century Church and English Society*, 1995; p. 191

5. *Sermon upon the Religious and Civil Education of Poor Children*, 1812. Quoted in Diana McClatchey, *Oxfordshire Clergy 1777–1869*; p. 142

6. Anthony Russell, *The Clerical Profession*, 1980; p. 46

7. *Sermon upon the Religious and Civil Education of Poor Children*, 1812. Quoted in Diana McClatchey, *Oxfordshire Clergy 1777–1869*; p. 142

8. A. B. Webster, *Joshua Watson, The Story of a Layman 1771–1855*, 1954; p. 36

9. Report of the National Society. Quoted in A. B. Webster, *Joshua Watson, The Story of a Layman 1771–1855*, 1954; p. 36

10. Thomas Mozley, *Reminiscences, Chiefly of Towns, Villages and Schools, Vol. 2*, 1885; p. 185

11. *Ibid.*; pp. 274–5

12. Revd J. C. Atkinson, *Forty Years in a Moorland Parish*, 1887; p. 46

13. Anthony Russell, *The Clerical Profession*, 1980; p. 138

14. M. K. Ashby, *Joseph Ashby of Tysoe 1859–1919*, 1961; pp. 22–3

15. Anthony Russell, *The Clerical Profession*, 1980; pp. 194–5

16. Edward Boys Ellman, *Recollections of a Sussex Parson*, 1912; p. 199

17. Bruce Wilson, *William Papillon; His Contribution to Wymondham Abbey*, 2005

18. J. C. Blomfield, *History of Finmere*; p. 66

19. John Prest, *The Most Difficult Village: Wheatley, England and the Church*, 2006; p. 42

20. Piers Brendon, *Hawker of Morwenstow: Portrait of a Victorian Eccentric*, 1975; p. 90

21. Brian Heeney, *Mission to the Middle Classes, The*

   Woodward Schools 1848–91, 1969

22. Anthony Russell, *The Clerical Profession*, 1980; p. 195

23. Committee of the Privy Council Report 1841–1842. Quoted in C. K. Francis Brown, *A History of the English Clergy 1800–1900*

24. Mary Sturt, *The Education of the People*, 1967; p. 118

25. Trevor Lloyd, *Suffragettes International*, 1971; p. 22

Chapter 7

1. Edward Boys Ellman, *Recollections of a Sussex Parson*, 1912; p. 167

2. Saba Holland, *A Memoir of the Rev. Sydney Smith*, 1855, Vol. I; p. 160

3. Diary of William Andrew, 5 December 1840, quoted in Owen Chadwick, *Victorian Miniature*, 1960; p. 53

4. Duff Hart-Davis (ed.), W. H. Thornton, *Reminiscences of an Old West Country Clergyman*, 2011; p. 121

5. William Plomer (ed.), *Kilvert's Diary, 1870–1879*, Readers Union 1944; entry for 14 October 1870

6. The other, more renowned Augustus Hare, biographer and travel writer, was his nephew.

7. Augustus Hare, *Memorials of a Quiet Life*, Vol. I, 1891; p. 307

8. *Ibid.*; pp. 342–3

9. *Ibid.*; p. 292

10. Anthony Russell, *The Clerical Profession*, 1980; p. 207

11. *Ibid.*; p. 210

12. Owen Chadwick, *The Victorian Church*, Part 1, 1966; p. 326

13. *Ibid.*; p. 327

14. John Prest, *The Most Difficult Village: Wheatley, England and the Church*, 2006; p. 43

15. G. Kitson Clark, *Churchmen and the Condition of*

England, 1832–1885, 1973; p. 212

16. Anthony Russell, *The Clerical Profession*, 1980; p. 225
    Owen Chadwick, *Victorian Miniature*, 1960; p. 55

17. Herbert B. J. Armstrong (ed.), *A Norfolk Diary. Passages from the diary of the Rev. Benjamin John Armstrong*, 1949

Chapter 8

1. John Wade (ed.), *The Extraordinary Black Book*, 1832

2. Asa Briggs, *Victorian Cities*; p. 61

3. Robert Gregory speaking at Cuddesdon 1865. Quoted in Alan Haig, *The Victorian Clergy*, 1984; p. 121

4. Alan Haig, *The Victorian Clergy*, 1984; p. 118

5. Owen Chadwick, *The Victorian Church*, Part 1, 1966; p. 331

6. Summary of Accounts and Papers, Religious Worship; p. 93

7. D. W. Bebbington, *Evangelicalism in Modern Britain*, 1989; p. 118

8. Jeffrey Cox, *The English Churches in a Secular Society*, 1982; p. 50

9. K. S. Inglis, *Churches and the Working Classes in Victorian England*, 1963; p. 7

10. Kathleen Woodroofe, *From Charity to Social Work in England and the United States*, 1962; p. 23

11. W. W. Champneys, *Spirit in the Word. Facts Gathered from a Thirty Years Ministry*, 1862; p. 150. Quoted in Bowen, *The Idea of the Victorian Church*, 1968; p. 290

12. C. F. Lowder, *A Biography*, 1881; p. 107

13. A. Clifton Kelway, *Memoirs of G. Rundle Prynne*. Quoted in Sabine Baring-Gould, *The Church Revival*, 1914; pp. 217–18

14. C. J. Stranks, *Dean Hook*, 1954; p. 36

15. S. C. Carpenter, *Church People, 1789–1889*, 1959; p. 393
16. Sabine Baring-Gould, *The Church Revival*, 1914; p. 91
17. A. Tindal Hart, *The Curate's Lot*, 1970; p. 167
18. G. B. Grundy, *Fifty-Five Years at Oxford*, 1945; p. 11
19. Peter Virgin, *The Church in an Age of Negligence*, 1989; p. 14
20. M. E. Bury and J. D. Pickles (ed.), *Romilly's Cambridge Diaries 1848–1864*, 2000; p. 231
21. William Addison, *The English Country Parson*, 1947; p. 216
22. *Ibid.*; p. 217
23. Piers Brendon, *Hawker of Morenstow: Portrait of a Victorian Eccentric*, 1975; p. 137
24. C. K. Francis Brown, *A History of the English Clergy 1800–1900*, 1953; p. 153
25. Sabine Baring-Gould, *Early Reminiscences 1834–1864*, 1922; p. 239
26. Owen Chadwick, *The Victorian Church*, Part 2, 1970; p. 153
27. Roger Wells (ed.), *Victorian Village: The Diaries of John Coker Egerton, Curate and Rector of Burwash, East Sussex 1857–1888*, 1992; pp. 28–9
28. Herbert B. J. Armstrong (ed.), *A Norfolk Diary. Passages from the diary of the Rev. Benjamin John Armstrong*, 1949; entry for 19 July 1868
29. Brenda Collons, *The Victorian Country Parson*, 1977; pp. 197–209
30. Augustus Jessop quoted in C. K. Francis Brown, *A History of the English Clergy 1800–1900*; p. 152
31. Sabine Baring-Gould, *The Church Revival*, 1914; p. 101
32. W. M. Jacobs, *A History of the English Clergy*; p. 91
33. A. Tindal Hart, *The Curate's Lot*, 1970; p. 170
34. Frances Knight, *The Nineteenth Century Church and English Society*, 1995; p. 159

35. Augustus Hare, *Memorials of a Quiet Life*, Vol. 1, 1891; p. 48

36. A. Tindal Hart, *The Curate's Lot*, 1970; pp. 136–7

37. *Ibid.*; pp. 163–4

38. *Ibid* ; p. 138

39. *Ibid* ; p. 143

40. Herbert B. J. Armstrong (ed.) *A Norfolk Diary. Passages from the diary of the Rev. Benjamin John Armstrong*, 1949; entry for 13 February 1875

41. *Ibid* ; entry for 16 September 1863

42. Revd John Breay, *A Fell-Side Parson*, 1995; p. 73

43. *Ibid* ; p. 76

Chapter 9

1. Owen Chadwick, *The Victorian Church*, Part 2, 1970; p. 151

2. Graham King, *The Spider Man of Dorset*, *Country*, August 1997

3. Francis Galton, *English Men of Science: Their Nature and Nurture*, 1970; p. 24

4. *Lords 1787–1945*, 1948. Quoted in C. K. Francis Brown, *A History of the English Clergy 1800–1900*, 1953; p. 233

Chapter 10

1. Basil Clarke, *Church Builders of the Nineteenth Century*, 1938; p. 225

2. C. J. Stranks, *Dean Hook*, 1954

3. *Ibid.*; p. 65

4. John Prest, The *Most Difficult Village: Wheatley, England and the Church*, 2006

5. Basil Clarke, *Church Builders of the Nineteenth Century*,

1938; p. 149

6. Rodney Bolt, *The Impossible Life of Mary Benson*, 2011

7. W. N. Yates, *Kent and the Oxford Movement*, 1983; p. 52

8. Nigel Yates, *Buildings, Faith and Worship: The Liturgical Arrangement of Anglican Churches 1600–1900*, 1991; p. 155

9. James Obelkevich, *Religion and Rural Society: South Lindsey 1825–1875*, 1976; p. 39

10. Joan Campbell, *The History of St Nicholas New Romney*, 2010; p. 16

11. Basil Clarke, *Church Builders of the Nineteenth Century*, 1938; p. 237

12. Sabine Baring-Gould, *Early Reminiscences 1834–1864*, 1922; p. 244

13. Pamela Bousfield, *A History of St Breward*, 1988; p. 22

14. Anthea Jones, *Tewkesbury Abbey: The Victorian Restoration Controversy*, 2012

15. Basil Clarke, quoted in *Church Builders of the Nineteenth Century*, 1938; p. 228

16. James Bettley, *In the Footsteps of William of Wykeham: Anglican Priest-Architect of the Nineteenth Century*, Ancient Monuments Society Transactions, Vol. 55, 2011; p. 10

17. *Ibid.*; p. 14

18. James Bentley, *Ancient Monuments Society Transactions*; Vol. 555, 2011

19. William Haslam, *From Death into Life, or, Twenty Years of my Ministry*, 1880; p. 232

20. Alan Savidge, *The Parsonage in England*, 1964; p. 116

21. Hayton to Bishop Kaye, 23 April 1827. Quoted in Francis Knight, *The Nineteenth Century Church and English Society*, 1995; p. 138

22. Hayton to Bishop Kaye, 26 May, 1832; *Ibid.* p. 139

23. William Plomer (ed.), *Kilvert's Diary, 1870–1879*, Readers

Union 1944; entry for 3 July, 1872

24. Edward Boys Ellman, *Recollections of a Sussex Parson*, 1912; p. 168
25. *Ibid.*; p. 191
26. Peter C. Hammond, *The Parson and the Victorian Parish*, 1977; p. 46
27. Alan Savidge, *The Parsonage in England*, 1964; p. 135
28. William Addison, *The English Country Parson*, 1947; p. 219

Chapter 11

1. Revd John Keble, *Sermons for the Christian Year*, 1875; p. 247
2. *Ibid.*; p. 38
3. *Sermons to a Country Congregation*
4. Charles Kingsley, *Twenty Five Village Sermons*, 1849
5. W. G. Elliot, *In My Anecdotage*, 1925; pp. 197–8
6. Alfred Blomfield (ed.), *A Memoir of Charles James Blomfield*, Vol. 1, 1863; pp. 78–9
7. M. E. Bury and J. D. Pickles (ed.), *Romilly's Cambridge Diaries 1848–1864*, 2000; p. 217
8. Anthony Trollope, *Barchester Towers*
9. William Addison, *The English Country Parson*, 1947; pp. 147–8
10. P. H. Ditchfield, *The Old-Time Parson*, 1908; p. 197
11. Alastair Johnson (ed.), *The Diary of Thomas Giordani Wright, 1826–29*, 2001; p. 247
12. William Plomer (ed.), *Kilvert's Diary, 1870–1879*, Readers Union 1944; entry for 14 July 1871
13. David Verey (ed.), *The Diary of a Cotswold Parson*, 1979; p. 87
14. *Fraser's Magazine*, 1869, quoted in *The Victorian Pulpit* by Robert H. Ellison, 1998; p. 49

15. Robert H. Ellison, *The Victorian Pulpit*, 1998; p. 34
16. *Church Quarterly Review*, 1887, quoted in *The Victorian Pulpit* by Robert Ellison, 1998; p. 40
17. Thomas Mozley, *Reminiscences, Chiefly of Towns, Villages and Schools*, Vol. 2, 1885; p. 297
18. Geoffrey Rowell, *Hell and the Victorians*, 1974; p. 108
19. *Ibid.*; p. 122
20. *Ibid.*; p. 171
21. M. E. Bury and J. D. Pickles (eds), *Romilly's Cambridge Diaries 1848–1864*, 2000; p. 177
22. C. T. Cook (ed.), *C.H. Spurgeon's Sermons for Special Occasions*, 1963; p. 97
23. Timothy Larson, *A People of One Book. The Bible and the Victorians*, 2011; p. 258
24. C. T. Cook (ed.), *C. H. Spurgeon's Sermons for Special Occasions*, 1963; p. 244
25. Herbert B. J. Armstrong (ed.), *A Norfolk Diary. Passages from the diary of the Rev. Benjamin John Armstrong*, 1949; entry for 12 January 1862; p. 89
26. *Ibid.*; entry for 12 February 1866; p. 120
27. Samuel Waldegrave, *Life of Archbishop Tait*, 1891. Quoted in Anthony Russell, *The Clerical Profession*, 1980; p. 95
28. M. E. Bury and J. D. Pickles (eds), *Romilly's Cambridge Diaries 1848–1864*, 2000; p. 273

Chapter 12

1. William Makepeace Thayer, *The True Woman*, 1893; p. 35
2. John Todd, *The Daughter at School*, 1853; p. 219
3. *Girl's Own Paper*, 26 December, 1885
4. *Ibid.*; 28 April, 1883
5. Thomas Gisborne, *An Enquiry into the Duties of the*

Female Sex, 1806; pp. 12–13

6. Isabel Reaney, *English Girls, Their Place and Power*, 1879; pp. 44–5
7. *Girls' Own Paper*, 16 April, 1892
8. Alan Walbank, *Queens of the Circulating Library*, 1950; p. 22

Chapter 13

1. James Obelkevich, *Religion and Rural Society: South Lindsey 1825–1875*, 1976; p. 131
2. *Ibid.*; p. 134
3. Herbert B. J. Armstrong (ed.), *A Norfolk Diary. Passages from the diary of the Rev. Benjamin John Armstrong*, 1949; entry for 9 October 1870; p. 156
4. Sabine Baring-Gould, *The Church Revival*, 1914; pp. 133
5. Dean D. Reynolds Hole, *More Memories*, 1894; p. 16
6. Peter C. Hammond, *The Parson and the Victorian Parish*, 1977; p. 95
7. Owen Chadwick, *The Victorian Church*, Part 1, 1966; p. 144
8. Revd J. C. Atkinson, *Forty Years in a Moorland Parish*, 1887; pp. 205–6
9. *Ibid.*; p. 458
10. Herbert B. J. Armstrong (ed.), *A Norfolk Diary. Passages from the diary of the Rev. Benjamin John Armstrong*, 1949; entry for 9 October 1870; p. 123
11. Duff Hart-Davis (ed.), W. H. Thornton, *Reminiscences of an Old West Country Clergyman*, 2011; pp. 122–3
12. Archdeacon Hope's Charge of 1841
13. Thomas Mozley, *Reminiscences, Chiefly of Towns, Villages and Schools*, Vol. 2, 1885; p. 275
14. M. E. Bury and J. D. Pickles (eds), *Romilly's Cambridge Diaries 1848–1864*, 2000; entry for 29 July, 1853

15. Roger Wells (ed.), *Victorian Village: The Diaries of John Coker Egerton, Curate and Rector of Burwash, East Sussex 1857–1888*; p. 99

16. William Plomer (ed.), *Kilvert's Diary, 1870–1879*, Readers Union 1944; entry for 17 December, 1870

17. Ian Bradley, *Abide With Me*, 1997; p. 197

18. William Plomer (ed.), *Kilvert's Diary, 1870–1879*, Readers Union 1944, entry for 17 April 1870

19. M. E. Bury and J. D. Pickles (eds), *Romilly's Cambridge Diaries 1848–1864*, 2000; entry for 24 July 1848

20. Roger Wells (ed.), *Victorian Village: The Diaries of John Coker Egerton, Curate and Rector of Burwash, East Sussex 1857–1888*, (entry for 17 August 1857), 1992; p. 27

21. *Ibid.*; entry for 24 October 1876; p. 179

22. Herbert B. J. Armstrong (ed.), *A Norfolk Diary. Passages from the diary of the Rev. Benjamin John Armstrong*, 1949; entry for 15 February 1855

23. *Ibid.*; entry for 6 August 1874

24. Roger Wells (ed.), *Victorian Village: The Diaries of John Coker Egerton, Curate and Rector of Burwash, East Sussex 1857–1888*, 1992; p. 263

25. Revd J. C. Atkinson, *Forty Years in a Moorland Parish*, 1887; p. 232

26. Anthony Russell, *The Clerical Profession*, 1980; p. 80

27. Herbert B. J. Armstrong (ed.), *A Norfolk Diary. Further Passages from the Diary of the Revd. Benjamin John Armstrong, Vicar of East Dereham, 1850–1888*, 1963; p. 96

28. Roger Wells (ed.), *Victorian Village: The Diaries of John Coker Egerton, Curate and Rector of Burwash, East Sussex 1857–1888*, 1992; p. 263

29. Duff Hart-Davis (ed.), W. H. Thornton, *Reminiscences, of an Old West Country Clergyman*, 2011; p. 29

Chapter 14

1. Revd J. C. Ryle, *Evangelical Religion: what it is and what it is not*, 1867

2. Sabine Baring-Gould, *Early Reminiscences 1834–1864*, 1922; p. 340

3. T. H. Huxley, *Essays Upon Some Controversial Questions*, 1892; p. 450

4. Terence Thomas (ed.), *The British, Their Religious Beliefs and Practices 1800–1986*, 1988; p. 65

5. *Ibid.*; p. 65

6. Mrs Humphrey Ward, *A Writer's Recollections*, 1918; p. 230

7. James Anthony Froude, *Short Studies on Great Subjects*, 1867; pp. 366–7

8. Owen Chadwick, *The Victorian Church*, Part 2, 1970; p. 67

9. Samuel Taylor Coleridge, *Confessions of an Enquiring Spirit*, p. 10

10. Derek Leon, *Ruskin: The Great Victorian*, 1949; p. 566

11. John Stuart Mill, *Diary* (13 January 1854)

12. Winwood Reade, *The Martyrdom of Man*, 1872

13. Thomas Mozley, *Reminiscences, Chiefly of Towns, Villages and Schools*, Vol. 2, 1885; p. 174

14. William James, *The Varieties of Religious Experience*, 1902; p. 89

Chapter 15

1. Michael Bateman (ed.), *This England*, 1969; p. 37

2. Owen Chadwick, *The Victorian Church*, Part 2, 1970; p. 41

3. Margaret Crowther, *Church Embattled: Religious Controversy in Mid-Victorian Britain*, 1970; p. 221

4. Brian Heeney, *A Different Kind of Gentleman*, 1976; p. 105

5. W. W. Champneys, *Parish Work*, 1866; p. 30

6. *The Church Times*, 17 November 1950

7. K. S. Inglis, *Churches and the Working Classes in Victorian England*, 1963; p. 284

8. Beatrice Webb, *Our Partnership*, 1948; p. 207

9. *The Times*, 2 April 1874

10. G. Kitson Clark, *Churchmen and the Condition of England, 1832–1885*, 1973; p. 181

11. *Macmillan's Magazine*, Vol. xxviii; p. 436

12. Owen Chadwick, *The Victorian Church*, Part 2, 1970; p. 193

13. Jeffrey Cox, *The English Churches in a Secular Society*, 1982; pp. 66–8

14. *Ibid.*; p. 76

15. *St Matthew's Yearbook, Brixton*, 1899; p. 14

16. Jeffrey Cox, *The English Churches in a Secular Society*, 1982; p. 93

17. Roger Scruton, *Our Church: A Personal History of the Church of England*, 2010; p. 129

18. *Ibid.*; pp .78 and 37

Bibliography

Addison, William, *The English Country Parson* (Dent, 1947)

Armstrong, Herbert B. J. (ed.), *A Norfolk Diary. Passages from the diary of the Rev. Benjamin John Armstrong* (Harrap, 1949)

Arnold, Thomas, *Principles of Church Reform* (Fellowes, 1833)

Ashby, M. K., *Joseph Ashby of Tysoe 1859–1919* (Cambridge University Press, 1961)

Atkinson, Revd J. C., *Forty Years in a Moorland Parish* (Rigg, 1887)

Aydon, Cyril, *Charles Darwin* (Robinson, 2002)

Baring-Gould, Sabine, *Church Revival* (Methuen, 1914)

Baring-Gould, Sabine, *Early Reminiscences 1834–1864* (Dutton, 1922)

Bateman, Michael (ed.), *This England* (Penguin, 1969)

Bebbington, D. W., *Evangelicalism in Modern Britain* (Unwin Hyman, 1989)

Bell, Alan, *Sydney Smith* (Oxford Paperbacks, 1982)

Best, Samuel, *Parochial Ministrations* (J. Hatchard, 1839)

Blomfield, Alfred (ed.), *A Memoir of Charles James Blomfield*, Vol. 1 (John Murray, 1863)

Bolt, Rodney, *The Impossible Life of Mary Benson* (Atlantic, 2011)

Bousfield, Pamela, *A History of St Breward* (1988)

Bowen, Desmond, *The Idea of the Victorian Church* (McGill

University Press, 1968)

Bradley, Ian, *Abide With Me. The World of Victorian Hymns* (GIA Publications, 1997)

Breay, Revd John, *A Fell-Side Parson 1826–1903* (Canterbury Press, 1995)

Brendon, Piers, *Hawker of Morenstow: Portrait of a Victorian Eccentric* (Jonathan Cape, 1975)

Brendon, Piers, *Hurrell Froude and the Oxford Movement* (Paul Elek, 1974)

Briggs, Asa, *Victorian Cities* (Penguin, 1968)

Briggs, Asa, *Victorian People* (Penguin, 1954)

Brooks, Chris, *The Gothic Revival* (Phaidon, 1999)

Brown, C. K. Francis, *The Church's Part in Education, 1833–1941* (SPCK, 1942)

Brown, C. K. Francis, *A History of the English Clergy 1800–1900* (The Faith Press, 1953)

Bury, M. E. and J. D. Pickles (eds), *Romilly's Cambridge Diaries 1848–1864* (Cambridge University Press, 2000)

Carlyle, Thomas, *Past and Present* (Oxford University Press World Classics, 1965)

Carpenter, S. C., *Church and People 1789–1889* (SPCK, 1959)

Chadwick, Owen, *The Secularization of the European Mind in the Nineteenth Century* (Cambridge University Press, 1975)

Chadwick, Owen, *The Victorian Church Part 1* (Black, 1966)

Chadwick, Owen, *The Victorian Church Part 2* (Black, 1970)

Chadwick, Owen, *Victorian Miniature* (Hodder & Stoughton, 1960)

Champneys, W. W., *Parish Work* (Seeley, 1866)

Church, Mary C. (ed.), *Life and Letters of Dean Church* (Macmillan, 1895)

Clark, G. Kitson, *Churchmen and the Condition of England, 1832–1885* (Methuen, 1973)

Clarke, Basil, *Church Builders of the Nineteenth Century* (SPCK, 1938)

Coleridge, Samuel Taylor, *Confessions of an Enquiring Spirit* (George Bell & Sons, 1901)

Collons, Brenda, *The Victorian Country Parson* (Constable, 1977)

Cook, C. T. (ed.), *C.H. Spurgeon's Sermons for Special Occasions* (Marshall, Morgan & Scott, 1963)

Cooper, Thomas, *The Life of Thomas Cooper* (Hodder & Stoughton, 1872)

Coupland, Sir Richard, *Wilberforce: A Narrative* (Clarendon Press, 1923)

Cox, Jeffrey, *The English Churches in a Secular Society* (Oxford University Press, 1982)

Crook, J. Mordaunt and C. A. Lennox-Boyd, *Axel Haig and the Victorian Vision of the Middle Ages* (Allen & Unwin, 1984)

Crowther, Margaret, *Church Embattled: Religious Controversy in Mid-Victorian Britain* (David & Charles, 1970)

Davies, G. C. B., *Henry Phillpotts, Bishop of Exeter* (SPCK, 1954)

Desmond, Adrian and James Moor, *Darwin* (Michael Joseph, 1991)

Ditchfield, P. H., *The Old-Time Parson* (Methuen, 1920)

Dodds, John W., *The Age of Paradox* (Gollancz, 1953)

Elliot, W. G., *In My Anecdotage* (Philip Allan, 1925)

Ellison, Robert H., *The Victorian Pulpit* (Susquehanna University Press, 1998)

Ellman, Edward Boys, *Recollections of a Sussex Parson* (Skeffington, 1912)

Fendall, C. P. and E. A. Crutchley (eds), *The Diary of Benjamin Newton: Rector of Wath 1816–18* (Cambridge University Press, 1933)

Fitzgerald, Penelope, *Edward Burne-Jones* (Michael Joseph, 1975)

Ford, Boris (ed.), *Victorian Britain: Cambridge Cultural History* (Cambridge University Press, 1989)

Fraser, Derek, *The Evolution of the British Welfare State* (Macmillan, 1973)

Froude, James Anthony, *Short Studies on Great Subjects* (Longmans, Green, 1867)

Galton, Francis, *English Men of Science: Their Nature and Nurture* (Frank Cass, 1970)

Gibson, A. Boyce, *Theism and Empiricism* (SCM, 1970)

Gisborne, Thomas, *An Enquiry into the Duties of the Female Sex* (T. Cadell & W. Davies, 1806)

Goldstrom, J. M., *Elementary Education 1780–1900* (David & Charles, 1972)

Gouldstone, Timothy Maxwell, *The Rise and Decline of Anglican Idealism in the Nineteenth Century* (Palgrave Macmillan, 2005)

Grisewood, Harman (ed.), *Ideas and Beliefs of the Victorians* (Sylvan Press, 1949)

Grundy, G. B., *Fifty-Five Years at Oxford* (Methuen, 1945)

Haig, Alan, *The Victorian Clergy* (Croom Helm, 1984)

Halevy, Elie, *History of the English People in the Nineteenth Century* (T. Fisher Unwin, 1923)

Hammond, Peter C., *The Parson and the Victorian Parish* (Hodder & Stoughton, 1977)

Hare, Augustus, *Memorials of a Quiet Life, Vol. I* (George Allen, 1891)

Hare, Augustus, *The Story of My Life, Vol. VI* (George Allen, 1896)

Hart, A. Tindal, *The Curate's Lot* (John Baker, 1970)

Haslam, William, *From Death into Life, or, Twenty Years of my Ministry* (Morgan & Scott, 1880)

Hecht, Jennifer Michael, *Doubt: A History* (HarperCollins, 2003)

Heeney, Brian, *A Different Kind of Gentleman* (Archon Books, 1976)

Heeney, Brian, *Mission to the Middle Classes, The Woodward*

Schools 1848–91 (SPCK, 1969)

Hibbert, Christopher, *Queen Victoria: A Personal History* (HarperCollins, 2000)

Higham, Florence, *Lord Shaftesbury* (SCM, 1945)

Hill, Rosemary, *God's Architect* (Allen Lane, 2007)

Hilton, Tim, *John Ruskin, The Early Years* (Yale, 1985)

Himmelfarb, Gertrude, *The De-Moralization of Society. From Victorian Virtues to Modern Values* (Vintage, 1996)

Himmelfarb, Gertrude, *Victorian Minds* (Knopf, 1968)

Hole, Dean D. Reynolds, *More Memories* (Macmillan, 1894)

Holland, Saba, *A Memoir of the Reverend Sydney Smith Vol. I* (Harper & Brothers, 1855)

Holmes, Richard, *Coleridge: Darker Reflections* (HarperCollins, 1998)

Holmes, Richard, *Coleridge: Early Visions* (Hodder, 1989)

Houghton, Walter E. *The Victorian Frame of Mind* (Yale, 1957)

Huxley, T. H., *Essays Upon Some Controversial Questions* (Macmillan, 1892)

Inglis, K. S., *Churches and the Working Classes in Victorian England* (Routledge & Kegan Paul, 1963)

Ingram, Kenneth, *John Keble* (Philip Allan, 1933)

Irving, Washington, *Old Christmas at Bracebridge Hall* (John Murray, 1822)

Jackson, Holbrook, *The Eighteen Nineties* (Penguin, 1939)

James, William, *The Varieties of Religious Experience* (Longmans, Green, 1902)

Jenyns, Revd Leonard, *Memoir of the Rev. John Stevens Henslow* (John van Voorst, 1862)

Johnson, Alastair (ed.), *The Diary of Thomas Giordani Wright, 1826–29* (Boydell Press, 2001)

Jones, Anthea, *Tewkesbury Abbey: The Victorian Restoration Controversy* (R. J. L. Smith, 2012)

Jordan, Robert Furneaux, *Victorian Architecture* (Penguin, 1966)

Keble, Revd John, *Sermons for the Christian Year* (James Parker, 1875)

Kingsley, Charles, *Twenty-five Village Sermons* (James Parker, 1849)

Knight, Frances, *The Nineteenth Century Church and English Society* (Cambridge University Press, 1995)

Larsen, Timothy, *A People of One Book, The Bible and the Victorians* (Oxford University Press, 2011)

Leon, Derrick, *Ruskin: The Great Victorian* (Routledge, 1949)

Lloyd, Trevor, *Suffragettes International* (American Heritage Press, 1971)

Long, David, *Ruskin* (Peter Davies, 1932)

MacCarthy, Fiona, *The Last Pre-Raphaelite* (Faber, 2011)

MacCarthy, Fiona, *William Morris: A Life for Our Time* (Faber, 1994)

McClatchey, Diana, *Oxfordshire Clergy 1777–1869* (Clarendon Press, 1960)

Maurice, F. D., *Has the Church or the State the Power to Educate the Nation?* (Rivington, 1939)

Meacham, Standish, *Lord Bishop: The Life of Samuel Wilberforce* (Harvard University Press, 1970)

Mozley, Thomas, *Reminiscences, Chiefly of Towns, Villages and Schools,* Vol. 2 (Longmans, Green, 1885)

Newman, John Henry, *The Arians of the Fourth Century* (Longmans, Green, 1890)

Newman, John Henry, *Thoughts on the Ministerial Commission, Respectfully Addressed to the Clergy* (Rivington, 1833)

Newsome, David, *Newman and the Oxford Movement in The Victorian Crisis of Faith* (Rivington, 1970)

Norman, E. R., *Church and Society in England 1770–1970* (Clarendon Press, 1976

Norwich, John Julius, *The Popes: A History* (Chatto & Windus, 2011)

Obelkevich, James, *Religion and Rural Society: South Lindsey*

1825–1875 (Clarendon Press, 1976)

Pemberton, W. Baring, *William Cobbett* (Penguin, 1949)

Plomer, William (ed.), *Kilvert's Diary, 1870-1879* (Readers Union, 1944)

Port, M. H., *Six Hundred New Churches: A Study of the Church Building Commission 1818–1856 and its Church Building Activities* (SPCK Press, 1961)

Prest, John, *The Most Difficult Village: Wheatley, England and the Church* (Prest, 2006)

Reade, Winwood, *The Martyrdom of Man* (Watts, 1872)

Reaney, Isabel, *English Girls, Their Place and Power* (Kegan Paul, 1879)

Rowell, Geoffrey, *Hell and the Victorians* (Oxford University Press, 1974)

Russell, Anthony, *The Clerical Profession* (SPCK, 1980)

Ryle, Revd J. C., *Evangelical Religion: what it is and what it is not* (William Hunt, 1867)

St Aubyn, Giles, *Souls in Torment* (New European Publications, 2010)

Savidge, Alan, *The Parsonage in England* (SPCK, 1964)

Scott, George Gilbert, *Personal and Professional Recollections* (General Books, 2009)

Scruton, Roger, *Our Church: A Personal History of the Church of England* (Atlantic, 2010)

Simon, Brian and Ian Bradley, *The Victorian Public School* (Gill & Macmillan, 1975)

Skinner, John, *Journal of a Somerset Rector 1803–1834* (Oxford University Press, 1984)

Southey, Robert, *Colloquies on the Progress and Prospects of Society* (John Murray, 1819)

Steegman, John, *Victorian Taste* (Nelson, 1970)

Stokes, Francis Griffin, *The Blecheley Diary of the Rev. William Cole 1765–67* (Constable, 1931)

Stranks, C. J., *Dean Hook* (Mowbray, 1954)

Sturt, Mary, *The Education of the People* (Routledge & Kegan Paul, 1967)

Symondsen, Anthony (ed.), *The Victorian Crisis of Faith* (SPCK, 1970)

Taylor, Miles and Michael Wolff (eds), *The Victorians Since 1901* (Manchester University Press, 2004)

Thayer, William Makepeace,*The True Woman* (Hodder & Stoughton, 1893)

Thomas, Terence (ed.), *The British, Their Religious Beliefs and Practices 1800–1986.* (Routledge, 1988)

Thompson, E. P., *William Morris: Romantic to Revolutionary* (Merlin Press, 1977)

Thornton, W. H. and Duff Hart-Davis, *Reminiscences of an Old West Country Clergyman* (Excellent Press, 2010)

Todd, Revd John, *The Daughter at School* (Nelson, 1853)

Tomkins, Stephen, *The Clapham Sect: How Wilberforce Transformed Britain* (Lion Hudson, 2010)

Trollope, Anthony, *Barchester Towers* (1857)

Verey, David (ed.), *The Diary of a Cotswold Parson* (Sutton, 1979)

Vidler, Alec R., *The Church in an Age of Revolution* (Penguin, 1961)

Virgin, Peter, *The Church in an Age of Negligence* (James Clarke, 1989)

Wade, John (ed.), *The Extraordinary Black Book* (Effingham Wilson, 1832)

Waithe, Marcus, *William Morris's Utopia of Strangers* (D. S. Brewer, 2006)

Walbank, Alan, *Queens of the Circulating Library* (Evans, 1950)

Ward, Mrs Humphy, *A Writer's Recollections* (Nisbet, 1918)

Warner, Oliver, *William Wilberforce* (Batsford, 1962)

Watt, Margaret, *The History of the Parson's Wife* (Faber, 1963)

Webb, Beatrice, *Our Partnership* (Longman, 1948)

Webster, A. B., *Joshua Watson, The Story of a Layman 1771–1855* (SPCK, 1954)

Wells, Roger (ed.), *Victorian Village: The Diaries of John Coker Egerton, Curate and Rector of Burwash, East Sussex 1857–1888* (Sutton, 1992)

Wiener, Martin J., *English Culture and the Decline of the Industrial Spirit, 1850–1980* (Cambridge University Press, 1981)

Wilberforce, William, *A Practical View of the Prevailing Religious System of Professed Christians* (Collins, 1829)

Wilson, A. N. (ed.), *Church and Clergy* (Faber, 1992)

Wilson, A. N., *God's Funeral* (John Murray, 1999)

Wilson, A. N., *The Victorians* (Hutchinson, 2002)

Woodforde, James, *Diary of a Country Parson 1758–1802* (Oxford University Press, 1978)

Woodroofe, Kathleen, *From Charity to Social Work in England and the United States* (Routledge & Kegan Paul, 1962)

Yates, Nigel, *Buildings, Faith and Worship: The Liturgical Arrangement of Anglican Churches 1600–1900* (Clarendon Press, 1991)

Yates, W. N., *Kent and the Oxford Movement* (Sutton, 1983)